THE EUROPEAN UNION SERIES

General Editors: Neill Nugent, William E. Paterson

The European Union series provides an authoritative library on the European Union, ranging from general introductory texts to definitive assessments of key institutions and actors, issues, policies and policy processes, and the role of member states.

Books in the series are written by leading scholars in their fields and reflect the most up-to-date research and debate. Particular attention is paid to accessibility and clear presentation for a wide audience of students, practitioners and interested general readers.

The series editors are **Neill Nugent**, Visiting Professor, College of Europe, Bruges and Honorary Professor, University of Salford, UK, and **William E. Paterson**, Honourary Professor in German and European Studies, University of Aston. Their co-editor until his death in July 1999, **Vincent Wright**, was a Fellow of Nuffield College, Oxford University.

Feedback on the series and book proposals are always welcome and should be sent to Steven Kennedy, Palgrave Macmillan, Houndmills, Basingstoke, Hampshire RG21 6XS, UK, or by e-mail to s.kennedy@palgrave.com

General textbooks

Published

Desmond Dinan **Encyclopedia of the European Union**
[Rights: Europe only]
Desmond Dinan **Europe Recast: A History of the European Union**
[Rights: Europe only]
Desmond Dinan **Ever Closer Union: An Introduction to European Integration** (4th edn)
[Rights: Europe only]
Mette Eilstrup Sangiovanni (ed.) **Debates on European Integration: A Reader**
Simon Hix and Bjørn Høyland **The Political System of the European Union** (3rd edn)
Dirk Leuffen, Berthold Rittberger and Frank Schimmelfennig **Differentiated Integration**
Paul Magnette **What is the European Union? Nature and Prospects**
John McCormick **Understanding the European Union: A Concise Introduction** (5th edn)
Brent F. Nelsen and Alexander Stubb **The European Union: Readings on the Theory and Practice of European Integration** (3rd edn)
[Rights: Europe only]
Neill Nugent (ed.) **European Union Enlargement**

Neill Nugent **The Government and Politics of the European Union** (7th edn)
John Peterson and Elizabeth Bomberg **Decision-Making in the European Union**
Ben Rosamond **Theories of European Integration**
Esther Versluis, Mendeltje van Keulen and Paul Stephenson **Analyzing the European Union Policy Process**
Hubert Zimmermann and Andreas Dür (eds **Key Controversies in European Integration**

Forthcoming

Laurie Buonanno and Neill Nugent **Policies and Policy Processes of the European Union**
Magnus Ryner and Alan Cafruny **A Critical Introduction to the European Union**
Sabine Saurugger **Theoretical Approaches to European Integration**

Also planned

The Political Economy of European Integration

Series Standing Order (outside North America only)
ISBN 9780333716953 hardback
ISBN 9780333693520 paperback
Full details from www.palgrave.com

Visit Palgrave Macmillan's
EU Resource area at
www.palgrave.com/politics/eu/

The major institutions and actors

The main areas of policy

The member states and the Union

Issues

Differentiated Integration

Explaining Variation in the European Union

Dirk Leuffen

Berthold Rittberger

and

Frank Schimmelfennig

© Dirk Leuffen, Berthold Rittberger and Frank Schimmelfennig 2013

First published 2013 by
PALGRAVE MACMILLAN

Palgrave Macmillan in the UK is an imprint of Macmillan Publishers Limited, registered in England, company number 785998, of Houndmills, Basingstoke, Hampshire RG21 6XS.

Palgrave Macmillan in the US is a division of St Martin's Press LLC, 175 Fifth Avenue, New York, NY 10010.

Palgrave Macmillan is the global academic imprint of the above companies and has companies and representatives throughout the world.

Palgrave® and Macmillan® are registered trademarks in the United States, the United Kingdom, Europe and other countries

ISBN 978–0–230–24643–0 hardback
ISBN 978–0–230–24644–7 paperback

This book is printed on paper suitable for recycling and made from fully managed and sustained forest sources. Logging, pulping and manufacturing processes are expected to conform to the environmental regulations of the country of origin.

A catalogue record for this book is available from the British Library.

A catalog record for this book is available from the Library of Congress.

10   9   8   7   6   5   4   3   2   1
22   21   20   19   18   17   16   15   14   13

Printed in China

Contents

PART II POLICIES

List of Figures, Tables and Boxes

Figures

Tables

Boxes

Preface

To the best of our recollection, it was in 2008 when Steven Kennedy, Palgrave Macmillan's publishing director for Politics, started chivvying us to produce a textbook on theories of European integration. At that time, this appeared to be an easy enough task because both the theory debate and the development of European integration appeared to have been stalled for some time. What should have amounted to a stock-taking exercise, combining European integration theory with the analysis of different policy areas, turned into a long journey, which offered surprising turns and 'discoveries' that made the research we put into this book so enjoyable and – partially – unpredictable. It also meant that the entire process of writing this book became more drawn out.

In this book, we seek to make two contributions to the study of European integration. First, we found that textbooks on European integration theory typically remain at the abstract, theoretical level and do not apply the assumptions and conjectures of integration theories comparatively to the analysis of concrete EU policies. One core objective of this book is to offer systematic, theory-guided explanations for EU integration outcomes across four different policy fields: the internal market, monetary and fiscal policy, security and defence, and – finally – domestic security policies. Second, we realized that theories of European integration had made relatively few efforts to come to grips with what we consider one of the fundamental features of European integration: the differentiation of integration across policy areas with regard to both the level of centralization (vertical differentiation) and the number of countries participating (horizontal differentiation). Mapping and explaining differentiation in the process of European integration required undertaking more research on our own than usually goes into a textbook.

In turn, we hope to have written a book that not only provides an introduction to European integration to advanced undergraduate and graduate students of Political Science and International Relations, but also elaborates our theorizing and understanding of European integration in a way that is interesting for European integration scholarship more generally. In our view, differentiated integration is likely to become a persistent feature of EU politics – probably even growing in importance. In addition, differentiated integration draws our attention to hitherto understudied and theorized variation inside the EU, a variation that seems useful for producing better explanations. We therefore hope that our book will serve as a catalyst for more activity in this exciting field of research.

Another potential benefit of our slow progress with the book is the fact that the euro crisis progressed in parallel. The crisis emphatically stresses the importance of understanding the mechanisms of European integration. Once again, Europe seems to stand at a crossroads; theories of European integration provide a ground for understanding, interpreting, and theoretically guiding us through this delicate situation. In addition, the crisis shows that the old dog of European integration theory is alive and well.

We are immensely thankful to the people who provided useful guidance during the process of writing this book. First, we would like to thank our publisher Steven Kennedy, the editors of this series, Neill Nugent and William E. Paterson, and the excellent anonymous reviewers who provided an extraordinary amount of patience, expertise, and outright enthusiasm. In addition, we would like to thank our students in Konstanz, Mannheim, Munich and Zurich on whom we 'tested' large parts of previous versions of this book. In addition, numerous colleagues provided valuable support and comments. In particular, we would like to thank Thomas Winzen, Jan Biesenbender, and the research group on differentiated integration at ETH Zurich and the University of Konstanz.

DIRK LEUFFEN
BERTHOLD RITTBERGER
FRANK SCHIMMELFENNIG

List of Abbreviations

AFSJ	Area of Freedom, Security, and Justice
CAP	Common Agricultural Policy
CEEC	Central and Eastern European country
CFSP	Common Foreign and Security Policy
EC	European Community
ECB	European Central Bank
ECJ	European Court of Justice
ECSC	European Coal and Steel Community
ECU	European Currency Unit
EEA	European Economic Area
EEAS	European External Action Service
EEC	European Economic Community
EFSF	European Financial Stability Facility
EFTA	European Free Trade Association
EMA	European Monetary Agreement
EMS	European Monetary System
EMU	Economic and Monetary Union
EP	European Parliament
EPC	European Political Cooperation
EPU	European Payment Union
ERM	Exchange Rate Mechanism
ESDP	European Security and Defence Policy
ESCB	European System of Central Banks
ESM	European Stability Mechanism
EU	European Union
EUMC	European Union Military Committee
EUMS	European Union Military Staff
GDP	Gross Domestic Product
HG	Headline Goals
HHG	Helsinki Headline Goals
IGC	Intergovernmental Conference
IMF	International Monetary Fund
IO	International Organization
IR	International Relations
JHA	Justice and Home Affairs
LI	Liberal Intergovernmentalism
MEP	Member of the European Parliament
NATO	North Atlantic Treaty Organization
OECD	Organisation for Economic Co-operation and Development

OEEC   Organization for European Economic Cooperation
OLP   Ordinary Legislative Procedure
PSC   Political and Security Committee
RI   Realist Intergovernmentalism
SEA   Single European Act
SGP   Stability and Growth Pact
TEU   Treaty on European Union
TFEU   Treaty on the Functioning of the European Union
US   United States
USA   United States of America
WEU   Western European Union
WHO   World Health Organization
WTO   World Trade Organization

Country codes for Figure 1.3

A   Austria
B   Belgium
D   Germany
E   Spain
EST   Estonia
F   France
FIN   Finland
GR   Greece
I   Italy
L   Luxembourg
M   Malta
NL   Netherlands
P   Portugal
SLO   Slovenia
SK   Slovakia
CY   Cyprus
IRL   Ireland
BG   Bulgaria
RO   Romania
UK   United Kingdom
CZ   Czech Republic
DK   Denmark
HU   Hungary
LT   Lithuania
LV   Latvia
PL   Poland
S   Sweden
N   Norway

IS	Iceland
TR	Turkey
CH	Switzerland

Chapter 1

The European Union as a System of Differentiated Integration

Jacques Delors, a former president of the European Commission, once called the European Union a UPO – an Unidentified Political Object. Already in the early 1970s, Donald Puchala (1971) likened students of European integration to blind men each examining a different body part of an elephant and, predictably, coming to divergent conclusions about the object of their study. Indeed, since its beginnings, scholars have debated the 'nature of the beast' without reaching consensus.

We argue that conceiving the EU as a 'system of differentiated integration' is an indispensable key to better understand its nature. In this chapter, we will make the case for this notion in two steps. First, we explore the nature of the EU by contrasting it with the two traditional and most widespread types of polities in the contemporary international system: the state and the international organization. This serves to show that the EU fits neither type and that it is like an international organization in some respects but more akin to a state in others. Second, we argue that this traditional comparison obscures the differentiated nature of European integration. We need three dimensions to understand the EU adequately: the level of centralization, the functional scope, and the territorial extension. Because the EU's centralization and territorial shape vary across policies, the EU is a system of differentiated integration.

In the second part of the chapter, we measure and map differentiated integration. For each policy area of the EU, we measure the level of centralization (vertical integration) and the territorial extension (horizontal integration) over time. This allows us to capture both integration and differentiation for the EU system and for individual policies. We find that vertical integration increases over time. The data further show that vertical and horizontal integration are less conflicting than often claimed. 'Deepening' and 'widening' go largely hand in hand in the history of European integration. Yet, the analysis also reveals that integration has been accompanied by differentiation. The difference in the level of centralization across policies (vertical differentiation) is pronounced and has increased, rather than shrunk, over time. So has horizontal differentiation: following the 1980s, the territorial extension of EU integration has begun to vary increasingly across policies.

1

Between International Organization and State

The European Union (EU) defies the classic dichotomous categories of public law, which distinguish two basic types of contemporary polities: the modern state and the international organization. Figure 1.1 contrasts the characteristics typically associated with the two types. Whereas there are differences in degree and individual exceptions, most states and international organizations cluster at either end of the spectrum. Figure 1.1 also shows where the EU fits in the picture. The further a cross ('X') is located to the right, the more the EU resembles an international organization; the further it is located to the left, the more it is akin to a state. The location of the EU on this spectrum is tentative and illustrative, it does not pretend to represent any exact measurement.

Membership

States are composed of citizens who mostly acquire their citizenship or nationality by birth. It is rare for individuals to change their citizenship or to be a citizen of more than one country. By contrast, the members of international organizations are states. The individual is not a subject of classic international law. Moreover, states become members of inter-

Figure 1.1   *The EU: between state and international organization*

	STATE	EU	IO
Membership			
Members	Citizens	—————X——	States
Acquisition	By birth	—————X—	Contractual
Delimitation			
Borders	Territorial, physical	—X————————	Functional, institutional
Issue scope	General	—X————————	Specialized
Authority			
Ordering principle	Hierarchy	————X———	Anarchy
Sovereignty	State sovereignty	——————X——	Sovereignty of MS
Legal order	Hard, highly legalized	—X————————	Soft, weakly legalized
Decision-making rule	Majoritarian	————X———	Non-majoritarian
Separation of powers	Yes	———X————	No, only executives
Governance capacity			
Coercive	Centralized	——————X——	Decentralized
Administrative	Centralized	—————X———	Decentralized
Fiscal	Taxation, large budget	——————X—	State contributions
Welfare provision	Interventionist, redistributive	—————X———	Regulatory
Legitimacy			
Cultural integration	National integration	—————X———	Multinationalism
Basis of support	Identity	—————X——	Efficiency

national organizations on a voluntary, contractual basis – usually by an international treaty. States are free to leave an international organization (although this is rather rare) and usually belong to many international organizations.

The EU's membership regime is clearly that of an international organization. Only states can become members. Accession is voluntary. It results from an accession treaty that needs to be accepted and ratified by all member states and the candidate state. The member states are also free, in principle, to leave the EU, even though this has not happened so far. In the most recent of the EU's treaty revisions, the Treaty of Lisbon, an exit procedure was formally introduced for the first time (Article 50). In contrast to other international organizations, however, the EU has citizens, too. Among other things, the EU accords them the right of free movement and residence throughout the EU, and the right to vote and stand in local and European elections in any member state. Yet, EU citizenship is derivative of and subordinated to national citizenship. Individuals acquire EU citizenship as an automatic consequence of citizenship in any of its member states, and the Treaty stipulates that EU citizenship shall supplement rather than replace national citizenship.

Delimitation

The system of states is a territorially ordered system. The borders between states are physical, geographical lines. State territories are also generally exclusive and exhaustive. It is rare for (land) territories to be governed by two or more states at the same time, or by no state at all. By the same token, states are functionally integrated. They possess the authority to deal with all areas of public policy on their territory: external and internal security, economy and welfare, individual rights and freedoms. By contrast, international organizations are typically functionally delimited. Their authority is task-specific: the North Atlantic Treaty Organization (NATO) is a security organization, the World Trade Organization (WTO) covers trade, the World Health Organization (WHO) deals with public health issues, and the Council of Europe focuses mainly on the rule of law and human rights protection. Obviously, the borders between these organizations are institutional rather than physical, and their competences are partially overlapping. For instance, both NATO and the United Nations Security Council may be involved in the same security issue either in cooperation or in competition, and both the WTO and World Intellectual Property Organization regulate intellectual property rights issues. Whereas states tend to integrate all task-specific competences on a single territory, (global) international organizations strive to regulate one specific issue for all territories.

In this respect, the EU is more like a state than an international organization. The EU has a clearly demarcated (and fairly contiguous) territory, as well as a physical border. People enter the EU much as they would enter the United States of America – and not as they would 'enter' the WTO or NATO. European integration has thoroughly transformed borders in Europe. Borders between two member states have largely lost their traditional functions as barriers to the free movement of persons and goods. In many places, they look more like borders between administrative districts within a state, rather than traditional borders between states. By contrast, the borders between member states and non-member states have become EU borders at which the EU's border regime is applied. Moreover, the EU covers all policy fields. Having started as an economic organization, it has expanded into all areas of public policy including foreign policy, internal and external security, and the protection of civil and social rights. Although its competences vary from issue-area to issue-area, there is hardly a field of policy-making that is not shaped in some way by the EU.

Authority

The modern state is sovereign – regardless of whether sovereignty ultimately rests with the people or an autocratic class or dictator. Its relationship to its citizen-members is hierarchical. The state alone has the authority to make and enforce laws that are binding for all people living on its territory. International organizations do not have these attributes of sovereignty. Their powers derive from the consent of the member states that do not give up their individual sovereignty upon founding or joining an international organization. The relationship between the international organization and its member states (as well as among the member states) is anarchical. Rather than being subordinated to an international organization, the member states coordinate their policies within its institutional framework. Decision-making is typically based on intergovernmental consensus. The member state executives that participate in international policy-making are not checked and balanced by parliamentary (citizen) representations, or by independent judiciaries at the international level. Adherence to the rules of an international regime is voluntary, and international law is typically soft law. Many rules are not legally binding and, even if they are, their interpretation and the settlement of disputes are subject to negotiations between the member states. Third-party adjudication is rare – and voluntary, where it exists.

To qualify as sovereign, the EU would have to be able to decide its constitutional order autonomously. Yet, its basic principles and rules remain treaty-based, and the member states remain the 'masters of the treaties'. Any change in the EU's 'constitution' needs to be negotiated among the member governments, agreed by unanimity, and ratified in each member state. This is typical for international organizations. At the same time, however, the member states have transferred some sovereign rights permanently to the EU, most notably in external trade and monetary policy. This is rare for an international organization.

Short of sovereignty, however, the EU's institutions resemble those of a state. First and foremost, its legal system is highly integrated. The EU produces law-like legal acts that take direct effect in the member states and are superior to competing domestic law. Cases of non-compliance and legal disputes are ultimately settled by an independent court, the European Court of Justice (ECJ), which makes binding decisions and is entitled to fine the member states, if need be. National courts refer cases involving European law to the ECJ for binding preliminary rulings. Second, the separation of powers is more similar to (liberal-democratic) states than to international organizations. The EU not only has an independent judiciary, but also a directly elected European Parliament (EP). Nevertheless, executives play an important role in legislation and jurisdiction as well. The most powerful chamber of the legislature, the Council, is composed of nation-state governments, and the European Commission is not only the EU's executive, but also formally initiates all legislation and monitors member state compliance. Third, decision-making in the EU is mainly majoritarian. Around 75 per cent of all EU laws result from the 'ordinary legislative procedure', which combines majority voting in the Council and the EP and covers virtually all areas of EU policy-making. However, EU decisions generally require large ('qualified') majorities, and the Council normally takes decisions by consensus in practice. In sum, the EU has arguably travelled half way from anarchy to hierarchy. Whereas rule-making and adjudication are clearly hierarchical, ultimately, the EU is not sovereign and cannot order the use of force against non-compliant member states. EU authority is characterized by hierarchy in the shadow of anarchy.

Governance capacity

International organizations have weak policy-making capacity. Whereas in states, including most federal states, the centre normally has the strongest administration and receives the biggest share of state revenues, the bureaucracies of international organizations are typically small, weak, and without independent income, let alone the power of taxation. Whereas the modern welfare state can use its powers to intervene in the economy and engage in redistribution, international organizations typically focus on regulatory policies: they make rules that coordinate and constrain the actions of states, rather than intervening directly in market or social relations. And whereas the state has the legitimate monopoly of the use of force, international organizations do not have the means physically to coerce their members into compliance with their rules.

The advanced legal integration of the EU stands in marked contrast to its limited governance capacity. First, it is not matched by any coercive powers. The use of force remains firmly with the member states; there is neither an EU police force nor an EU army. Second, the administrative capacity of the EU is strong for an international organization but weak by comparison with the states of Europe. The European Commission has approximately 38,000 staff, roughly the same number as the federal administration of Switzerland, a highly decentralized European country. But whereas the Swiss federal administration serves a population of 7.7 million, the European Commission deals with half a billion. It is therefore not surprising that the EU relies strongly on the administrations of its member states to implement EU legal acts. Third, the EU has weak fiscal capacity. It cannot directly tax the EU citizens, it is not allowed to run deficits, and its expenses are limited to little more than 1 per cent of the EU's GDP. This contrasts starkly with the public expenditure quota of more than 45 per cent of GDP that the average member state spends. Given its limited budget, it is clear that the EU cannot engage in the same kind of interventionist, redistributive economic and welfare policies for which the member states use many of their revenues. In line with typical international organization activity, its policy-making activities are predominantly regulatory. It is in the area of economic regulatory policy that the EU has its most impressive powers: market integration, monetary policy, and competition policy.

Legitimacy

The modern state is, or aspires to be, a nation-state. With the help of institutions such as schools and the media, it promotes the idea that its citizens form a distinct community (a 'nation') that shares a common and distinctive history and destiny, language, culture, and/or religion. Ideally, the state rests on a common identity of its citizens, who regard and support it as the political form of their community. By contrast, international organizations do not have strong identity and cultural underpinnings. They are composed of states that represent multiple national communities with diverse cultures and do not establish direct relations of political loyalty with the citizens of these states. Their legitimacy therefore depends predominantly on efficiency: the production of benefits that the nation-state could not provide autonomously.

The EU's sources of support are more typical for an international organization. European identity is weak. According to *Eurobarometer* surveys, less than 10 per cent of the respondents identify themselves primarily as Europeans. This pattern of national identification has proved extraordinarily stable in the past decades – and is likely to remain so, given that crucial resources and institutions of nation-building remain bound to the nation-state: mass media, education, and language. On the other hand, the EU's identity basis is stronger than that of most international organizations. It possesses a European regional and cultural identity, and the fact that its member states are exclusively liberal democracies creates a community of political values and norms. Hence, whereas the EU cannot rely on a 'thick' national identity as a diffuse source of loyalty, it benefits at least from a 'thin' civic identity based on abstract transnational values.

In sum, William Wallace's (1983) characterization of the European Community as 'less than a federation – more than a regime' certainly still holds at the time of writing. But it amounts to a purely negative definition: it tells us what the EU is *not*. In addition, the analysis has also shown that the EU does not end up uniformly on either the international organization or the state side of the spectrum. It is not simply a strong international organization or a weak state, but is similar to a state in some respects and an international organization in others. Whereas its constitutional foundations (state membership and sovereignty) and its social legitimacy (weak citizenship and identity) are typical for an international organization, the EU's territoriality, issue-scope, and policy-making process (separation of powers, majority voting, and law enforcement) are similar to those of a state. Another remarkable feature is the coexistence between strong legal integration and regulatory policy-making, on the one hand, and weak (administrative, coercive, and fiscal) governance capacity and redistributive policy-making, on the other (Bartolini 2005).

Whether and why the EU will remain more like an international organization or become more like a state is also the traditional core question and debate of integration theories. Supranationalism claims that the momentum created by initial, small steps of integration may lead to an expansion of the Community's tasks, competences, and capacities, and finally to a shift in citizens' identity and loyalty away from the nation-state and toward the new centre. Intergovernmentalist theory, by contrast, argues that member state governments will remain in control of European integration and guard their ultimate sovereignty. In addition, the weakness in capacity and identity will remain a structural obstacle blocking the EU's trajectory toward state-building.

Differentiated Integration

So far, we have looked at the EU as a whole and compared it with the typical state and the typical international organization. We have seen that the EU cannot be unequivocally subsumed under either type. This comparison, however, obscures further complexity in European integration: the variation among areas of EU policy and among European territories. Whereas it is true that the EU now deals with virtually all fields of policy, the nature and degree of integration in each area of EU policy differs significantly. And whereas the EU has a demarcated and rather contiguous territory with a physical EU border, there is variation in integration among, and even beyond, its member state territories.

In order to better grasp this differentiation, let us think about European integration as a multi-dimensional process. To begin, we propose an understanding of polities more generally as three-dimensional configurations of authority.

- The *level of centralization* is the first dimension. It is on this dimension that the variation between the state, with its hierarchical authority and centralized governance capacity, and the anarchical and decentralized international organization is located. In abstract terms, polities where all authority is vested in one place (the centre) have the maximum level of centralization, whereas competences dispersed equally across a multitude of organizations indicate a low level of centralization.
- The *functional scope* of a polity is the second dimension. It varies between authority over a single issue (minimum functional scope) and authority over the entire range of policies (maximum functional scope). The state, with its all-encompassing policy competence, and the functionally specialized international organization differ strongly on this dimension as well.
- The third dimension is *territorial extension*. The authority of a polity can be limited to a single political territory (minimum territorial extension) or encompass the entire world (maximum territorial extension). Here again, the state and the (global) international organization (with universal membership) are potentially at the opposite extremes of the dimension.

Figure 1.2 illustrates different types of polities resulting from variation in the configuration of authority. Territorial extension is shown on the horizontal x-axis, the level of centralization on the vertical y-axis, and functional scope on the z-axis. The classical configurations are the (unitary) state and the international organization. In the unitary state, all policies are made at the same (central) level and cover the same (limited) territory. In addition, the state traditionally has maximum functional scope: it covers all policies. By contrast, international organizations are typically decentralized and task-specific, but cover more territories.

The lower three shapes represent more complex configurations of authority. Here, we need to distinguish between policies (A, B, and C

Figure 1.2   *A three-dimensional representation of polity-types*

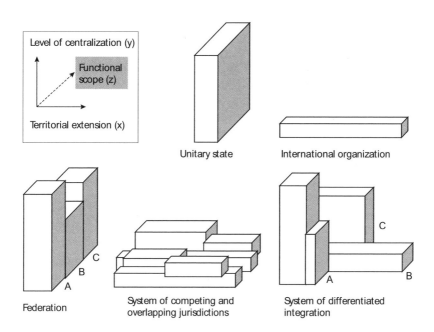

Unitary state

International organization

Federation

System of competing and overlapping jurisdictions

System of differentiated integration

in the figure) because the level of centralization and/or the territorial extension varies across the functional scope of the polity. The *federation* is the most familiar complex configuration. It differs from the unitary state in that at least one policy is governed at the subnational (regional) level (here: sector B) or co-governed by subnational and national authorities (sector C), whereas other policies are fully centralized (A). Federal states typically have areas of exclusive federal competences, areas of mixed or shared competences, and areas of exclusive subnational competences. Defence is normally 'a federal competence whereas education is often a subnational one. The territorial extension and functional scope of the federation, however, is of the same order as that of unitary states. It deals with all policies on a closed territory. This is also the basic model of federalist conceptions of European integration, which assume a set of member states that form a union and allocate the authority over policy sectors to themselves, to the union or, as mixed competences, to both states and the union.

The second and much 'messier' configuration of authority is the *system of competing and overlapping jurisdictions*. We take this concept from Bruno Frey and Reiner Eichenberger, who developed the idea of functional overlapping competing jurisdictions (FOCJ) as 'the new democratic federalism for Europe' (Frey and Eichenberger 1996). In this configuration, each jurisdiction focuses on a single policy or function, each policy is provided or offered by several jurisdictions that compete with each other, and the membership of the jurisdiction varies in size. In the international domain, the coexistence of hundreds of international organizations, most of them highly specialized, some working in the same policy fields, with variable and overlapping membership and different regional focus, is an (imperfect) approximation of this type. In the discussion about the form and future of European integration, Philippe Schmitter (1996: 136) called this type of polity '*condominio*' and describes it as 'many Europes', in which 'there would be multiple regional institutions acting autonomously to solve common problems and produce different public goods'. Liesbet Hooghe and Gary Marks (2003) label this configuration of task-specific jurisdictions with intersecting memberships 'type-2 multi-level governance' and contrast it with 'type-1 multi-level governance', which is exemplified by the federation.

In our view, however, the EU is a hybrid type. In contrast to federal type-1 governance, the territorial extension of the EU varies by policy or task. The EU has different borders for the eurozone, 'Schengenland', or the single market. On the other hand, categorizing the EU as functional type-2 governance ignores the extent to which the EU has developed an institutional centre and a membership core that reaches across the EU's policies with their variation in centralization and territorial extension. This institutional core is constituted, first, by the Treaty on European Union. It covers all policies of the EU and – in the Lisbon Treaty – defines the EU as a single legal entity. The institutional core is furthermore constituted by the EU's institutions. The European Council, composed of the member states' heads of state and government, gives general directions for all policies of the EU and for treaty revisions. The Council, the Commission, the EP and the ECJ are also present (albeit to differing degrees and with varying competences) across the board of EU activities and across the territories into which the EU's external relations reach. Finally, there is a core group of member states, mostly the original six member states, that takes part in all the policies of the EU at the highest level of centralization. The EU is not 'many Europes' with task-specific jurisdictions each having their own organization. It is one Europe with *an organizational and member state core but with a level of centralization and territorial extension that vary by function*. This is how we define a 'system of differentiated integration'.

A representation of a system of differentiated integration is depicted in the lower right corner of Figure 1.2. It has the same functional scope as the state and the different levels of centralization for the policy areas A–C that characterize a federal state. In addition to variation in the level of centralization, however, the territorial extension varies by policy as well. In this example, the highly centralized sector A is limited to a few territories, resembling a state's authority pattern, whereas sector B is similar to an international organization. Sector C combines medium–high centralization with extended territorial coverage. Policy sector A is more complex than sectors B and C, since there are a few territories that accept a high level of centralization in this sector but one does not. An example would be Denmark and EMU – it participates in the Exchange Rate Mechanism but has not adopted the euro.

Measuring Differentiated Integration

If the EU is best understood as a system of differentiated integration, its development needs to be measured and mapped accordingly. Scholars of European integration have traditionally focused on the level of centralization and the functional scope. Leon Lindberg and Stuart Scheingold (1970) were the first to undertake a systematic categorization and mapping of the scope of the EU's system of decision-making. Their work focused on the *extension* of policy areas where the EU can claim authoritative decision-making power, and the *intensity* of EU decision-making. This enabled them to capture the relative importance of EU-level decision-making compared with domestic processes in a given policy area (Lindberg and Scheingold 1970: 66–70). Many scholars have built on and updated Lindberg and Scheingold's pioneering work (see, among others, Börzel 2005; Donahue and Pollack 2001; Hix 2005; Schmitter 1996). Whereas their assessments of the progress and extent of European integration capture the level of centralization and the functional scope, they do not take into account the horizontal dimension of territorial extension, which is crucial for a system of differentiated integration.

Our focus in this book is on primary law. In the EU, primary law is constituted by the treaties (including accession treaties). Treaty changes are negotiated in intergovernmental conferences (IGCs), and they need to

Box 1.1   *Timeline: major steps of integration*

1952	ECSC	1993	Maastricht Treaty
1954	EDC (not ratified)	1995	EU 15
1958	EEC & Euratom	1999	Amsterdam Treaty
1967	Merger Treaty	2003	Treaty of Nice
1973	EC 9	2004	EU 25
1981	EC 10	2007	EU 27
1986	EC 12	2009	Treaty of Lisbon
1987	Single European Act		

be signed and ratified by all member states. Similarly, the accession of new states to the EU requires the approval of all member states. Box 1.1 displays the major milestones of European integration understood as changes in the EU's primary law. The creation of the European Coal and Steel Community (ECSC), the ensuing failure to establish the European Defence Community, and the establishment of the European Economic Community (EEC) and Euratom, commonly referred to as the Treaties of Rome, in the 1950s, reflect the major steps of the first decade of European integration. The Single European Act (SEA) marks the first major revision of the EEC Treaty and was rapidly followed by the Maastricht, Amsterdam, Nice and Lisbon Treaties. Treaty changes in the EU generally entail advances of integration. For instance, the SEA introduced a new legislative procedure known as the 'cooperation procedure', the treaties signed in Maastricht and Amsterdam launched and amended yet another legislative procedure, the 'co-decision procedure'. Since these reforms have upgraded the EP to a central institution of the EU, they advance vertical integration. By establishing the second and third pillars (Common Foreign and Security Policy, and Justice and Home Affairs, respectively) the Maastricht Treaty has come to include new policy areas in the treaty framework. Before Maastricht, the member states possessed virtually exclusive competence in these areas. Box 1.1 also lists the different enlargement rounds, starting with the accession of Denmark, Ireland, and the United Kingdom in 1973, followed by Southern enlargement in the 1980s, the second Northern enlargement of 1995 and, finally, the two rounds of Eastern enlargement in 2004 and 2007.

We explore how integration and differentiation have developed in the history of the EU along these milestones of formal integration. In line with our stylized representation of a 'system of differentiated integration' in Figure 1.2, we start from the assumption that the EU potentially covers the entire range of policies, but that each policy varies with regard to the level of centralization and the territorial extension. We call integration along the y-axis 'vertical integration'. It refers to the centralization of EU decision-making in different policy areas. Integration along the x-axis is 'horizontal integration'. It captures the territorial extension of the EU's jurisdiction in each policy area. Horizontal integration thus gives us a more fine-grained understanding of territorial integration than the broader concept of enlargement, which is usually associated with the uniform extension of the EU's jurisdiction to new EU member states. In sum, as the combination of levels of vertical and horizontal integration is likely to differ across policy areas, we will see both vertical and horizontal differentiation in the EU.

For vertical integration, we build on Tanja Börzel's (2005) measurement of the 'depth' of integration. She operationalizes 'depth' by coding the 'procedures according to which policy decisions are taken focusing on the involvement of supranational bodies and Council

Table 1.1   *Measurement of vertical and horizontal integration of European states*

		Vertical integration		Horizontal integration (%)
	Coordination	*Delegation*	*Pooling*	
0	No EU-level policy coordination	None	None	0
1	Intergovernmental coordination	None	None	20
2	Intergovernmental cooperation	Minimal	None	40
3	Joint decision-making I	'Community method'	Limited pooling	60
4	Joint decision-making II	'Community method'	Pooling	80
5	Supranational centralization	Full delegation to supranational bodies		100

Source: Börzel (2005: p. 221) for vertical compilation.

voting rules'. Depth thus refers to the level of centralization and, hence, the degree to which member states pool their sovereignty (e.g. deciding on policy by qualified majority or unanimity), or delegate decision-making authority to supranational institutions, such as the European Commission, the EP and the ECJ. Börzel (2005: 211) distinguishes six categories of depth that vary in terms of decision-making rules and the involvement of supranational organizations.

Category 0 displayed in Table 1.1 refers to the absence of any policy coordination at the EU level. In this instance, a policy is exclusively decided at the level of the state. Examples are taxation (since the EU has no independent right to tax), or certain aspects of research and education policy (where national or regional governments zealously guard their prerogatives, for instance, to fund universities, define university entrance requirements, or define school curricula).

Category 1 refers to situations in which there is some form of 'intergovernmental coordination', which implies that the member states acting through the Council decide by unanimity while supranational actors, such as the Commission, the EP and ECJ, have neither agenda-setting, nor legislative decision-making or adjudicatory powers. For instance, any form of policy-making in the field of social security and social protection would have to meet unanimous agreement of the EU member states. Until the Treaty of Maastricht, low levels of policy coordination also characterized most policy decisions in the area of external and internal security: the authority to take decisions rested exclusively with the member states deciding by unanimity on whether or not to make use of common European prerogatives.

Category 2 'intergovernmental cooperation' differs from 'intergovernmental coordination' in that it allows for limited supranational involvement. While the prevalent decision-making rule in the Council remains unanimity, the Commission, EP, and ECJ exercise very circumscribed decision-making power, e.g. the Commission may share the right of initiative with the Council, and the EP may be consulted in legislative decision-making process. Prior to the entry into force of the SEA, this form of intergovernmental cooperation was the predominant decision-making mode. Based on the so-called 'Luxembourg Compromise', an informal decision rule adopted to end the 'empty chair crisis' which paralyzed legislative decision-making in the Community between July 1965 and January 1966, every piece of legislation could be vetoed by a single member state if 'vital' national interests were deemed to be at stake. At present, it is in the area of security and defence policy where member states continue to accord only very limited influence to the Commission and the EP, even though a wide set of policy competencies are shared between EU and national levels.

Börzel's categories 3 and 4 capture what is commonly referred to as the 'community method' of decision-making. Following a Commission proposal, both the Council and EP bargain over the final legislative outcome, while the ECJ exercises judicial review over legislation. Börzel discriminates between two forms of the community method: 'joint decision-making I' and 'joint decision-making II'. The main difference between the two is that, according to the former, the Council decides by unanimity while, in the latter case, the Council voting rule is qualified majority voting. In both cases, the EP can exercise legislative influence by proposing amendments to legislative proposals, which the Council has to take into account. All policies where the co-decision procedure (with qualified majority voting in the Council) applies fall into the 'joint decision-making II' category. As a result of the entry into force of the Lisbon Treaty, this mode of decision-making is the dominant legislative procedure in the EU, hence its name 'ordinary legislative procedure' (OLP). By its reach, the OLP extends to the policy areas traditionally covered by the co-decision procedure, such as environmental policy, consumer protection, and legislation relating to the realization of the internal market, to include most issues in the field of justice and home affairs, ranging from border protection, asylum, and immigration policies to judicial cooperation in criminal matters. Moreover, the OLP applies to the area of external trade and the conclusion of international agreements, as well as to the EU's big spending policies (agriculture, structural, cohesion and research policies).

Category 5 of vertical integration refers to a fully centralized decision-making mode labelled 'supranational centralization'. This mode of decision-making precludes legislative involvement of member state governments and gives precedence to unilateral action on behalf of 'non-majoritarian institutions', such as the Commission, the European Central Bank (ECB) or the ECJ, which operate at arm's length from governments. The paradigmatic – and, at the time of writing, only – case in this category is monetary policy and the dominant role attributed to the ECB in this context. Table 1.1 lists the six categories of vertical integration. While 'delegation' refers to the involvement of supranational actors in decision-making, 'pooling' captures the application of super-majoritarian voting rules in the Council.

Turning to horizontal integration, we find that the territorial dimension of European integration is increasingly becoming a charged and salient issue in the debate about the future of the European integration project. Eastern enlargement has received great scholarly attention and, since there is a continuous demand for membership (with Turkey being the most prominent candidate for accession) the issue is likely to remain important. The tricky question concerning horizontal integration is that EU member states do not equally partake in all EU activities. Various countries 'opt out' from specific policies, other countries (and even some non-member states) 'opt in'. All this renders the boundaries of the EU fuzzy, and such fuzzy boundaries need to be taken into account when discussing differentiated integration.

How do we go about measuring horizontal integration? To assess different levels of horizontal integration, individual policy areas need to be scrutinized with a view to determining how many states formally subject themselves to the rules governing a particular policy area at a particular point in time. Note that horizontal integration not only includes states formally members of the EU, but is also open to the possibility that non-EU member states adopt EU rules. Therefore, we first count the number of countries participating in different EU-related policy 'regimes' no matter whether they are EU member states or not. In order to align the measurement of horizontal integration with that of vertical integration, we propose a scale ranging from 0 to 5. For every policy sector, we divide the number of participating states by the total number of European states at the time and multiply the result by 5. At the extremes of this scale, no European state participates (0) or all European states participate (5). Put differently, we translate the percentages of participating states into our scale ranging from 0 to 5.

Table 1.2 shows the countries we include as 'European states', when they were included in the dataset, and when they acceded to the EU (if they did). Because the political borders of Europe in the East are ill-defined or disputed, we only include those countries in the Eastern half of the continent that have an agreed accession perspective, i.e. we exclude Belarus, Moldova, Russia, and Ukraine from the dataset.

Table 1.2   *European states and their accession dates*

Country	European state	Accession	Country	European state	Accession
Belgium	1950	1952	Lithuania	1991	2004
France	1950	1952	Malta	1964	2004
Germany (FR)	1950	1952	Poland	1950	2004
Italy	1950	1952	Slovakia	1993	2004
Luxembourg	1950	1952	Slovenia	1991	2004
Netherlands	1950	1952	Bulgaria	1950	2007
Denmark	1950	1973	Romania	1950	2007
Ireland	1950	1973	Croatia	1991	(2013)
United Kingdom	1950	1973	Iceland	1950	In negotiations
Greece	1950	1981	Turkey	1950	In negotiations
Portugal	1950	1986	Macedonia	1992	Candidate
Spain	1950	1986	(FYROM)		
Austria	1950	1995	Montenegro	2006	Candidate
Finland	1950	1995	Albania	1950	
Sweden	1950	1995	Serbia (Yugoslavia)	1950	Candidate
Cyprus	1960	2004	Bosnia-Herzegovina	1992	
Czech Republic	1993	2004	Norway	1950	
Estonia	1991	2004	Switzerland	1950	
Hungary	1950	2004	(Czechoslovakia)	1950–1992	
Latvia	1991	2004	(Germany (DR))	1950–1990	

Kosovo is also disregarded because it is not recognized by all EU member states. Moreover, we do not take the European micro-states into consideration. As a result, we currently count 37 European states (starting from 27 states in 1950).

We further distinguish four qualitatively different constellations of horizontal integration. During the first four decades of European integration, it was an almost unquestioned assumption that all EU rules should uniformly apply to all EU member states (see [a] in Table 1.3). The prospect of differentiation was equated with fragmentation and considered to pose a threat to the integration project. In the eyes of ardent Euro-Federalists, differentiation and European unification were incompatible with the postulate of achieving an 'ever closer union'. Nonetheless, the idea of horizontal differentiation was floated as early as in the mid-1970s by politicians such as Willy Brandt and Leo Tindemans in an era often characterized by stagnation of the integration process. And even though there are some early examples of horizontal differentiation, such as the Schengen Agreement (initially not part of EU law), horizontal differentiation was, until the 1990s, by and large non-existent. Since then, commentators and scholars have begun to claim that the 'nature of European integration is undergoing a piecemeal revolution' with the 'process of differentiated integration ...

Table 1.3   *Types of horizontal differentiation*

[a]	No horizontal differentiation (uniform application)
[b]	External differentiation
[c]	Internal differentiation
[d]	Internal and external differentiation

replacing the erstwhile process of unified integration' (de Neve 2007: 503; Stubb 1996, 2002).

If EU rules apply uniformly to all member states but outsiders also adopt these rules, we observe an externalization of the *acquis communautaire* (*external* differentiation). Take the free movement of goods and services as an example. From the entry into force of the Treaty establishing the EEC in 1958, all six founding member states were subject to the rules governing this particular policy area. Following different enlargement rounds, all 27 members of the EU are also subject to the provisions governing the free movement of goods and services. Hence, we would conclude that there is no horizontal differentiation since the Treaty rules apply to all member states uniformly. However, the non-EU member states of the European Economic Area (EEA) – Iceland, Liechtenstein, and Norway – have also enacted EU legislation on the free movement of goods and services. The EU's internal market is thus effectively extended to the whole of the EEA. Switzerland, which is not a member of the EEA, has negotiated bilateral agreements with the EU, one of which covers trade in industrial goods. One could thus argue that the provisions governing the free movement of goods and services extend beyond the circle of EU member states, to cover 30 states (or even 31, if we also account for Switzerland).

A second form of horizontal differentiation is *internal* differentiation. EU rules cease to apply uniformly to all EU member states, since individual member states decide to 'opt-out' from membership in a particular policy area. The Treaty of Maastricht marks a milestone in this regard as it paved a legal avenue for this form of differentiation. The euro is often considered a paradigmatic case. Two member states, Denmark and the UK, negotiated concessions so that they could 'opt out' from taking part in the third stage of EMU, the single currency. Presently, only 17 out of 27 EU member states have renounced their domestic currencies in favour of the single currency.

The Treaty of Maastricht equally marked a watershed for foreign policy cooperation by deepening vertical integration in the area and embedding CSFP in the EU Treaty as its 'second pillar'. At the same time, Denmark was granted an 'opt out' from defence-related matters. The trend that started in Maastricht continued in the Treaties of Amsterdam, Nice and Lisbon, which formally enshrined and extended the possibility for horizontal differentiation in matters of common security and defence policy: 'Enhanced Cooperation' allows subgroups of EU member states to march ahead on security and defence-related matters. The Lisbon Treaty continues to highlight the formal possibility to form subgroups of the 'willing'. Thus far, however, individual subgroups of member states have refrained from taking up this possibility, even though most commentators argue that 'the question of a differentiated integration approach to the CFSP [Common Foreign and Security Policy] has increasingly become one of when, rather than if' (De Neve 2007: 510).

Finally, *external* and *internal* differentiation can be combined. We have to conceive of such a situation as one where 'insiders' (one or more EU member states) decide to 'opt out' from a certain policy while 'outsiders' (one or more non-EU member states) 'opt in' by subjecting themselves to EU rules. A prominent example is the Schengen border regime. The Schengen Agreement was signed between France, Germany, and the Benelux countries in 1985 outside the EU legal framework and it was only formally incorporated into EU law with the Amsterdam Treaty. Schengen provides for the removal of border controls between the participating countries and the harmonization of visa, immigration, and asylum policies. During the following decades, many EU member states have joined the border regime (with the exception of Bulgaria, Cyprus, Ireland, Romania, and the UK), as well as four non-EU member states (Iceland, Liechtenstein, Norway, and Switzerland). At the time of writing, the Schengen zone, an area without internal border controls and with uniform external border policies, thus consists of 26 states. Monetary policy shows a similar pattern of external and internal differentiation. Two non-EU countries, Kosovo and Montenegro, have unilaterally adopted the euro, even though they are not part of the European System of Central Banks (ESCB). Similarly, the euro is the official currency in Andorra, Monaco, San Marino and the Vatican.

In Figure 1.3, we provide an overview of differentiated membership in the EU and major EU-based regimes in 2011. The core membership of European integration consists of 15 countries that participate in all regimes. Another 16 countries, members and non-members alike, participate selectively.

Mapping Differentiated Integration

Having set the conceptual stage, we will now provide an overview of vertical and horizontal integration, covering a broad range of public policies spanning six decades of European integration from 1950 to

Figure 1.3   *Differentiated membership in the EU*

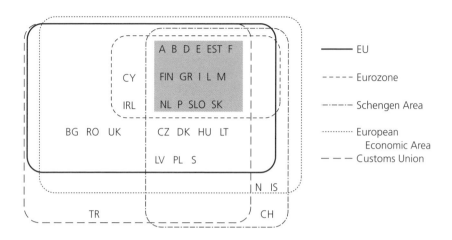

Note: Map represents selected policies at the end of 2011 and excludes micro-states. The abbreviations for the countries are in full on pages xv–xvi.

Source: Mapping design inspired by Kölliker (2001).

2010. We distinguish regulatory policies (which are aimed at market-making and market-correcting measures), economic and monetary policies, expenditure policies (which involve the distribution of financial resources), and the areas of internal and external security. Internal security-related policies cover police and security cooperation and civil matters; external security refers to cooperation in questions of security and defence. The scores for vertical integration are mostly adopted from Börzel's analysis (2005), updated where needed. For some policies, we provide our own coding. The values for horizontal integration are also based on our own calculations (see Table 1.3).

Some general trends can be discerned from these data. Table 1.4 displays the average values over all policy areas of vertical and horizontal integration from 1950 to 2010. It shows an unambiguous trend towards further integration on both dimensions of integration. Both dimensions start at zero in 1950. The average value of vertical integration across all our policy areas almost reaches the level of 4, i.e. joint decision-making II. The 'ordinary legislative procedure' thus deserves its name. Similarly, on average, almost 75 per cent of all European states participate in the EU's policies in 2010 (on our scale we reach a value of 3.7). The two processes more or less go 'hand in hand' at this aggregate level. The trajectory of vertical integration is characterized by a period of stagnation during the 1960s and 1970s. The 1980s witnessed the *relance européenne*, and we see a continuous trend towards deepening culminating, with the entry into force of the Lisbon

Table 1.4   *Vertical and horizontal integration across EU policies at the time of treaty changes*

	1958	1987	1993	1999	2003	2010
Foreign policies:						
Political external relations	0.0/0.0	1.0/2.1	1.5/1.5	2.0/1.9	2.0/1.9	2.5/3.5
Economic external relations	1.5/1.1	1.5/2.1	3.5/1.7	3.5/2.1	3.5/2.1	3.5/3.6
Interior policies:						
Criminal/domestic security	0.0/0.0	0.0/0.0	1.0/1.5	2.0/1.9	3.0/1.9	4.0/3.5
Civil	0.0/0.0	0.0/0.0	3.0/1.7	3.5/2.1	4.0/2.1	4.0/3.6
Economic and monetary union:						
Macroeconomic policy and employment	1.5/1.1	1.5/2.1	1.5/1.7	3.5/2.1	3.5/2.1	3.5/3.6
Monetary policy	1.0/1.1	1.0/1.4	4.0/1.1	5.0/1.5	5.0/1.7	5.0/2.2
Tax	1.5/1.1	1.5/2.1	1.5/1.7	1.5/2.1	1.5/2.1	1.5/3.6
Regulatory policies:						
Economic freedoms	2.0/1.1	4.0/2.1	4.5/1.7	4.5/2.5	4.5/2.5	4.5/4.1
Competition and industry	2.0/1.1	2.0/2.1	3.0/1.7	3.0/2.5	4.0/2.5	4.0/4.1
Environment/consumer protection	0.0/0.0	3.0/2.1	3.75/1.7	3.75/2.5	3.75/2.5	3.75/4.1
Occupational health and safety standards	0.0/0.0	4.0/2.1	4.0/1.7	4.5/2.5	4.5/2.5	4.5/4.1
Energy and transport	2.0/1.1	2.0/2.1	2.0/1.7	2.0/2.5	2.0/2.6	4.0/4.2
Labour	1.0/1.1	1.0/2.1	3.5/1.7	4.0/2.5	4.0/2.5	4.0/4.1
Expenditure policies:						
Culture	0.0/0.0	0.0/0.0	1.0/1.7	1.0/2.1	1.0/2.1	4.5/3.6
Welfare	0.0/0.0	0.0/0.0	3.0/1.7	4.0/2.1	4.0/2.1	4.0/3.6
Research and development	0.0/0.0	3.5/2.1	3.5/1.7	4.0/2.1	4.0/2.2	4.0/3.8
Agriculture	3.0/1.1	3.0/2.1	3.0/1.7	3.0/2.1	3.0/2.1	4.5/3.6
Territorial, economic and social cohesion	1.5/1.1	3.9/2.1	3.25/1.7	3.75/2.1	4.0/2.1	4.0/3.6

Notes: Values range from 0 to 5 according to categories in Table 1.1. The first value in each cell represents the level of vertical integration; the second, the level of horizontal integration. Following Börzel (2005), in this table a vertical integration of 3.5 captures a situation of unanimity and co-decision or majority voting and consultation of the European Parliament; 4.5 accounts for the usage of co-decision (OLP) in joint-decision-making II.

Source: Partly based on Börzel (2005: 222–3).

Figure 1.4   *Vertical and horizontal integration, all policies, 1950–2010*

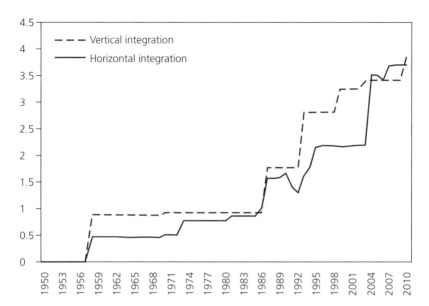

Treaty in 2010. We also find a steep increase in horizontal integration since the 1980s and, especially, in the 2000s. Note that the dent in horizontal integration in the early 1990s and other less striking drops in horizontal integration are artefacts due to the increase in the number of European states. The number of new states has increased sharply after the fall of the 'Iron Curtain'.

The aggregate data suggest that integration has grown over the past 60 years in a stop-start process. Phases of steep growth (in the 1950s and the late 1980s through the 1990s) have been followed by periods of relative stagnation (the 1960s and 1970s, as well as the 2000s until the Treaty of Lisbon). What is also noticeable is that vertical integration has not decreased throughout the history of European integration. Setting aside the fact that some countries moved in and out of the European currency arrangements during the 1970s and 1980s, states have also never withdrawn from policy integration once they decided to participate. Moreover, it is remarkable that the two dimensions of integration have largely moved in parallel, with horizontal integration taking the lead when vertical integration stagnated. The evidence thus seems to suggest that the widely debated dilemma between 'deepening' and 'widening', vertical and horizontal integration, does not exist. Apparently, the EU has not expanded geographically at the cost of further institutional integration, and competence transfer to 'Europe' has not deterred countries from joining. The picture of joint growth in vertical and horizontal integration, however, masks other important patterns of European integration: vertical and horizontal differentiation. Vertical differentiation is the variation in the level of centralization across policies. Horizontal differentiation is the variation in territorial extension across policies. Differentiation becomes visible when we move from aggregate data averaging across policy areas to disaggregated data for individual policies.

Figure 1.5 illustrates vertical integration for selected policy areas. Whereas we observe a deeper integration over time in all policy areas, it is also clear that there is marked variation in their level of centralization. The selected policies are representative for the more general trend of regulatory policy (economic freedoms, and occupational health and safety standards), foreign policy (external relations), internal policy (criminal/domestic security), and economic and monetary policy (monetary policy). The individual policies that we classified under expenditure policies vary substantially (cf. Table 1.4). While the EU's budget mainly provides financial assistance (to farmers, economically weaker regions, and funds for research and development (R&D) projects), decision-making authority (vertical integration) for the 'big' spending policies (health, social and welfare provisions) continues to be a national prerogative. The same holds for the right to tax, which also remains an exclusive right of national parliaments.

Figure 1.5   *Vertical differentiation across selected policies*

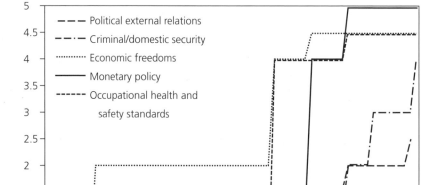

We find clear differences in the trajectories and levels of integration of the different policies depicted in Figure 1.5. Regulatory policy serves well to illustrate the general trend towards increased levels of vertical integration. When the European integration project was launched in the 1950s, the majority of policy areas still resided at the national level. Economic or 'market-making' regulation was the chief occupation of the EU in its first 30 years of existence. The EU held some (albeit very limited) competencies and decision-making prerogatives for those policies aimed at dismantling national barriers to the free movement of goods and services, and securing undistorted competition. In the context of the single market programme, the regulatory competencies were extended. Vertical integration in the area of social or 'market-correcting' regulation took off: 'Since national standards on environment, consumer protection, industrial health and security, or labour markets often work as non-tariff barriers to trade, the need for harmonization at the EU level became increasingly evident' (Börzel 2005: 221). At the time of writing, there is no area of economic and social regulation escaping EU-level involvement. It is in this context that scholars refer to the EU as a 'regulatory state' (Majone 1996).

Most other policy areas depicted in Figure 1.5 became subject to European level decision-making as a result of the SEA and after the entry into force of the Maastricht Treaty. The trajectory of monetary policy integration is particularly impressive. Beginning in the 1980s, this policy reaches the top level of vertical integration, supranational centralization, by the end of the 1990s. A noticeable difference or 'disparity' of integration can be seen in the case of internal and external security policies (see Börzel 2005: 225–6). Not only have security policies trailed behind regulatory policy-making and some of the expenditure policies, when vertical integration in these policies had finally increased in the 1990s, the level of vertical integration climbed noticeably higher for internal than for external security policies. The area of external security is dominated by 'intergovernmental cooperation' with strongly circumscribed involvement of the Commission (no ECJ adjudication and merely EP consultation), while vertical integration in internal security policies conforms to what has been labelled 'joint decision-making II'. Following the Lisbon Treaty, visa, asylum, and immigration policies, as well as issues relating to policing, judicial cooperation, and criminal prosecution, will be decided under the 'ordinary legislative procedure', which endows the Commission with the right of initiative, the Council and EP with co-equal legislative powers, and the ECJ with an adjudicating role. In fact, with the sole exception of foreign and security policies, the policies displayed in Figure 1.5 are solidly subject to the 'Community method' of decision-making after Lisbon.

Similarly, both horizontal integration and horizontal differentiation have also increased over time. From the 1970s onwards, we see a rising

Figure 1.6   *Horizontal differentiation across selected policies*

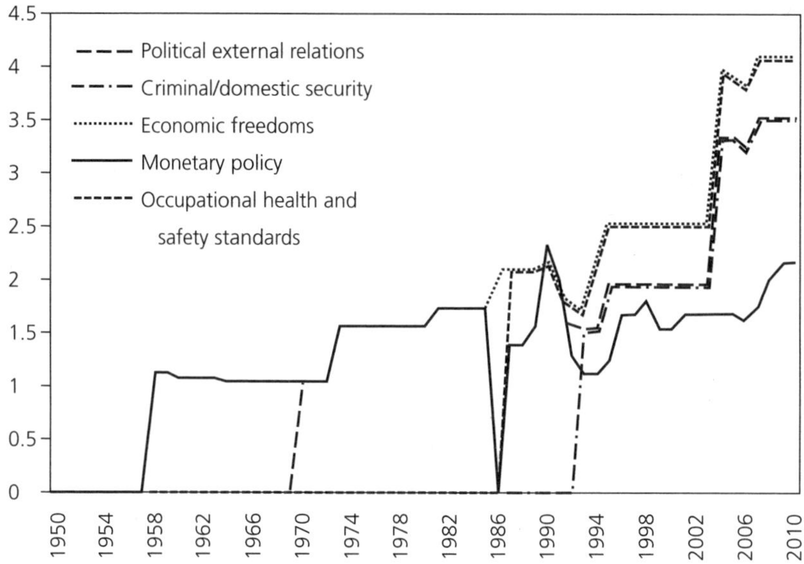

proportion of states participating in European integration over the different accession rounds (Figure 1.6). Eastern enlargement has led to a sharp rise in the number of member states. An exception is monetary policy, since the new member states were initially excluded from the eurozone. Others such as the UK, Sweden, or Denmark have chosen to stay out. Perturbations in the early 1990s – such as the 'Black Monday' of 1992 – have provoked abrupt changes in the number of states participating in the exchange rate mechanism. But the pattern for the other policies is more stable. Monetary policy is also the one policy in which the levels of vertical and horizontal integration clearly diverge. Whereas it is vertically the most integrated policy in our selection, it is at the same time the least integrated horizontally. All other policies are clearly more equal with regard to vertical and horizontal integration (see also Table 1.4), and contribute to the overall pattern of balanced deepening and widening.

Our data enable us to discern even more nuanced patterns of horizontal differentiation. Figure 1.7 shows the number of policy areas per decade that fall under the different categories of horizontal differentiation introduced above. In the first decades of European integration, uniformity was the rule and differentiation was ruled out. Horizontal differentiation only developed during the 1980s, and it has become more prominent and diverse since then. Less than half of the 18 policy areas still conform to the idea of uniform integration among all member states and member states only.

Figure 1.7   *Types of horizontal differentiation over time*

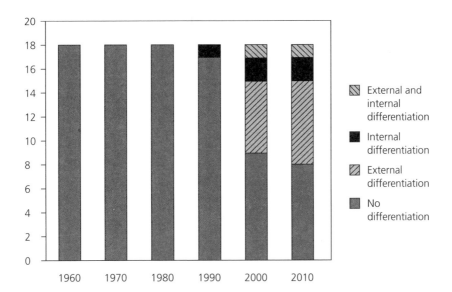

Starting with the area of regulatory policies, horizontal differentiation assumes a particular quality. While EU rules continue to apply uniformly across all EU member states, we can witness an increasing trend towards *external* differentiation. This means that EU rules apply uniformly to all EU member states. Yet, non-EU member states have, for example, adopted 'market-correcting' EU policies – such as environmental or health and safety standards – as a result of their participation in the single market. Since the 1990s, the 'regulatory state' has thus expanded beyond the borders of the EU. While our selected expenditure policies vary in their vertical integration, they display only very limited horizontal differentiation. The lack of internal horizontal differentiation appears unsurprising, given that all member states want to participate in the distribution of the financial 'spoils'. In transport and research policies, we can also witness EU 'outsiders' taking part in the EU money game.

In the area of monetary policy, horizontal differentiation takes on yet another quality: internal differentiation. For instance, several EU member states have decided to 'opt out' from accepting the euro as legal tender and, consequently, from abiding by the monetary policy decisions set by the ECB. The use of the single currency displays an even higher degree of differentiation. In addition to internal differentiation, non-EU member states have adopted the euro as legal tender in their respective territories: Andorra, Kosovo, Monaco, Montenegro, San Marino, and the Vatican. Horizontal differentiation displays similar characteristics in the area of internal security, where the uniform application of EU rules is challenged by internal as well external differentiation. This applies to areas such as border controls, immigration, and asylum, as well as policing. In the area of external security, horizontal differentiation is weak even though treaty provisions allow for 'enhanced cooperation'.

Differentiation: A Persistent Feature of European Integration

The preceding analysis has demonstrated that vertical integration (Figure 1.5) displays not only significant variation across policies, but also an increase in the range of levels of vertical integration over time. In the first decades of European integration, even the most integrated policies were only at the level of intergovernmental cooperation and only two levels above national policies. Following the SEA and in the 1990s, the difference between national policies and some of the integrated policies covers the full range of levels of vertical integration from intergovernmental coordination to supranational centralization. In addition, we observe increasing variation across policy areas. Whereas in the 1970s the difference between economic and external policies was only one point on our five-point scale, it amounted to three points in the 1990s. This variation has not contracted over time. Thus, aggregate increases in vertical integration across all policies have been accompanied by heightened vertical differentiation.

Variation in horizontal integration across policies has also increased over time (see Figure 1.6). Until the mid-1990s, the territorial extension of the integrated policy areas has been very similar. The gap widens slightly in the second half of the 1990s and significantly with Eastern enlargement. Since the mid-1990s, each policy area has had its own specific territorial extension. Whereas almost all policies displayed no horizontal differentiation at the beginning of the integration process, this only remains true for half of the policies at the time of writing. In addition, the types of horizontal differentiation have diversified. Initially, internal differentiation was the only form of horizontal differentiation. Since the 1990s, however, external differentiation and a mix of internal and external differentiation have become more frequent than differentiation among member states only (see Figure 1.7).

In sum, the evidence shows that differentiation has increased rather than diminished in the course of European integration. The beginnings of European integration in the 1950s were limited territorially and functionally, but highly unified. A process of horizontal differentiation set in as soon as the Community began to conclude association agreements of various kinds with third countries in Europe and beyond.

Vertical differentiation progressed when new policies (such as monetary policy and foreign policy, in the early 1970s) were introduced at a less centralized, intergovernmental level. A major leap in differentiation occurred in the 1990s. The Schengen Agreement, which came into force in 1990, was the first major integration agreement that was concluded between a limited group of forerunner countries, rather than all member states. It established an 'opt in mechanism' of integration, i.e. it was open for other countries to join later. By contrast, monetary integration allowed Britain and Denmark to 'opt out'. In addition, the pillar structure of the EU established by the Treaty of Maastricht formally institutionalized the policy-specific vertical differentiation of decision-making competences and procedures.

These developments of the early 1990s have proven durable. First, 'opt ins' and 'opt outs' have continued to be used in the EU since that time. In 1997, the Treaty of Amsterdam even officially introduced a so-called Enhanced Cooperation procedure that permits a minority group of member states to move ahead with integration within the EU structures. Under the threat of non-ratification, recent treaties include or are accompanied by exemptions or other special clauses for individual member states. Second, in spite of changes within the 'pillars' and movement of policies from the third to the first 'pillar', the 'pillar' structure has remained intact. The Lisbon Treaty abolishes the 'pillars' in name, but continues to differentiate between policy-specific decision-making procedures. Finally, the EU has vastly expanded and differentiated its institutional relations with third countries since the early 1990s. The EEA, the Bilateral Agreements with Switzerland, Stabilization and Association Agreements with the Balkans, and the European Neighbourhood Policy extend EU rules and policies beyond EU borders.

None of the developments that have brought about and sustained differentiation is likely to go away in the foreseeable future. For one, the functional and territorial expansion of the EU has greatly increased the diversity of policies, actors, and interests in the EU. In addition, political identities and loyalties have remained predominantly national. There is no consensus on the direction that European integration should take, or the final institutional form that it should have. Whereas some member state governments and parties aspire to some form of the United States of Europe, others think that integration has gone too far already. The increased use of referendums has added to the complexity of the EU. Since top-down coercion is not an option in the EU, divergent preferences need to be accommodated through flexibility and differentiation if European integration is not to come to a standstill, and if the EU is not to break apart.

The picture of a both more integrated and more differentiated EU that emerges from this analysis poses a challenge for theories of European integration. Ideally, they should be able to explain both the growth and the differentiation in vertical and horizontal integration at the same time. Which policies are taken up by the European enterprise and when? Why do these policies differ in the ways they are negotiated and decided between Brussels, Strasbourg and national capitals? Why do certain policies only address EU member states whereas others invite outside actors? Why do some outside actors demand participation while others are more reluctant? Why does differentiation increase over time? And how can we explain the temporal dynamics of European integration more generally? Such are pertinent questions that we need to understand when analyzing the processes and structures of European integration. In order to shed light on these questions, we now turn to the major theories of European integration.

PART I

THEORY

In the early days of European integration, 'integration theory' was equivalent to theorizing about the origins, development and trajectory of the European Community. Moreover, neofunctionalism, developed mainly by Ernst B. Haas, was *the* theory of European integration. Since then, theory-driven explanations for European integration have strongly diversified. On the one hand, neofunctionalism has been rivalled by intergovernmentalist theories of European integration since the 1960s, and by constructivist and postmodernist approaches more recently. On the other hand, theories of European integration have been complemented by theories of European politics and policies. We propose to distinguish three families of integration theories: supranationalism, intergovernmentalism, and constructivism. In the introduction to Part I, we first recapitulate briefly how integration theory has developed over time, and then outline a framework for integration theories and the major propositions and differences of the three theories. In the subsequent chapters, we go into the details of each theory and derive propositions on differentiated integration.

We can distinguish two general sources of development and change in the theory of European integration (see also Rosamond 2007). On the one hand, theoretical change can be inspired by *theoretical* developments in the discipline of Political Science and, above all, the field of International Relations (IR). Theoretical innovations and refinements tend to be tried out in, and adapted to, the study of European integration sooner or later. On the other hand, theoretical change may reflect *political* developments in European integration itself. Dynamic growth in specific areas of European integration is likely to trigger increased scholarly interest for these areas and a focus on the driving forces of integration, whereas periods of stagnation favour reflection on the obstacles to integration and the European Union (EU) as a stable system. Histories of European integration theory usually draw on both sources of theoretical change to account for the development of integration theory (see e.g. Battistelli and Isernia 1993; Caporaso and Keeler 1995).

As a starting point for the subsequent discussion, Figure PI.1 maps the development of integration theory chronologically onto the development of European integration and indicates how theories of European integration have responded over time to theory develop-

29

Figure PI.1   *Developments in European integration and integration theories*

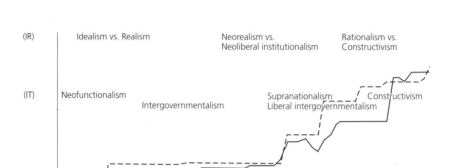

ments in IR and to real-world developments in European integration. The figure also displays the development of vertical and horizontal integration in the EU (see Chapter 1), and contrasts it with the theoretical development in IR theory (top) and European integration research (centre). Finally, we also place research trends that focus on the analysis of the EU as a political system (PSA) in their temporal order (bottom). This helps in visualizing how, over time, the paradigmatic debates of IR, as well as the periods of upswing and stagnation in European integration, have influenced theoretical developments in the study of the EU.

Neofunctionalism, belonging to the supranationalist school of thought, was the dominant theory of integration in the early periods of integration theorizing. Prominent scholars such as Ernst B. Haas, Leon Lindberg, Joseph Nye and Philippe Schmitter defined the neofunctionalist research agenda. The mid-1960s saw the birth of intergovernmentalism to mark a counter-point to neofunctionalism, with Stanley Hoffmann being its most prominent proponent. The debate between supranationalism and intergovernmentalism mirrors the paradigmatic debate between 'idealism' and 'realism' in IR. Neofunctionalism drew on and elaborated the functionalist theories of international cooperation and organization at the core of IR idealism. They stipulated ways to overcome the balance of power behaviour and recurrent warfare that realists considered to be endemic features of international politics. The initial dominance of neofunctionalism in integration theory reflected the upswing of supranational economic integration in the

1950s. In line with the functionalist model, first, the six original member states of the EU proceeded to integration in technical economic areas and transferred competences to a supranational authority. This development appeared to contradict realist assumptions about the primacy of state autonomy and power in an international system characterized by anarchy.

By contrast, the rise of intergovernmentalism in the mid-1960s coincided with the De Gaulle era and the ('empty-chair') crisis in integration. These developments discredited the idea of a linear integration process ending up in a federal European state and inexorably driven by 'spillovers' from one policy to another and from the original member states to further countries. Rather, De Gaulle's vision of a 'Europe of Fatherlands', and his rejection of a further delegation and pooling of national sovereignty, was more in line with realist theory. The ensuing 'doldrums era' (Caporaso and Keeler 1995: 13), which was characterized by the absence of big leaps in integration, reoriented research on the European Community away from integration theory altogether. It was at that time that Ernst Haas, the most influential neofunctionalist, declared regional integration theory 'obsolescent' (Haas 1975). By contrast, Leon Lindberg and Stuart Scheingold (1970) turned towards analyzing the European Community as a special political system. Others focused on the individual policies of the Community and policy-making within the existing institutional framework (Wallace *et al.* 1983).

The *relance européenne* of the 1980s revived integration theory. The Internal Market programme and Economic and Monetary Union (EMU) overcame the unanimity constraint of decision-making in the Community, included many new policy areas, and led to unprecedented sovereignty transfers to supranational institutions. These developments were duly followed by a new wave of theorizing on European integration in the 1990s, which reproduced the supranationalist–intergovernmentalist divide, albeit in a modified form. Both sides started from different strands of institutionalism in political science (Aspinwall and Schneider 2000; Hall and Taylor 1996). Supranationalist theorizing of the 1990s drew heavily on 'historical institutionalism' and the notion of 'unintended consequences' to explain the momentum in European integration (Pierson 1996; Stone Sweet and Sandholtz 1997), whereas Andrew Moravcsik's 'liberal intergovernmentalism' (1993, 1998) applied central assumptions of 'neoliberal institutionalism' in IR, with its focus on international institutions facilitating and stabilizing cooperation among rational state actors. Neoliberal institutionalism (Keohane 1984; Keohane and Nye 1977) had established itself as the major challenger to the (neo)realist paradigm in IR theory during the 1980s.

Just as stagnation in the 1970s brought about a turning away from integration theory, so did the relative saturation that set in around the mid-1990s. The British opt-out from monetary union, the failed Danish referendum on the Treaty of Maastricht, and the nearly failed referendum in France, signalled new constraints on integration. A series of further treaty negotiations (Amsterdam, Nice, and Lisbon) produced further vertical integration but did not meet expectations. At the end of the 1990s, the debate between intergovernmentalism and supranationalism largely subsided. Rather, both rational institutionalists drawing on theories of American and Comparative Politics (e.g. Hix 1994, 2005) and students of 'multi-level governance' (e.g. Hooghe and Marks 2001; Jachtenfuchs and Kohler-Koch 1996; Marks *et al.* 1996) concurred in the view the EU had reached a more or less stable set of institutions and policies that would change only marginally and incrementally. Therefore, research on the EU was advised to move away from studying the EU as a 'system of integration' and to focus instead on politics and policy-making within a stable set of institutions.

At the same time, however, the new paradigmatic debate between rationalism and constructivism spilled over from IR and gave rise to the first constructivist analyses of European integration. Whereas rationalist theories assume that international politics is fundamentally driven by the strategic and economic self-interest of states and other actors, and shaped by bargaining processes, constructivists accord primacy to identities, ideas, and ideational processes in explaining international relations. Intergovernmentalism and supranationalism in integration theory share rationalist assumptions. By contrast, constructivist approaches analyze European integration as a process of community formation driven by identities, values, norms, and policy ideas. The development of integration theories has followed the debate between rationalism and constructivism in the field of IR with a lag of a few years. At least since the publication of the *Social Construction of Europe* (Christiansen *et al.* 2001), constructivist research has gained momentum in European integration research. The constructivist research programme in the study of European integration was further spurred by several political developments that appeared to defy a rationalist logic: the enlargement of the EU to the East (Schimmelfennig 2001); the progressive democratic constitutionalization of the EU (Rittberger and Schimmelfennig 2006); and the increasing relevance of mass-level identity politics for European integration (Hooghe and Marks 2008).

These events also signalled the need to broaden the explanatory foci of integration theory to horizontal integration, democratization, and domestic politics.

- Whereas vertical integration slowed down after the mid-1990s, *horizontal integration* made an unprecedented leap forward in the 'big bang' enlargement to ten new member states in 2004, and a further two in 2007. These events demonstrated clearly that the predominant focus of integration theories on issues of 'deepening' or vertical integration was no longer tenable. The ensuing theoretical debate on enlargement (Schimmelfennig and Sedelmeier 2005) built on the rationalist–constructivist debate, rather than following the older lines of supranationalism versus intergovernmentalism in integration theory.

- The same theoretical controversy applied to another striking development of this period: the increasing empowerment of the European Parliament (EP) (Rittberger 2005) and, more generally, the *democratic constitutionalization* of the EU. Even in the absence of major changes in the distribution of policy competences between the states and the EU, the shift in power among the institutions of the EU strengthened vertical integration.

- Finally, the frequency and relevance of referendums in European integration indicated that neither the intergovernmentalist focus on governments and domestic interest groups, nor the supranationalist focus on supranational institutions and transnational interest groups captured the full range of relevant actors in European integration any longer. It became obvious that, without bringing *domestic politics* and domestic ratification back into the equation, integration theories would miss an important part of the integration process and would not be able to explain the integration outcomes adequately (Finke 2009; Hobolt 2009; Leuffen 2007, 2009).

Differentiation is another development in European integration that integration theories have largely neglected in the past. While early integration theory may be excused because differentiation was negligible in the 1960s and 1970s, the renewed debate of the 1990s between (liberal) intergovernmentalism and supranationalism took place at a time when differentiation had become politically salient and an important feature of European integration (Kölliker 2006: 38). Intergovernmentalist analyses of the treaty revisions of the 1990s described instances of differentiation, and Andrew Moravcsik and Kalypso Nicolaïdis even called for elaborating integration theory to deal adequately with exclusion and opt-outs (1999: 93). Yet, differentiated integration has not been treated systematically in general intergovernmentalist analyses (but see Gstöhl 2000; Kölliker 2006), let alone by supranationalist theories with their focus on centralization and institutionalization in European integration. This neglected area of integration is where the following chapters seek to make a theoretical contribution.

Theories of European integration stipulate the conditions and mechanisms under which competencies and boundaries shift in the

European multi-level system. They explain the scope and dynamics of integration and allow us to formulate expectations as to when and under what conditions integration will progress (or stall). We seek to go beyond explaining (further) integration versus no (further) integration, however. We are interested in both vertical and horizontal integration, as well as in vertical and horizontal differentiation. For this reason, we study integration at the level of individual policies rather than the EU as a whole. In other words, the individual policy area is the 'unit of analysis' that varies with regard to the level of centralization and the territorial extension.

Furthermore, we ask four questions:

1. What explains the level of *vertical integration* of a policy? Under which conditions do policies become more vertically integrated?
2. What explains the extension of *horizontal integration* of a policy? Under which conditions do policies change their territorial extension?
3. Why is a policy more, or less, vertically integrated than another (*vertical differentiation*)?
4. Why does a policy have a greater territorial extension than another (*horizontal differentiation*)? Why is there internal or external differentiation (or both)?

Integration theories typically tell us about the 'demand for' and the 'supply of' integration. *Demand* refers to the needs and preferences of actors. Depending on their interests or ideas, governments, interest groups, parties, and other types of actors form preferences for the extent of vertical and horizontal integration in a policy area. They may see (further) integration as a solution to their policy problems, as a way to increase their welfare, others as a desirable way of ordering regional international relations. Conversely, they may regard integration as the source of policy problems; some fear losing their power, wealth, or identity from policy integration; others regard integration as an undemocratic or otherwise problematic political order. The *analysis of integration preferences* is the first step of explanation in any integration theory.

Integration preferences can be distinguished in three areas:

- First, the relevant or dominant integration preferences can originate from different actors: the *governments*, *national societies*, *transnational society*, or *supranational organizations*.
- Second, integration preferences may be *exogenous* or *endogenous*. Exogenous preferences are informed and constrained by events and developments outside the European integration process, whereas endogenous preferences emerge from within the Community and as

the result of previous steps of integration.

- Finally, integration preferences may be *material* or *ideational*. Material preferences are oriented towards security, power, and wealth, whereas ideational preferences are based on ideas, culture, identity, and community.

Whether demand for integration can be realized and preferences can be attained has to do with supply conditions. *Supply* depends on the constellation of actor preferences, their resources and power, and the institutional and cultural context of integration. Demand can be realized if actor preferences 'match', or if one actor is able to persuade other actors to agree to its preferred level and extension of integration. Reaching agreement is facilitated or impeded under certain institutional and cultural conditions. Whether demand is met, and at which level of integration, depends on negotiations between the actors. The *analysis of integration negotiations* is therefore the second explanatory step in any theory of European integration.

The characteristics of integration negotiations can also be distinguished in several areas:

- Concerning the relevant or dominant actors in negotiations, we distinguish intergovernmental negotiations from those that are nationally or supranationally embedded. Integration theories assume that governments are always relevant in integration negotiations. The question is whether they are the only relevant actors. In *purely intergovernmental* negotiations, only governments are relevant. In *nationally embedded* negotiations, domestic actors (such as parties, parliaments, constitutional courts or electorates) also play a relevant role, formally or informally. In *supranationally embedded* negotiations, supranational organizations such as the Commission or the EP facilitate or constrain intergovernmental negotiations.
- The mode of negotiations varies between hard bargaining, soft bargaining, and arguing. *Hard bargaining* means that integration negotiations consist in the pursuit of individual goals and the exchange of threats to veto or exit. In *soft* (or cooperative or integrative) *bargaining*, the actors pursue collective goals and the common interest, seek consensus, and forego exit or veto threats. *Arguing* refers to the exchange of information and arguments designed to persuade the partners of one's policy options.
- The integration outcome can be determined by the relative *power* of the actors, or shaped by the *institutional* or *normative context* of negotiations. Depending on the mode of negotiations, power consists in bargaining power (having to do with the credibility of the actors' threats and alternative options) or arguing power (emanating, for instance, from the actors' authority or legitimacy). This

power can be constrained or reinforced by the rules and norms of the organization.

Demand and supply result in an integration outcome: not only a specific level of vertical and horizontal integration, but also a specific extent of vertical and horizontal differentiation. This outcome feeds back into demand and supply at a later stage of integration. The outcome may, for instance, add new actors: a notable example being supranational organizations such as the European Central Bank or the EU Military Staff created in the previous round of integration. It may also strengthen the endogeneity of preferences or shape future negotiations – in particular, if integration constrains the range of options that governments have, triggers learning processes, or changes the rules of negotiation. Integration theories differ, however, on the importance of this feedback mechanism. Whereas intergovernmentalism tends to regard it as largely irrelevant, supranationalism (and, to a lesser extent,

Figure PI.2   *Analytical framework of integration*

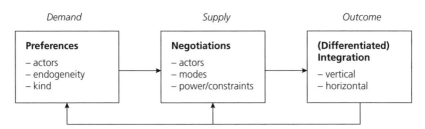

constructivism) argues that it is the most important driving force of integration. The integration–theoretic analytical framework that results from these considerations is depicted in Figure PI.2.

The framework is sufficiently general to apply to all integration theories we present in this book. We distinguish three major theories of European integration: intergovernmentalism, supranationalism, and constructivism. Certainly, the three theories are schools of thought or theory families united by core assumptions rather than single, consistent theories. They have developed and changed over time – e.g. from traditional, realist intergovernmentalism to liberal intergovernmentalism, and from neofunctionalism to supranational institutionalism – and each consists of several strands or approaches. For the purposes of this book, however, we will concentrate on the basic assumptions and propositions that constitute the core of each school of thought. Each theory offers answers to the main questions presented in our analytical framework. For the demand side, each theory stipulates who the main *actors* of

Table PI.1 *Keywords of integration theories*

Demand: integration preferences

	Actors	*Endogeneity*	*Kind*
Intergovernmentalism	Governments, domestic society	Exogenous	Material
Supranationalism	Transnational society, supranational organizations	Endogenous	Material
Constructivism	Not specified/open	Endogenous	Ideational

Supply: integration negotiations

	Actors	*Modes*	*Power/constraints*
Intergovernmentalism	Intergovernmental	Hard bargaining	Bargaining power
Supranationalism	Supranationally embedded	Soft bargaining	Institutionally constrained bargaining power
Constructivism	Supranationally and nationally embedded	Arguing	Normatively constrained bargaining power

European integration are and what factors shape their integration *preferences*. For the supply side, the theories tell us how these actors negotiate and what determines the outcomes. We now summarize the core assumptions and propositions of each theory that we will develop in much greater detail in subsequent chapters. Table PI.1 provides the keywords for each theory at a glance.

Intergovernmentalism distinguishes itself from supranationalism mainly by its assumptions about the relevant actors and the distribution of power between governments, on the one hand, and transnational and supranational actors, on the other. As the name of the theory indicates, it regards national governments as the main actors in European integration. In its liberal variant, intergovernmentalism holds that domestic interest groups play an important role in forming national preferences. For intergovernmentalists, European integration is, at its core, driven by the national interest. In its original, realist version, this interest consists in preserving national autonomy and promoting national power through integration. Liberal intergovernmentalism regards integration as an instrument with which to maximize national economic benefits under conditions of international interdependence. Integration decisions are made in intergovernmental negotiations in which national governments bargain hard to further the national interest, and in which the powerful governments prevail. The institutional and cultural context of negotiations can be neglected, and so can the capacities of supranational organizations. According to intergovernmentalism, the process of integration remains under the control of member state governments, which collectively determine the speed and substance of any further steps of integration. It thus denies a transformative impact of European integration on the state system.

Supranationalism considers actors and processes above and beyond the nation-state to be the mainspring of European integration. Supranational actors and transnational interest groups increasingly gain autonomy throughout the integration process and attempt to push the integration process in their preferred direction. Integration preferences become increasingly endogenous, i.e. shaped and reshaped by the progress in integration. In order to achieve their goals, transnational interest groups rely on their lobbying power. Supranational organizations use their formal institutional competences, as well as informal institutional resources (such as expertise), to affect integration processes and outcomes. Processes of institutionalization at the supranational level support supranational organizations, induce soft bargaining, and constrain the power of states. Under certain conditions, the institutions created by member state governments trigger a self-reinforcing process which begets further integration and escapes member state control. Integration thus has a transformative impact on the state system and state actors.

Finally, in the *constructivist* perspective, European integration is about community-building. Community-building is driven by ideational preferences and processes: the dissemination and distribution of common, 'European' identities, values, norms, and policy beliefs determines the strength of the community and, consequently, the speed, extent, and direction of integration. Processes of arguing and persuasion characterize the negotiations. Together with the consolidation of European ideas in supranational institutions, these processes promote community-building. Traditionally, the main actors in the European community-building process have been national and supranational elites but citizens have become more relevant over time – in particular, as a result of Euro-sceptic mobilization.

In the chapters that follow, we present the three integration theories in greater detail. First, we describe the basic assumptions and general theories on which they are based. We identify three 'institutionalisms' as the theoretical foundations of the integration theories: rational institutionalism for intergovernmentalism, historical institutionalism for supranationalism, and sociological institutionalism for constructivism. Second, we show how the basic assumptions about how institutions develop, work and translate into propositions about European integration. Finally, we show how the integration theories can be applied to differentiated integration. Each theory chapter concludes with two core hypotheses.

Chapter 2

Intergovernmentalism

From Realist to Liberal Intergovernmentalism

The origins of intergovernmentalism are tightly linked to the first period of stagnation in European integration. In the mid-1960s, the presidency of General de Gaulle and the 'empty chair crisis' – France's representatives refused to attend any intergovernmental meetings because of a conflict over the financing of the Common Agricultural Policy – appeared to mark the limits of supranational integration, and the resilience of state interests and power. It was then that Stanley Hoffmann (1966, 1982) formulated the major assumptions and expectations of intergovernmentalist integration theory. Intergovernmentalism, however, is not confined to explaining the limits of integration. Historian Alan Milward (1984, 1994; Milward and Brennan 1992) later argued that European integration had worked as an intergovernmentalist project from the very start. In his view, it was designed as the 'rescue of the nation-state' from the shambles of World War II, and Andrew Moravcsik's liberal intergovernmentalism (1993, 1998) claimed to explain the new momentum of European integration in the 1980s and 1990s.

These are the core tenets of traditional intergovernmentalism:

- States are, and will remain, the dominant actors in the process of European integration. They shape European integration according to national goals and interests.
- The extent of European integration is limited by the states' interest in autonomy, the interest in self-preservation of nation-state bureaucracies, the diversity of national situations and traditions, the dominance of national identities, and by external actors and influences (such as the United States or NATO).
- European integration does not undermine the European nation-state but has strengthened it during post-World War II reconstruction, and in the global competition with other economic powers and emerging markets.
- Integration is limited to the economic sector and related 'low politics'. States anxious to preserve their autonomy will prevent the core functions of the sovereign state (the 'high politics' of internal and external security or foreign policy) from being integrated.

- For the same reason, the supranational organizations of the EU are, and will remain, weak. They lack the expertise, the resources, and the popular support to expand their power at the expense of the member states.

Because the unitary state, its power, and its quest for autonomy – core assumptions of realism in International Relations – is placed at the centre of theorizing about European integration, we will refer to this traditional version of intergovernmentalism as 'realist intergovernmentalism' (RI).

Intergovernmentalism has received fresh impetus from the renewed interest in European integration since the mid-1980s. It has also reflected recent developments in IR theory. In the 1990s, Moravcsik (1993, 1998) developed the theory of 'liberal intergovernmentalism' (LI), which follows in the footsteps of the realist variant insofar as it puts states, state interests, and state bargaining centre stage, but attributes to societal actors and international institutions a more prominent theoretical role. LI is based on 'neoliberal institutionalism' in IR (Keohane 1984; Keohane and Nye 1977). In line with the *liberal* component of this IR theory, LI assumes that the foreign policy of the state results from a domestic policy process and reflects the issue-specific interests of the dominant domestic groups. In line with its *institutionalist* component, LI emphasizes the relevance of international institutions for facilitating and stabilizing cooperation between states. In his book *The Choice for Europe* (1998), Moravcsik analyzes the major

Table 2.1 *Building blocks of intergovernmentalism*

General assumptions	Rationalist institutionalism in International Relations Rational states in an interdependent and anarchical international system	
Explanatory theory	Endogenous trade theory Bargaining theory Club theory	Functional theory of institutions
Factors explaining integration	Interdependence, state preferences and state power	Governmental interests and collective action problems
	LI: sector-specific societal preferences and bargaining power	LI: severity of enforcement problems
	RI: geopolitical preferences and overall power	RI: state autonomy

steps in European integration 'from Messina to Maastricht', i.e. from the establishment of the EEC to the founding of the EU.

Because Moravcsik's approach is the most prominent, up-to-date, complete, and theoretically elaborate intergovernmentalist integration theory, our presentation will be mainly based on LI, but highlights the differences from RI where appropriate. Table 2.1 presents the main building blocks of intergovernmentalist integration theory, which will be discussed in greater detail in the coming sections.

In this chapter, we will descend the ladder of abstraction in three steps. We begin our presentation of intergovernmentalism by explicating its theoretical roots in rationalist institutionalism in IR, and by identifying four more middle-range rationalist theories that intergovernmentalism uses to explain international cooperation. We then apply this framework to European integration in general, and specify liberal and realist intergovernmentalist hypotheses. Finally, we extend intergovernmentalism to the phenomenon of differentiated integration.

Rationalist Institutionalism

General assumptions: international interdependence and rational choice

Intergovernmentalism starts from the assumption that European integration is similar enough to general international politics, and the EU is sufficiently like other international institutions, that it can be profitably studied and explained from an IR perspective. Indeed, Moravcsik maintains that the 'EC is best seen as an international regime for policy co-ordination' (1993: 480; cf. Hoffmann 1982: 33) and that European integration represents 'a subset of general tendencies among democratic states in modern world politics' (Moravcsik 1998: 5). IR theories traditionally assume that states are the central actors in international politics and that they act in a context of anarchy, i.e. in the absence of a centralized authority making and enforcing political decisions. Policy-making in international politics generally takes place in intergovernmental negotiations, and agreements require the consent of all state participants.

The second building block is a rationalist framework that puts actors centre stage and explains collective outcomes such as integration as a result of the interaction of rational individual choices. (Bounded) rational choice means that, on the basis of their knowledge about the world and their preferences, actors calculate the utility of alternative courses of action and choose the one that maximizes (or satisfies) their utility under given circumstances. Rationalist institutionalism in IR theory, then, seeks to explain the establishment of international cooperation and international institutions as a collective outcome of inter-dependent ('strategic') rational state choices and intergovernmental negotiations in an anarchical context.

The fundamental starting point for rationalist institutionalism in IR is international interdependence. An international constellation is characterized by interdependence, if states are unable to fulfil their security or welfare needs alone – or if it would be inefficient for them to act autonomously. Take, for instance, the case of global warming. The reduction of carbon dioxide emissions by a single country would be futile if all other countries increased their emissions at the same time. Or consider trade. According to liberal economic theory, societies as a whole are generally better off if they open up for international trade and allow for a division of labour in which they can concentrate on their most efficient economic sectors. In sum, in a situation of international interdependence, states are better off collectively if they cooperate.

Yet, international cooperation can be problematic for at least three reasons. First, there is a transaction cost problem. It is costly for states to obtain information about the preferences and capabilities of other states in order to determine the most efficient cooperative solution, and it is costly to negotiate this solution. Under unfavourable circumstances, these transaction costs can be so high that states prefer not to cooperate at all. Second, even if states find an efficient solution that benefits all participants, they are often faced with the problem of how to distribute the gains and costs of cooperation among them. States try to maximize their own share of the gains, and they might forgo a deal that they consider unfair or lopsided. For instance, developing countries have for a long time refused to participate in the costly efforts to reduce CO_2 emissions with the argument that the industrialized world has become rich by burning fossil fuels. The Doha round of trade negotiations in the World Trade Organization has also failed so far because developing and emerging economies reject a deal that they perceive to benefit the North disproportionately. Third, international cooperation is complicated by the problem of enforcement. It is often rational for a state to 'free-ride', i.e. defect from cooperation and exploit the cooperative behaviour of others. For instance, states would benefit from continuing with their greenhouse gas emissions while all others bear the cost of emission reductions, and it would be rational for them to protect their own unproductive economic sectors against foreign competition while all others open up their markets.

Explanatory theories: the functional theory of institutions, endogenous trade theory, bargaining theory, and club theory

Rationalist institutionalism offers four substantive theories that specify how and under which conditions rational state actors cooperate in an anarchical, interdependent, international system. The functional theory of institutions shows how international institutions help states overcome the transaction costs and enforcement problems of international cooperation. Endogenous trade theory accounts for the policy preferences of states. Bargaining theory explains the substantive outcomes of international negotiations. Finally, club theory explains the size of international institutions.

Functional theory of institutions. States establish international institutions because they are functional in dealing with fundamental problems of international cooperation. Efficient, welfare-maximizing solutions to international interdependence require reliable information on the state of the world, cause–effect relationships, and other actors' preferences and capabilities. For instance, how bad is global warming? What causes it and how can it be stopped? What are other states willing and able to do to reduce emissions? International organizations are often better at providing this information than governments alone. Furthermore, they reduce transaction costs by offering a forum for multi-actor negotiations and services for effective and efficient communication. Finally, the enforcement problem requires effective monitoring and sanctioning. Again, international institutions are established because they fulfil these tasks more effectively and efficiently than individual states. Different institutional designs then reflect the need to deal with different problems of collective action (Koremenos *et al.* 2001). Generally speaking, the demand for centralization increases with uncertainty about the preferences of other states or about the (future) state of the world, and with the severity of the enforcement problem caused by incentives to free-ride.

Endogenous trade theory. The preference of a state for or against an international policy depends on the effect that this policy has for the state. For the paradigmatic case of trade policy, 'endogenous trade (or tariff) theory' (see Nelson 1988) tells us under which conditions states prefer free trade arrangements (low or no tariffs) to protectionist policies (high tariffs). This has mainly to do with the state's economic endowments and structure. According to the Heckscher–Ohlin model, trade liberalization benefits the relatively abundant factor, i.e. capital-owners gain and workers lose when capital is abundant, whereas workers gain but capital-owners lose in labour-abundant countries. If we assume that the factors are specific to industries (the Ricardo–Viner model), e.g. capital cannot easily move from one industry to another in pursuit of higher returns, it is industries rather than factors that gain or lose from trade liberalization. Export-oriented industries gain from trade liberalization whereas import-competing industries lose. In both cases the winners will lobby for free trade, whereas the losers will lobby for protection. The success of lobbying in turn depends on how well the groups can organize. Small groups with concentrated gains or losses are better able to organize and lobby than large groups with dispersed gains or losses. This is the reason why producers are usually better lobbyists than consumers, and why highly concentrated industries do better than those with a large number of small enterprises. Finally, the theory tells us that the power of large and small countries differs. Whereas large countries (with large domestic markets) can affect the world market unilaterally with their domestic policies, small countries are unable to do so. This argument leads us to bargaining theory.

Bargaining theory. The substantive outcomes of international negotiations – how the gains from international cooperation are distributed among the actors – depend on the actors' relative bargaining power. Bargaining power results from the asymmetrical distribution of information and of the benefits of a specific agreement (compared with those of alternative outcomes or 'outside options'). Generally, actors that have more and better information are able to manipulate the outcome to their advantage (Schneider and Cederman 1994). In addition, actors that are less in need of a specific agreement, because they are more satisfied with the status quo or have alternative options, have more bargaining power: they are able to threaten the others credibly with non-agreement and thereby force them to make concessions. Provided that all actors benefit from cooperation, those with the highest bargaining power can impose their preferred distribution of the costs and gains of cooperation on the others.

Club theory. Finally, club theory deals with the issue of organizational size. A club is a voluntary association deriving mutual benefit from producing and sharing collective goods, such as a common market or a clean environment. Membership in clubs can be limited and often needs to be because new members are not only additional contributors to the club goods, but can also become rival consumers who restrict the old members' access to the club goods (causing socalled 'crowding costs'). When states integrate their markets and economies, they produce external effects for non-member countries (for instance, by diverting trade and investments away from them). However, third countries can also produce externalities for the integrated states. For example, lower taxation or less social and environmental regulation attract business away from the integrated market and thus bring its rules and policies under pressure. If this is the case, it becomes useful to enlarge the club. In addition, a larger size might produce economies of scale and increase the budget of the international organization. Thus, from a rationalist perspective, the question is whether a given integrated area already has optimal size, or whether collective welfare may be maximized by admitting further countries. The core hypothesis of club theory therefore posits that a club will expand (only) until the marginal costs of admitting a new member equals the marginal benefits. Since clubs are voluntary associations, all old and new members must derive a positive utility from expansion lest they use their veto.

Liberal intergovernmentalism draws on all four theories to analyze European integration. Endogenous trade theory accounts for state preferences on integration (not on issues of commercial policy alone); bargaining theory explains who gets what in intergovernmental negotiations on integration; the functional theory of institutions tells us when and why governments delegate power and competences to European supranational organizations; and club theory sheds light on the conditions of enlargement.

Intergovernmentalism and European Integration

Which specific propositions on European integration does intergovernmentalism derive from these general rational-institutionalist assumptions and theories? Moravcsik proposes a three-stage analysis: domestic politics generates national preferences, intergovernmental negotiations produce substantive bargains, and, after agreement has been reached on substance, further international negotiations on the choice of institutions lead to decisions to pool and delegate state competencies. In its most condensed form, Moravcsik's argument is that

> EU integration can best be understood as a series of rational choices made by national leaders. These choices responded to constraints and opportunities stemming from the *economic interests of powerful domestic constituents*, the *relative power of each state* in the international system, and the role of institutions in bolstering the *credibility of interstate commitments*. (Moravcsik 1998: 18, emphasis added)

National preferences

Realist intergovernmentalism assumes that there is a 'national interest' defined by the state. It most fundamentally consists in preserving and increasing the autonomy, security, and influence of the state. National preferences on the EU thus depend on how beneficial or detrimental integration is to national autonomy. From this perspective, small states are more integration-friendly than large states. Larger states need international cooperation less than smaller states because their autonomy and security is less threatened in an interdependent world. In particular, integration offers smaller states the possibility to bind larger states to collective rules and to increase their limited power by joining forces with others (Grieco 1996). In addition, integration follows the realist logic of alliance formation. European states are more willing to integrate the more they feel threatened externally. Traditional realist intergovernmentalism does not need to consider domestic politics. The state defines the national interest on its own, and integration preferences vary only with the power of (and threats to) the state.

By contrast, liberal intergovernmentalism follows a liberal theory of foreign policy preference formation. Liberalism as a theory of foreign policy assumes that governmental preferences vary between policy issues, and reflect the interests and power of societal groups (intermediated by domestic political institutions). Because European integration has focused on economic policies, state preferences have also been predominantly economic. While general demand for European integration results from interdependence, the pressure to cooperate for mutual benefit in an expanding and 'globalizing' international economy, concrete integration preferences emerge primarily from 'the commercial interests of powerful economic producers' (Moravcsik 1998: 3). As a consequence, governments pursue integration as 'a means to secure commercial advantages for producer groups, subject to regulatory and budgetary constraints' (Moravcsik 1998: 38). Depending on how competitive these powerful producers are on the European market, states either demand the opening and deregulation of markets or protectionist policies. This is in line with endogenous trade theory.

In policies that deal with non-economic issues or affect business only indirectly, other societal actors have a stronger role and state preferences will be more strongly shaped by their concerns. In public policies (such as environmental policy or immigration policy), the strength of environmental or immigration interest groups, and the distribution of environmental and immigration preferences in the electorate, complement – and may even override – economic interest. In addition, domestic economic interests most clearly shape state preferences, the 'more intense, certain, and institutionally represented and organized' they are (Moravcsik 1998: 36) and the less 'uncertainty there is about cause-effect relations' (Moravcsik 1999: 171). This applies, for instance, to agricultural policy with its concentrated, well-organized, and well-informed producer lobby. Conversely, 'the weaker and more diffuse the domestic constituency behind a policy' (Moravcsik 1999: 171) and the more uncertain and modest 'the substantive implications of a choice', the less predictable are national preferences and the more likely ideological preferences will be influential (Moravcsik 1998: 486–9; Moravcsik and Nicolaïdis 1999: 61). According to Moravcsik, this is the case, among others, for macro-economic policies such as monetary integration, where preferences are based on 'the macro-economic preferences of ruling governmental coalitions' (Moravcsik 1998: 3).

Liberal intergovernmentalism regards interest groups as the relevant domestic constituency of European integration. Mass publics only become relevant under two conditions: that European integration creates strong and concrete costs and benefits affecting large groups of society, and that these groups find a way to affect the government's integration policy and decisions. According to Moravcsik, this is unlikely in the EU's core commercial policies because the interests of consumers and taxpayers are too diffuse to become effectively mobilized (Moravcsik 1993: 488). It is more likely in the case of 'public goods issues' such as environmental or social policy, about which mass publics care more strongly and where powerful societal organizations exist (Moravcsik 1993: 493).

Even in these policy-areas, however, Moravcsik does not expect effective political pressure, because the public policies that voters care about most (welfare state policies) are not integrated, and because European integration strengthens national governments and weakens the influence of democratic politics (Moravcsik 1993: 514–15). First, the lack of transparency of EU politics dilutes the domestic accountability of national governments. Second, national parliaments are only weakly involved in European-level policy-making and have few opportunities to decide on EU issues. Such input as national parliaments are allowed, as in treaty ratification, permits them only to say 'yes' or 'no' – and in a parliamentary system, the government can usually rely on the majority to support the European deals it has negotiated. Finally, voters only get a chance to ratify European decisions if these are put to a referendum, and referendums are only used in a few countries on the occasion of treaty changes.

These conditions have partly changed since the early 1990s. As the functional scope of European integration has expanded, it has come to affect the autonomy and welfare of citizens in many more ways than in the early days of the Community, and it has created losers and adversaries. In addition, referendums have become a persistent feature of European treaty-making since the early 1990s and have delayed or derailed several intergovernmental agreements. These developments do not create a problem for LI as such, but require stronger attention to domestic politics and ratification in theorizing European integration. On public goods issues that create clear and strong costs and benefits, and mobilize relevant mass-level constituencies, governments are strongly constrained in defining and pursuing the 'national interest'.

Interstate bargaining

Intergovernmentalism describes the most *relevant negotiation processes in European integration as processes of intergovernmental bargaining* concerning the *distribution* of gains from cooperation. Because the costs and benefits of any cooperative arrangement are likely to differ across member states, the national preferences of the member states usually diverge, and because integration decisions often have binding and substantial material consequences for governments and market actors, the stakes are high. Negotiations therefore consist in *hard* bargaining

> in which credible threats to veto proposals, to withhold financial side-payments, and to form alternative alliances excluding recalcitrant governments carried the day. The outcomes reflected the relative power of states – more precisely patterns of asymmetrical interdependence. Those who gained the most economically from integration compromised the most on the margin to realize it, whereas those who gained the least or for whom the costs of adaptation were highest imposed conditions. (Moravcsik 1998: 3)

This account has two negative implications for the impact of supranational organizations. First, Moravcsik argues that efficiency is not a serious collective action problem in European integration. Transaction costs are generally low, information is plentiful and symmetrically distributed among states (Moravcsik 1998: 479–80) so that intergovernmental negotiations reliably produce efficient outcomes. In other words, governments normally do not need supranational organizations such as the Commission to help them find a feasible and efficient deal. Second, and as a corollary, the bargaining power of supranational organizations is low because they are deprived of their main potential bargaining resource: scarce and asymmetrically distributed information. Supranational entrepreneurship is not necessary to reach efficient agreements, and supranational organizations lack the power to bargain successfully for concessions by the member states. For these reasons, governments remain in control of the integration process. The EU does not hold more power than the states want it to have and deem necessary to provide for stable intergovernmental cooperation.

By contrast, the liberal-intergovernmentalist analysis of interstate bargaining is open to the effects of domestic politics on intergovernmental negotiations (Moravcsik 1993: 514–17). These are captured by the metaphor of the 'two-level game' (Putnam 1988). In the two-level game, national governments negotiate simultaneously at two tables – one with other governments and the other with domestic veto-players. In order to reach an agreement, governments need to find terms that are acceptable both to the other governments and to those domestic actors that need to ratify the agreement. In doing so, they face a trade-off. A large domestic 'win-set', i.e. the set of domestically acceptable agreements, facilitates intergovernmental agreement because it makes it easier for governments to accommodate the divergent interests of other states. At the same time, the agreement may be far away from their preferences. By contrast, a narrow domestic win-set makes it more difficult to reach international agreement but increases the government's bargaining power. If a government can credibly threaten other governments with the non-ratification of an agreement that they value highly, these governments will accommodate the preferences of the constrained government in order to secure ratification. By the same token, the constrained government will achieve a negotiation outcome that is close to its ideal. This is also known as Schelling's 'paradox of weakness'. Under conditions of uncertainty, governments can also exploit the ratification constraints strategically (see Schneider and Cederman 1994). Since a government usually knows better than other governments what its own domestic win-set is, it can present its ratification constraints as more severe than they really are in order to obtain a more beneficial deal.

In their analysis of the Amsterdam treaty negotiations, Simon Hug and Thomas König (2002) argue against the backdrop of the Danish rejection of the Maastricht Treaty, that governments sought to minimize the chances of a failure, tried to anticipate challenges that could arise at the ratification stage, and dropped those issues that created the strongest ratification constraints. Moreover, countries face different institutional ratification requirements. In the order of decreasing constraints, they range from a mandatory referendum via qualified parliamentary majorities to simple parliamentary majorities. In line with the paradox of weakness, Hug and König (2002) show that countries with higher domestic ratification constraints performed better in the negotiations.

Institutional choice

Institutional choice is again driven by governments and by their concern about each other's future compliance with the substantive deals reached. In other words, whereas EU governments do not need or want supranational organizations to define their preferences, to provide them with the information necessary to reach efficient substantive agreements, or to devise the rules of distribution, they rely on supranational actors to solve the problems of monitoring and sanctioning. Even in this respect, however, the supranational organizations remain instruments and agents of the governments rather than autonomous actors.

Whether such enforcement problems arise, depends first of all on the nature of the collective action problem at hand (Scharpf 1999: 165–6; Schimmelfennig and Moravcsik 2009: 72). On the one hand, there are issues of *coordination*. Here, actors need to agree on a common standard but have no incentive to defect unilaterally once this standard is in place. In these cases, there is no enforcement problem, and governments delegate decisions to common decision-making or supranational organizations, mainly in order to reduce transaction costs. By contrast, when states do have an incentive to defect and an *enforcement* problem exists, governments are willing to centralize decision-making and delegate more extensive powers of monitoring and compliance to supranational organizations such as the Commission, the Court of Justice, or – in the case of monetary policy – the ECB.

By transferring sovereignty to international institutions, governments remove issues from the influence of domestic actors, which might build up pressure for non-compliance if their costs deriving from integration increase. They also remove them from decentralized intergovernmental control, which may be too weak to secure compliance in particular if powerful member states violate the rules (Moravcsik 1998: 9, 73). The degree to which governments favour the pooling (voting by procedures other than unanimity) and the delegation of sovereignty to supranational institutions depends on the value they place on the issues and substantive outcomes in question, and on their uncertainty about the future behaviour of other governments. The more a government benefits from a cooperative agreement, and the higher the risks of non-compliance by other governments, the higher is its readiness to cede competences to the EU to prevent potential losers from revising the policy (Moravcsik 1998: 9, 486–7).

In contrast with the liberal variant, realist intergovernmentalism assumes that states are primarily concerned about autonomy and influence in institutional choice – and not so much about issue-specific welfare. They only consent to transferring competencies to the EU if they expect net gains in overall autonomy and influence. This is the essence of Joseph Grieco's 'voice-opportunity' thesis, which posits that weak states are particularly interested in European integration and willing to sacrifice formal sovereignty because they see it as a way to bind the stronger states and to enhance their influence on international outcomes (Grieco 1996).

The intensity, clarity, and predictability of a state's institutional preferences depend on the certainty or strength of their welfare or autonomy implications. When institutional effects are uncertain or weak, governments' institutional preferences will also be weak, or follow ideological attitudes. According to Moravcsik, this has been the case, for instance, with regard to the powers of the EP. Since the powers of the EP have long been weak, and the future composition and policy positions of the EP are highly uncertain, states did not care, or were unable, to calculate their utility from reforming the EP. Therefore, they relied on ideological attitudes. As a result, conflict between federalist (in favour of more EP powers) and anti-federalist governments (against) dominated the negotiations on institutional reform (see Rittberger 2005).

General hypotheses

Intergovernmentalism assumes that states (governments) are the relevant actors in European integration. They initiate, steer, and control the process of European integration as an instrument to realize national preferences under conditions of international interdependence. The level of centralization and the territorial extension of European integration result from intergovernmental negotiations, and reflect the extent of interdependence, the severity of collective action problems, and the intergovernmental constellation of preferences and power. Indeed, integration is fundamentally driven by patterns of interdependence, which trigger not only a general demand for international cooperation, but also shape state preferences, bargaining power, and institutional choice.

- The strength of interdependence explains how much demand there is for cooperation.
- The position (e.g. stakes and competitiveness) of domestic society in international interdependence explains state preferences.
- The asymmetry of international interdependence (and of domestic ratification constraints) produces differential bargaining power.
- The nature of the collective action problem generated by interdependence shapes institutional choice.

Demand for integration increases with the strength of interdependence. When international interdependence increases in an issue-area and promises to increase the utility of member state governments from integration, demand for extending the scope of integration will rise. In addition, the more uncertain governments are about the future state of the world and the future rule-compliant behaviour of their cooperation partners (relative to the utility of cooperation), the more willing they are to centralize decision-making and enforcement powers in the EU. Likewise, whenever the situation that a state is not integrated generates externalities and expectations of gains from integration, member governments and non-member governments will demand an increase in the territorial extension of integration. Conversely, there be will no integration in the absence of interdependence because states will not derive any utility from cooperating.

In the case of LI, utility is defined by the issue-specific interests of powerful domestic actors. In the case of RI, utility is defined by the overall interest of the state in autonomy and security. The higher the expected gains from integration, the stronger the demand for integration. Whether and how this demand for integration will be translated into actual integration, however, depends on several supply conditions: the constellation of preferences and bargaining power, as well as the availability of adequate institutions.

The likelihood of integration increases with the convergence of national preferences. Agreement on integration requires that all states reap net benefits from it, otherwise they would use their veto. The more that preferences for integration converge, i.e. the win-set of the negotiations expands, the easier it is for the states to find a point of agreement.

The substantive terms of integration result from the international distribution of bargaining power. The most powerful actor determines the terms of integration according to its interests. This actor is able to make the other actors accept its preferred sectoral regulation (e.g. its preferred degree of market liberalization, amount of emissions reduction, or monetary policy guidelines), the distribution of gains from territorial expansion, and the level of centralization. For LI, bargaining power increases with the availability of outside options and the strength of domestic ratification constraints. It decreases with the intensity of issue-specific societal preferences for European integration. By contrast, in the realist perspective, bargaining power increases with overall power resources.

Intergovernmentalism and Differentiated Integration

How does differentiated integration come about? If differentiated integration was not an option, the extent of vertical and horizontal integration, i.e. the level of centralization and territorial extension, would be determined by the lowest common intergovernmental denominator. Under conditions of international treaty-making, in which each state has veto power, the extent of integration would be decided by the state with the strongest bargaining power, i.e. the best outside-options, or the highest interest in the status quo. This state would block any further vertical or horizontal integration that is not in its interest. It would block vertical integration beyond its own needs for third-party monitoring and sanctioning, or for autonomy maximization, and it would prevent the accession of states that would not increase its utility. Integration is still possible if the veto player is offered adequate concessions or side-payments but such compensation may either not suffice, or become too costly for the other states.

Beyond the lowest common intergovernmental denominator, the EU would be subject to severe trade-offs. If it wanted to engage in further vertical integration, it would lose, or have to exclude, those states that do not benefit from transferring policy competences to the EU, or from strengthening the EU's decision-making and enforcement powers. If, on the other hand, it wanted to increase its membership, it might have to reduce its level of centralization in order to accommodate the least integration-friendly state. This is known and debated as the 'widening-deepening dilemma' of integration.

From an intergovernmentalist perspective, differentiated integration can solve this dilemma by overcoming the rigidities of uniform integration and creating opportunities for policies to be integrated at different levels of centralization, and for different groups of countries to cooperate among each other separately at the level of integration that they prefer. It is thus an efficient strategy for accommodating international diversity and avoiding deadlock when intergovernmental consent is required. In line with its general assumptions and hypotheses, intergovernmentalism explains differentiated integration by differences in interdependence and cooperation problems, state preferences, bargaining power, domestic ratification constraints, and – in the case of RI – autonomy costs and benefits.

Realist intergovernmentalism: autonomy-driven differentiated integration

From the realist perspective, differentiated integration results from different autonomy costs across sectors and countries. In contrast to LI assumptions, according to which states have no problem trading their autonomy for increasing their welfare, realists assume that states value their autonomy for its own sake and would rather accept reduced welfare than compromising autonomy, in particular those autonomy rights that constitute the core of their sovereignty.

In the 1960s, Stanley Hoffmann introduced the distinction between 'high politics' and 'low politics' to explain the limits of integration and spillover. We refer to this variable as 'politicization'. 'High politics' include those policy areas that concern the security and status of a state in the international system. In these policy areas, it is hard to identify a common good that could be furthered through integration. Rather, the logic of the zero-sum game and relative gains dominates: one state's gain is another state's loss. By contrast, in the areas of 'low politics', states can pursue a common good and realize mutual gains without compromising their national sovereignty, security, and power status. In general, foreign policy, internal policy, and security policy are the core domains of high politics but taxation, energy, and monetary policy can also be considered key areas of national sovereignty (Hoffman 1966). Later, however, Hoffmann conceded that absolute-gains or common-good issues and relative-gains or zero-sum issues could be found, in principle, across the entire range of policies (Hoffman 1982: 29). It is thus the nature of the collective action problem, rather than the substantive policy area that determines whether high or low politics apply.

In line with this reasoning, we should expect a high level of vertical integration, first and foremost, in areas of 'low politics', whereas highly politicized areas are unlikely to be integrated at all, or will be integrated later than the 'low-politics' areas. Moreover, if high-politics areas are integrated, the level of centralization will be lower than in sectors dominated by 'low politics'. Finally, horizontal integration is likely to vary with the level of centralization and the policy characteristics of a sector. 'High-politics' sectors, and/or those with higher levels of centralization, will be less territorially extended than decentralized and/or 'low-politics' sectors. The reason is that those states that can afford to do so will shy away from integration, if autonomy costs are high. This should mainly be the case for the large and powerful member states, which, in general, are less affected by international interdependence, possess higher autonomy as well as a higher status in the international system, and are more capable of providing for their own security. Small states have less *de facto* sovereignty in the first place and stand to gain autonomy through integration, rather than lose it.

From the RI perspective, then, vertical and horizontal differentiation across policies reflects variation in politicization. 'High-politics' areas are less vertically and horizontally integrated than 'low-politics' areas, and small or weak countries are more likely to be integrated (at a higher level of centralization) than large and powerful countries. As a corollary of these considerations, we are likely to find external differentiation in 'low-politics' areas, which attract non-member states that shy away from the autonomy costs of full membership, and internal differentiation in 'high-politics' areas in which some member states are reluctant to commit to deep vertical integration.

Liberal intergovernmentalism: interest divergence and externalities of differentiation

Liberal intergovernmentalism hypothesizes that the likelihood of integration increases with the homogeneity of national interests. If interests converge, there is no need for differentiation, because all countries will be able to agree on the same level of integration. Yet, if interests diverge, the state whose interests are the closest to the status quo has the highest bargaining power and determines the outcome. This outcome leaves many governments dissatisfied that would have preferred a different extent of integration. These governments have an incentive to seek differentiation in order to move closer to their preference.

Why would interests diverge? According to liberal intergovernmentalism, demand for integration results, first, from international *interdependence*. International interdependence is not the same, and does not develop at the same time, across all policy sectors, and between all states. Demand for differentiated integration can correspondingly be explained by differences in interdependence across policies and states.

Even if international interdependence affects all countries, divergence may still result because dominant societal actors or governments are differentially affected and have different preferences on how to deal with it. Groups that stand to benefit from increased international interdependence (e.g. internationally competitive producers) typically ask for negative integration, i.e. the opening up of international markets. By contrast, those that come under pressure from international interdependence (e.g. non-competitive producers) will ask for positive integration or market-correcting measures. Depending on the distribution of societal preferences and power, governments may seek more or less regulation, protection, or redistribution in order to cope with interdependence. This heterogeneity in preferences produces demand for differentiated integration, too.

Let us first consider demand for vertical differentiation. Policies with early and high international interdependence are likely to be integrated earlier than those sectors in which interdependence is weaker or develops later. That trade policy was integrated earlier than immigration policy and that defence policy is only weakly integrated, would therefore be explained by earlier and stronger critical interdependence in trade (in comparison with migration), and by the absence or weakness of security interdependence. Second, even similarly interdependent policies may lead to vertical differentiation if they vary with regard to the homogeneity of member states preferences. The weakness of vertical defence integration might thus not only result from weak interdependence, but also from divergent preferences on the form and substance of integration. Finally, vertical differentiation may be a response to variation in enforcement problems. Policies with a high free-riding potential should generate higher demand for centralization than policies characterized by coordination problems.

Regarding horizontal integration and differentiation, the reasoning is similar. Two countries that are highly interdependent develop a stronger demand for integration than two countries with low interdependence. In this perspective, the fact that the EC-6 integrated first would have to be explained by the fact that interdependence among them was high, and higher than their interdependence with the non-member countries. According to the same reasoning, countries that applied for membership later did so after their interdependence with the EU had risen substantially. European countries that do not want to join the EU should typically be those that are least dependent on the EU in a policy area.

At the level of individual policies, horizontal differentiation varies with the territorial extension of interdependence. Where the territorial reach of critical interdependence is smaller than that of the EU, we should see internal differentiation; external differentiation is present where the territorial reach of critical interdependence extends beyond the EU. Demand for the external differentiation of the internal market would thus be explained by the reach of significant market interdependence beyond the organizational boundaries of the EU. Similarly, horizontal differentiation reflects patterns of interest homogeneity. States with similar interests are integrated in the same policies and at the same level of centralization. Two groups of states each having compatible interests inside but unable to reach agreement between the two of them are likely to be integrated in different policies or at different levels of vertical integration in the same policy. From this perspective, the differentiated membership of member states in EMU would reflect either different levels of interdependence or different preferences in monetary policy.

Differentiated integration as a remedy for deadlock caused by heterogeneous state preferences works under the condition that all participating states regard differentiation as more beneficial than the uniform status quo. Generally, all states can choose a level of sectoral and vertical integration that is in line with their level of interdependence and their integration preferences, and all states benefit from not having to accommodate states with incompatible interests. This demand may, however, not be met because of two supply conditions: transaction costs and externalities.

Differentiation makes integration more complex, cumbersome, and time-consuming. Negotiations in different policies and at different levels of centralization involve different sets of governments and supranational actors. The supranational organizations of the EU need to deal with different sets of countries, some members, some non-members, and they need to work with different decision-making and administrative rules and competences across policies. The costs of reaching and implementing agreement are clearly higher than in a system in which the same actors negotiate on all policies according to the same rules. If transaction costs exceed the benefits of differentiation, especially if a system of differentiated integration threatens to become paralyzed, governments stop or block the process.

In addition, differentiated integration may be subject to negative externalities. Negative externalities result from negative interdependence between differentiated policies. The fact that one policy is more integrated than another may create costs for the more or the less integrated policy. And the fact that two groups of countries cooperate at different levels of integration may affect at least one of the groups negatively. As an example of negative externalities in vertical differentiation, take the freedom of movement of persons (strong vertical integration) and weakly integrated police competences. The effectiveness of the national police is undermined if criminals can easily cross borders but police officers in their pursuit cannot. In this case, the more integrated policy creates negative externalities for the less integrated one. The

combination of a supranational monetary policy and an intergovernmental fiscal policy is often seen as an example of a less integrated
policy undermining the more integrated policy. Since the EU cannot
strictly enforce fiscal discipline, the fiscally weaker or more profligate
eurozone countries have an incentive to free-ride on the fiscal strength
and discipline of others by expanding sovereign debt and hoping for a
bailout if they head toward bankruptcy.

To illustrate negative externalities in horizontal differentiation, take
again the freedom of movement of persons. If one group of member
states were willing to integrate their police forces whereas another
group were not, transnational organized crime would have an incentive to move its activities to the less integrated countries. Conversely,
we may also find constellations in which the less integrated group
free-rides on the more integrated one. Imagine that one group of
member states had a common asylum and refugee policy based on
liberal rules, whereas the other group kept its restrictive national
rules, the flow of refugees would be channelled towards the more integrated group. Alkuin Kölliker (2001, 2006) explains negative externalities by the characteristics of the goods produced in the more
integrated group of countries, in particular by their excludability.
Excludable goods encourage the group of countries wanting more
integration to move ahead but create incentives for the reluctant
group to veto (if they feel discriminated) or to join (if they want to
participate). The example of differentiated police integration is a case
in point. By contrast, non-excludable goods create incentives for free-
riding behaviour. They do not create an incentive for the reluctant
group to join and are likely to deter the group seeking higher integration from moving ahead. If you can participate in the club goods
without having to join and to pay, why become a member? From an
intergovernmentalist perspective, differentiated integration with negative externalities is unlikely to be realized or sustainable. The states
that choose not to suffer from these externalities will either forego or
veto differentiation. Differentiation with negative externalities will
only be established and upheld if the losers are compensated or lack
bargaining power.

The bargaining power required for differentiation with negative
externalities may not only result from superior material capabilities,
but also from institutional factors. First, countries with higher ratification constraints can more easily attain 'opt outs'. To achieve the higher
level of integration that they desire, states are more willing to let countries with credible non-ratification threats free-ride rather than jeopardize the entire agreement. This explains the concessions made to
countries such as Denmark or Ireland after the negative referendums
on the Maastricht and Lisbon Treaties. Second, non-member or new
member states are more easily discriminated against than (old) member

states. As Plümper and Schneider (2007) show, the EU has repeatedly used its superior bargaining power in accession negotiations to impose discriminatory transition arrangements on new member states in order to reduce the costs of enlargement for the old member states. In Eastern enlargement, for instance, the movement of labour from the Central and Eastern European countries to the old member states was initially restricted, and agricultural subsidies to the new members were phased in over a ten-year period.

Conjectures

According to liberal intergovernmentalism, the main factors driving integration are interdependence, preference homogeneity, and compliance problems. In addition, realist intergovernmentalism considers the autonomy costs of integration to be relevant. In the case of differentiation, transaction costs and externalities are also relevant. We distinguish conjectures at the level of policies (Conjecture 1) from those at the level of states (Conjecture 2).

Conjecture 1

The *vertical and horizontal integration* of a policy increases with:

(i)   international interdependence;
(ii)   the homogeneity of state preferences; and
(iii) the severity of the compliance problems;

and decreases with:

(iv)   the autonomy costs of integration.

Whereas conditions (i) to (iii) follow from liberal intergovernmentalist assumption, condition (iv) is derived from realist intergovernmentalism. This conjecture also has implications for the development of integration over time, policies characterized by:

(i)   higher international interdependence;
(ii)   more preference homogeneity;
(iii) less severe compliance problems;

or

(iv)   lower autonomy costs are integrated earlier.

We can further derive expectations regarding vertical and horizontal differentiation from this hypothesis. In addition, differentiation is affected by transaction costs and externalities.

Vertical differentiation. The extent of vertical differentiation in European integration increases with the variation of:

(i)   interdependence;
(ii)   preference homogeneity;
(iii)   compliance problems; and
(iv)   autonomy costs across policies;

and decreases with:

(v)   transaction costs; and
(vi)   negative externalities across policies.

Horizontal differentiation. With horizontal differentiation, policies are characterized by:

(i)   higher international interdependence;
(ii)   more preference homogeneity;
(iii)   less severe compliance problems;
(iv)   less politicization;
(v)   higher transaction costs; and
(vi)   more negative externalities are less horizontally differentiated.

At the level of states, intergovernmentalist conjectures refer to the likelihood of a state participating in integration.

Conjecture 2

The likelihood that a state participates in the integration of a particular policy increases with:

(i)   the extent of its interdependence with the other participating states; and
(ii)   the proximity of its preferences to those of the other participating states;

and decreases with:

(iii)   compliance costs;
(iv)   domestic ratification constraints; and
(v)   the state's size.

Again, this conjecture has implications for the timing of a state's integration, as well as its propensity to seek 'opt outs'. Countries that:

(i)   are more dependent on their international environment;
(ii)   have more mainstream preferences;
(iii) have weaker compliance problems;
(iv)   are subject to weaker ratification constraints; and
(v)   are smaller

integrate themselves earlier and are less likely to seek 'opt outs'.

Because small states are usually more dependent on their international environment and compliance problems are usually reflected in the state preferences, conditions (i) and (v) and conditions (ii) and (iii) are likely to be correlated.

Chapter 3

Supranationalism

From Neofunctionalism to Supranationalism

Supranationalist and intergovernmentalist theories have always been the main competitors in integration theory. In the early phase of European integration, neofunctionalism and realist intergovernmentalism shaped the debate; in the 1990s, supranational institutionalism and liberal intergovernmentalism opposed each other. Whereas intergovernmentalism claims that European integration is shaped by the preferences and power of states, and remains under their control, supranationalism argues that transnational society and supranational organizations are relevant actors, too, and that the initial steps of European integration build sufficient momentum to push its functional scope, level of centralization, and territorial extension beyond the level governments had originally intended. Whereas intergovernmentalism emphasizes the continuity of European integration as a form of international organization, supranationalism stresses its transformative potential: how it grows out of the domain of international relations and develops into a new kind of polity. In one of the phrases most often cited by students of European integration, Haas defines integration as a 'process whereby political actors in several distinct national settings are persuaded to shift their loyalties, expectations, and political activities toward a new and larger center, whose institutions possess or demand jurisdiction over pre-existing national states' (Haas 1961: 366–7).

Among the supranationalist theories, neofunctionalism was the dominant theory of integration in the early periods of integration theorizing. Prominent scholars such as Ernst Haas, Leon Lindberg, Joseph Nye, and Philippe Schmitter defined the neofunctionalist research agenda from the late 1950s until the 1970s. Since the late 1980s, the supranational institutionalism of Wayne Sandholtz and Alec Stone Sweet has marked a major refinement of neofunctionalism. Supranational institutionalism differs from its neofunctionalist predecessor in noticeable ways.

First, the original formulation of neofunctionalism sought to explain the ultimate formation of a European federal state. Once this prospect seemed to be robustly undermined by the crises and stagnation of

Table 3.1   *Building blocks of supranationalism*

General assumptions	Historical institutionalism Rational national, transnational, and supranational actors Unintended consequences and path dependency of institution-building
Explanatory theory	Dynamic theories of integration and institutionalization: – pluralism – transactionalism – principal–agent and incomplete contracting theory – path dependence
Factors explaining integration	Intensity of transnational exchanges Autonomy of supranational actors Rule density

political integration in the mid-1960s, scholars such as Sandholtz, Stone Sweet, Fligstein, and their collaborators were less interested in explaining the trajectory towards a particular *finalité* or end-point of the integration project. Instead, they directed their focus to studying processes and outcomes of *institutionalization*, the emergence and evolution of supranational rules, the capacity of supranational and transnational actors to shape and interpret these rules, and the effect of such rule-governed activity on cross-border transactions and the re-shaping of the EU's authority structure (Stone Sweet *et al.* 2001: 3; Stone Sweet and Sandholtz 1998: 16–20).

Second, supranationalists have broadened the range of objects studied. While neofunctionalism mainly focused on 'spillover' processes in the economic realm to explain the expansion of integration to new policy sectors, supranationalists also study processes and shifts towards increased centralization; something we have labelled vertical integration. In doing so, they have addressed a diversity of topics, ranging from the empowerment of the EP, or the expansion of the ECJ's jurisdiction to the institutionalization of policy areas such as internal and external security (e.g. the contributions in Stone Sweet *et al.* 2001).

In the next section, we present supranationalist assumptions and key theoretical arguments in more detail, before we discuss supranationalism as a theory of European integration. In the final section, the phenomenon of differentiated integration is illuminated from a supranationalist perspective. We conclude with the presentation of a set of supranationalist conjectures on differentiated integration. To set the stage for theory discussion, Table 3.1 gives an overview of the main building blocks of supranationalism.

Historical Institutionalism

General assumptions: rational actors in a path-dependent process of institutionalization

As intergovernmentalism, supranationalism has its origins in IR theory. In the 1950s and 1960s, the theories of neofunctionalism and transactionalism were the main challengers of the then dominant realist theory. These theories did not dispute the realist assumption that states are rational actors in an anarchical international system but, rather, questioned the conclusions that realists drew from this assumption. They held that, under the right social conditions, the international system was not bound to be characterized by recurring wars, permanent insecurity, and the dominance of great powers, but could be transformed into a rule-governed system through processes of institutionalization.

Supranationalism is similar to intergovernmentalism in that it assumes (boundedly) rational actors. 'Societal actors, in seeking to realize their value-driven interests, will choose whatever means are made available by the prevailing democratic order' (Haas 2004: xv). It also shares the starting point of intergovernmentalist theorizing: dense international interactions create a situation of international interdependence, in which unilateral state action is inefficient. Moreover, international cooperation is needed but difficult to realize in an anarchical system. States therefore agree on international rules and establish international organizations in order to facilitate and stabilize international cooperation for the benefit of all participants. Furthermore, supranationalism does *not* dispute that governments are central and powerful actors in the integration process, and that (hard) bargaining constitutes an important mode of interaction among the member states (Pierson 1998: 29; Stone Sweet and Sandholtz 1997: 134).

In two fundamental respects, however, supranationalism differs from intergovernmentalism. First, it extends the list of relevant actors. Whereas realist intergovernmentalism regards states as unitary actors and as the only actors that matter in European integration, liberal intergovernmentalism adds powerful domestic interest groups. Supranationalism includes transnational and supranational actors, too. Multinational corporations (i.e. firms that are not solely based in a single country) and transnational interest groups (ranging from business, professional, and labour associations to issue-specific associations representing environmental, educational, or civil rights interests) proliferate in the course of integration and act autonomously from the states. They demand supranational rules and the abolition of national rules, if supranational rules help them realize their objectives. In addition, supranationalism regards supranational organizations such as the Commission, the ECJ, and the EP as actors in their own right, rather than as mere instruments of the member states. They also seek to pursue their individual and collective interests in an instrumental fashion. This brings us to the second fundamental difference.

Supranationalism questions the rational-institutionalist assumption that states can design institutions to perform efficiently and reliably according to their preferences. This is also a core insight of historical institutionalism. The theory of historical institutionalism constitutes an important counter-point to functional theories of institution-building, which are prominent in the liberal intergovernmentalist account of integration (see Chapter 2). Functional theories of institution-building explain institutional choices by imputing these choices from the effects which states wish these institutions to produce (Keohane 1984). Hence, institutional choices are explained by their (expected) effects. Historical institutionalists reject this conjecture for three reasons (Pierson 1996, 2000, 2004). First, historical institutionalists doubt that political actors are as far-sighted as suggested by functional theorists; instead, they assume that political actors have rather short time horizons (given, for example, re-election constraints) and do not always take into account the potential long-term consequences of institutional choices. Second, historical institutionalists dispute that actors are able to foresee all possible contingencies and consequences of their actions, believing that initial institutional choices can thus have unintended consequences. Complex social processes that involve a large number of actors are likely to produce feedback loops and interaction effects that cannot possibly be foreseen or understood by even the most farsighted of actors (Pierson 1998: 39). Third, historical institutionalists contend that political actors can only marginally correct certain institutional developments, given often insurmountable obstacles to change induced by prohibitive decision-rules or the presence of veto players.

Supranational organizations not only monitor the rules that member states have agreed on, but also reformulate and reshape these rules. Supranationalists argue that the process of integration creates 'gaps' (Pierson 1996) in the subsequent treaty settlements, which prove to be enabling for some actors (interest groups; supranational actors, such as the Commission, the ECJ, or the EP) while they are difficult to reverse for others (most notably the member state governments). Consequently, integration may engender unintended consequences for the EU governments, which inhibit self-reinforcing dynamics. In the medium term, the process of integration deviates from the purpose governments had intended it to have, and forces them to adapt their preferences and behaviour in order to avoid high costs. Haas's (1961, 366–7) 'process whereby political actors ... are persuaded to shift their loyalties, expectations, and political activities toward a new and larger center' is thus not the result of a deliberate choice at the beginning of the integration project. It is the unintended result of a series of incremental decisions to shift competences from the national to the European level, each of them motivated by the imperfections and inefficiencies of previous integration steps and by the calculation that, ultimately, preserving the *status quo*, cutting back integrated competences, or exiting from the Union would have been more costly than moving ahead.

Explanatory theories of integrative dynamics

On the basis of these general assumptions on actors and institutions, supranationalists have employed different sets of theories that highlight driving forces and structural conditions conducive to integrative dynamics. First, the supranationalist assumption that transnational social groups play an important role in the integration process is rooted in a pluralistic understanding of politics, stressing the importance of interest groups in competing for access and influence on political decisions. Second, supranationalism emphasizes the importance of cross-border exchanges among societal actors (dubbed 'transnational exchange') as a precondition for political integration. In this context, we will take a brief look at transactionalism. Third, the problems of delegation highlighted by principal-agent theory are relevant for supranationalist theorizing in order to understand the mechanisms underpinning what Pierson (1996) has referred to as 'gaps' in member state control. Finally, we will briefly elaborate on the historical-institutionalist mechanism of path-dependence.

Pluralism. Haas argues that integration is most likely to proceed in highly industrialized economies characterized by the mobilization of society 'via strong interest groups and political parties, and leadership by elites competing for political survival and dominance under rules of constitutional democracy' (Mattli 2005: 329–30). Supranationalism is thus rooted in a theory of pluralism: groups, not states, are the central actors in the integration process. In modern, economically interdependent societies it is the competition among interest groups – striving to maximize the utility of their individual group – that drives the political process. Policy outcomes are the result of the differential pressure exercised by various interest groups (Haas 1961: 374, 378; 1968: xxxiii–xxxvi). What is the link between integration, industrialization and pluralism in liberal democratic states? Haas argues that 'the modern "industrial-political" actor' has most to win from integration, because he 'fears that his way of life cannot be safeguarded without structural adaptation' and hence 'turns to integration' (Haas 1961: 375). Integration is therefore in the interest of those social and political interest groups – such as export-oriented manufactures and producers, or highly qualified and mobile white-collar workers – who realize that expanding their activities beyond the confines of the nation state may be conducive to securing socio-economic benefits and objectives. The potential for transnational exchanges among these groups further increases if the pluralistic structures displayed by different countries resemble each other, a condition Mattli refers to as 'symmetrical regional heterogeneity' (Mattli 2005: 330). Parallel pluralistic structures (or socio-economic cleavages) in a region greatly facilitate the potential for social and political interest groups to join forces with their transnational counterparts in order to foster economic ties and hence promote integration (Mattli 2005: 330).

Transactionalism. Supranationalism is congruent with theoretical approaches, which put socio-economic exchanges or transactions, and the resulting interdependence, among political units (i.e. states) at centre stage. One theory linking cross-border transactions (ranging from inter-personal communications to trade) to community building is Karl Deutsch's theory of transactionalism. According to Karl W. Deutsch (1954), the increasing density of cross-border communication and social exchanges among individuals will result in a closer community among states, held together by common loyalties and sentiments. Deutsch argues that the more intense and dense transactions between two states, the more important (or interdependent) these two states will be to one another. Moreover, if these transactions and communications are deemed to be beneficial, they will promote trust, foster loyalties between the two states (Rosamond 2000: 44), and even lead to the development of a new 'amalgamated' community. Deutsch's theory of transactionalism and supranationalism departs from the postulated effects of social cross-border exchanges on the 'quality' of the emerging community: While transactionalism points at the potential formation of a 'security community' sharing a common sense of solidarity and common institutions, supranationalism is more concerned with the creation of supranational rules and governance structures (Stone Sweet and Sandholtz 1997: 300). To explain supranational governance supranationalists argue, akin to transactionalism, that cross-border transactions are integral as they create 'demand' for supranational rules, destabilizing and eventually replacing those at the national level.

Principal–agent and incomplete contracting theory. Principal–agent theory can be considered a further building block of supranationalism. According to the functional theory of institutions, governments, acting as 'principals', delegate considerable decision-making authority to 'agents' to fulfil certain collective tasks effectively and efficiently (Pollack 1997). Yet, several problems come with the delegation of tasks to agents. The first problem is adverse selection: how can principals be sure that they have selected the 'right' agent? The second problem is one of moral hazard: once an agent is selected, how can principals be sure that the agent does not develop an agenda of his or her own? In both instances, the principal faces the problem of asymmetrical information: in the case of adverse selection, principals are uncertain about the true motives of the agent *prior* to establishing the contractual relationship. In the case of moral hazard, the principal is uncertain about the activities of the agent once the contractual relationship is in place.

In both instances, principals establish an ample set of control mechanisms to prevent the potential for 'agency slippage' or 'bureaucratic drift'. We can distinguish a variety of so-called *ex ante* and *ex post* control mechanisms, which can be employed by principals to limit the agents' discretion. *Ex ante* control mechanisms are often dubbed 'administrative procedures', which 'define more or less narrowly the scope of agency activity, the legal instruments available to the agency, and the procedures to be followed by it' (Pollack 2003: 27). *Ex post* control mechanisms, in contrast, are geared towards oversight of the agent's activities and include procedures to monitor agency behaviour to rectify information asymmetries, or to influence the agent's behaviour through the application of sanctions (e.g. cutting the budget, dismissing agency personnel, overriding agency behaviour with new legislation). In spite of elaborate control mechanisms to hold agents at bay, however, agents 'will seek to use grants of authority for their own purposes, and especially to increase their autonomy' (Pierson 1998: 35).

The 'incomplete' nature of contracts, such as international treaties, tends to exacerbate the problem of agency slippage and bureaucratic drift. The notion of an 'incomplete contract' stipulates that the process of contracting is fraught with uncertainties. It is hard for the contracting parties to anticipate contingencies arising in the future, which prompt parties subject to the contract to offer conflicting interpretations over the initial contract. Moreover, asymmetric or incomplete information raises the costs of negotiating, which may result in a contract or treaty that represents a second-best option for the parties involved. As a result, contractual imperfections tend to force the contracting parties to renegotiate aspects of the initial bargain (Cooley and Spruyt 2009: 26). Moreover, contractual incompleteness tends to increase agents' discretion and hence their autonomy *vis-à-vis* their principals.

Path dependence. Institutional path dependence (Pierson 1996: 2000) refers to the idea that institutions are difficult to reform once they have been created – even if they develop in unintended ways, they become inefficient due to changing circumstances, or contradict the preferences of the principals. Paul Pierson (2000: 252) defines path dependence as a process 'in which preceding steps in a particular direction induce further movement in the same direction'. Actors that have decided to take one of several paths at an intersection are more likely to continue on this path in the future, rather than returning to the intersection to explore alternative paths. The mechanism of 'increasing returns' captures the rational behaviour that generates and supports path dependence.

Put positively, the benefits of continuing on the chosen path (relative to switching to another path) increase the further one walks. Actors become ever more experienced in dealing with an institution as time passes. Conversely, the 'sunk costs' and 'exit costs' rise (Pierson 2000: 252). When new institutions are introduced, actors make personal investments to adapt to the new institutions. These investments are often so high that, as a consequence, actors stick to these institutions even if new and more efficient alternatives appear. Unless major 'exogenous shocks' occur (such as wars, revolutions, or economic crises) the institutional route, once taken, becomes increasingly resistant to change. Exit costs further increase with the number of relevant other actors in the same institution. Either it is too costly for a single actor to exit if everybody else stays in, or it becomes too difficult to agree on how to change the institution.

In its analysis of European integration, supranationalism draws on pluralism and transactionalism to explain demand and support for European integration beyond the group of governments; and it draws on principal-agent theory and path dependence to explain the self-reinforcing dynamic of the integration process.

Supranationalism and European Integration

When it comes to explaining the initial steps of European integration, supranationalist and intergovernmentalist accounts do not differ to any appreciable extent. Supranationalists may give a more prominent role to transnational societal interactions and organizations in producing and voicing demand for integration, but will otherwise agree with a story of how governments agree on a particular level of centralization, and territorial extension based on the intergovernmental constellation of preferences and bargaining power. Supranationalist and intergovernmentalist explanations diverge once supranational institutions have been created and started to work.

Spillover

How do the mechanisms of transnational exchange and activism of social groups, agency discretion, and institutional path dependence feature in supranationalist theories of European integration? How do they work together to produce progressive vertical and horizontal integration? Supranationalists have traditionally subsumed mechanisms of transformative change under the label of 'spillover'. Ernst Haas saw the logic of spillover as the central mechanism to explain the expansive logic of European integration (Haas 1968: 283–317). Later works have categorized the factors and conditions producing integration's expansive logic into *functional, political,* and *institutional* spillover mechanisms (Schmitter 1969; Tranholm-Mikelsen 1991: 15–16).

Functional spillover results from the connectedness of different policy sectors. The functional spillover mechanism postulates that there will be a demand for further integration if the gains resulting from integration in policy sector A remain sub-optimal, unless adjacent policy sectors B and C will also be integrated, or when integration of A has negative effects on sectors B and C, unless they are all being integrated collectively (Lindberg and Scheingold 1970: 117). Put differently: the externalities of integrating a particular policy sector incite governments to undertake further, previously unplanned, steps of integration in adjacent policy sectors in order to prevent welfare losses. A similar logic is behind what Haas calls 'geographical spillover' as a trigger of horizontal integration – enlargement (Haas 1968: 313–15). States, which may be initially reluctant to join the EU, will feel pressured to join eventually, given the negative externalities of staying outside the Community.

Political spillover occurs as a reaction to initial integrative steps once interest groups, bureaucrats, and other domestic political actors direct their expectations and activities to the new, supranational level of decision-making. To the degree that integration improves the likelihood that the actors will realize their political aims at the supranational rather than the national level, we are likely to observe the formation of transnational coalitions and the development of common problem-solving perspectives (Haas 1968: xxxiv). Even though this process does not necessarily have to be harmonious (Schmitter 1969: 166), political actors will – in the course of time – develop new loyalties that transcend the nation state. Lindberg and Scheingold (1970: 199) characterize this process as actor socialization, thereby underlining the proximity of political spillover to constructivism (see also Haas 2001; Niemann and Schmitter 2009). Interest groups, bureaucrats, and other domestic actors will – on the basis of these newly acquired identities, attitudes, and coalitions – exercise pressure and influence on governments, and press them to advance the process of integration.

Institutional spillover is triggered by the activities of the EU's supranational actors, the Commission, the ECJ and the EP. On one hand, these actors contribute to the processes of functional and political spillover: they allude to connections between different policy sectors and point to the potential positive externalities of further integration. Conversely, they highlight the negative externalities and consequences of potential failures to advance sector integration (Nye 1971: 59). For the same reason, supranational actors support the formation of transnational coalitions. On the other hand, supranational actors – first and foremost, the Commission – help the governments of EU member states to discover their common interests and opportunities for efficient cooperation. Furthermore, they play a crucial role in helping the member states to 'upgrade their common interest' (Haas 1961) in finding bargaining solutions that are considered optimal from an integration perspective. This argument, however, is founded on the condition that supranational organizations – such as the Commission – possess an information advantage *vis-à-vis* the member state governments, which they are willing to exploit fully.

More recent supranationalist analyses have taken up and refined the notion of spillover as the core mechanism generating the expansionary dynamic of integration. Alec Stone Sweet and Wayne Sandholtz argue that European integration progresses as a result of the interplay of three developments: the expansion of transnational exchange, the political influence of groups that benefit from this exchange, and supranational actors' capacity to pursue an integrative agenda.

- As transnational economic exchange expands, the costs of adopting separate national rule-structures increase, as does the demand of transnational actors – interest groups, transnational corporations, producer and consumer groups – for supranational rule-making and policy coordination with the objective of destabilizing disparate national rule-structures, which hinder the free flow of goods and services. This demand will be stronger, the more these actors expect to profit from cross-border exchange and, hence, the larger the perceived advantage of uniform EU level rules *vis-à-vis* different national rules is. This process is in line with the idea of functional spillover.
- Transnational actors direct their demands for uniform EU-level rules to facilitate cross-border exchange at their respective national governments; yet, if these prove reluctant to advance the agenda for more uniform EU-level rules, transnational and societal actors turn to supranational organizations to voice their demands. This is evidence for political spillover.
- Finally, and corresponding with the logic of institutional spillover, the Commission and the ECJ use the powers and information at

their disposal to expand the scope of EU-level rules to facilitate cross-border exchange and, thus, help to increase collective transnational utility (Stone Sweet 2004; Stone Sweet and Sandholtz 1997: 299, 306; 1998: 4).

In addition, however, the supranational-institutionalist analyses of European integration that developed in the 1990s drew explicitly on historical institutionalism, focused more strongly on judicial and constitutional developments, and elaborated a process of institutionalization as the main cause of progressive integration.

Institutionalization and path dependence in European integration

Fligstein and Stone Sweet (2002) argue that market-making and polity-building processes are not merely interrelated but can be characterized as self-reinforcing processes. As transnational economic exchanges increase, legal or technical problems and obstacles may arise that hinder the free flow of trade in goods, services, and capital. Firms that lose business or incur costs as a result turn to policy-makers and courts to demand rules that solve these problems. If these demands are met, markets are likely to expand since the rules provide market actors with new opportunities to engage in market transactions: 'If market actors adapt their activities to exploit these new opportunities, then the feedback loop will be completed, and the cycle will begin anew' (Fligstein and Stone Sweet 2002: 1213). Fligstein and Stone Sweet demonstrate empirically that the long shadow cast by European law on national regulations and administrative practices tends to empower those private (economic) actors that are actively engaging in transnational exchanges, while firms with a domestic orientation are facing harder times. When those actors advantaged by EU-wide rules and institutions

> pushed for more integration through lobbying and litigation, EC legislators found that the search for Eurowide solutions to the problems posed by the expansion of transnational society and economic interdependence were the only feasible response. As the EC's rule structure became more dense and differentiated, so did the grounds for legal action, and actors moved to push the Commission and the ECJ to establish or interpret new rules in their favour. (Fligstein and Stone Sweet 2002: 1226)

In *The Judicial Construction of Europe*, Stone Sweet (2004) employs this theoretical framework to account for the gradual *constitutionalization* of the EU, exemplified by the establishment and acceptance of the ECJ's doctrines of direct effect and supremacy of European law. He shows that these doctrines had a profound impact on patterns and density of transnational exchanges: as private actors were enabled to plead rights bestowed by EU law before national courts, and as national judges applied EU law and prioritized it over (competing) national law, private actors made use of their opportunity to go to national judges and ask them to remove domestic (legal) obstacles to trade. And as transnational activities mounted, 'the pool of potential litigants expands, as does the number and diversity of situations likely to give rise to conflicts between traders and states' (Stone Sweet 2004, 15). Consequently, there is a constant and self-reinforcing process linking transnational exchange, litigation, and rule-making that feeds back onto traders and private actors seeking (further) opportunities to realize their socio-economic interests.

Stone Sweet and collaborators also find that social groups that are not directly engaged in economic activities, such as environmentalists or advocates of women's rights, 'would use the courts to destabilize or reform national rules and practices they find disadvantageous' (Stone Sweet 2004: 15). For example, in 1976 the ECJ declared that Art. 141, which posits that men and women shall receive equal pay for equal work, also implies that the EU is not merely an economic community 'but is at the same time intended ... to ensure social progress and seek the constant improvement of the living standards and working conditions of [its] people' (*Defrenne II*, ECJ 43/75). While the founding members of the EEC Treaty inserted Art. 141 to discourage social dumping, 'over the course of twenty-five years, private litigants and national judges helped the Court transform the provision into a basic right to sex equality in the workplace' (Stone Sweet 2004: 148). The ECJ developed 'a rights-oriented interpretation of the Treaty ..., which further empowered women, *vis-à-vis* national governments, within processes governments could not directly control' (Stone Sweet 2004: 148). According to supranationalists, intergovernmentalism fails to acknowledge that the institutional bases of the ECJ's powers are those of a trustee or fiduciary court and not those of a more-or-less faithful agent of the member states (Carrubba *et al.* 2008; Garrett *et al.* 1998). The effective insulation of the ECJ from member state control was crucial to engendering the further institutionalization of the EU (Fligstein and Stone Sweet 2001: 31; Sweet and Sandholtz 1997: 310–12).

Even though the EU's primary law initially reflects the preferences of member states and their respective bargaining power, the application of the EU treaties developed in directions unforeseen or unintended by member state governments. First, actors who operate under the treaty rules adapt to them and use the opportunities offered by them to realize their own preferences, which may not be congruent with those of the member states who enacted the rules in the first place (Lindner and

Rittberger 2003: 451–5). Second, treaty rules never represent a complete contract that caters for every possible contingency, since rules are open to interpretation; rules (obviously) may offer controversial interpretations, and sometimes they may not even offer clear prescriptions for action. In situations like these, supranational organizations such as the ECJ and the Commission – who have been endowed by the member states with the onus of applying and interpreting these rules – may exploit this grey zone for their own advantage. The process of rule-modification and rule-interpretation is a continuous process:

> As they interpret and apply the rules, courts, legislators, and administrators necessarily modify them by establishing their effective meaning. The new or changed rules then guide subsequent interactions, as the actors which act under these rules adapt their behaviours to the rules. The disputes that arise thereafter take shape in an altered rule structure and initiate the processes that will again reinterpret and modify the rules. The new rules guide actor behaviour, and so on. (Stone Sweet and Sandholtz 1997: 310)

The unanticipated institutionalization of intergovernmental treaties has not only spawned legal integration, but has also benefited the EP. Since the 1990s, the EP has been extremely successful in interpreting the formal rules laid down in the treaties to further its own institutional prerogatives, against the will of many member state governments (e.g. Farrell and Héritier 2003, 2004; Héritier 2007; Hix 2002). The starting point of the argument is similar to the argument on judicial empowerment. The treaty and its rules on legislative procedures represent an incomplete contract, and governments lack complete information as to how the EP will interpret the formal treaty rules. Members of the EP (MEPs) have two crucial advantages over governments: a longer time horizon relative to the Council members and the Council Presidency in particular, which finds itself under pressure to deliver results during its short six-month tenure, and a lower sensitivity to failure because governments (rather than MEPs) will be blamed if the EU does not deliver. These advantages translate into EP bargaining power in day-to-day decision-making, which it can use to delay or veto important decisions unless governments consent to giving the EP informal competences in practice that go beyond the formal powers conferred by the treaties. These informal rules effectively shift the balance of power from the member states to the EP's benefit and are often formalized in the next round of treaty revisions (Hix 2002).

From a supranationalist point of view, these processes show that the intergovernmental treaty negotiations on which intergovernmentalist analyses focus are effectively embedded in transnational and supranational contexts. They take place in an environment that undergoes significant changes in the period between two intergovernmental conferences. In this respect, the conferences are convened against the background of new demands by transnational actor coalitions and an institutional context shaped by the self-reinforcing dynamic of the process of institutionalization. The demand for further integration is thus less the result of 'exogenous shocks' (manifestations of increased international interdependence) but, rather, springs from endogenous, path-dependent processes, and intergovernmental negotiations are less the generators of integration but, instead, its product (Caporaso 1998: 350; Stone Sweet and Sandholtz 1998: 16, 20).

Supranationalists expect that once a certain level of integration is reached, it will be almost impossible for governments to reverse it (Fligstein and Stone Sweet 2001: 38, 55). As stated, supranationalism takes recourse to the mechanisms of high institutional thresholds and sunk costs postulated by historical institutionalism in order to explain the (near) irreversibility of an institutional path once taken (Pierson 1998: 43–7). First, the rules to amend or change the treaties are very restrictive, since they demand unanimous agreement among governments, plus ratification in each member state; furthermore, policy changes within the treaties require at least a qualified majority. When only a minority of states benefits from a particular rule, the majority will do everything it can to block change.

Second, over the course of the period since the 1960s, national political systems have become increasingly penetrated by rules originating at EU level. The sunk costs of adapting national rules and policy-making processes to the exigencies of EU politics render the mere existence of a state outside the EU increasingly unattractive. In this sense, 'exit' is also becoming an ever more unlikely policy option for an EU member state. Thus, the threat of leaving the Union is unlikely to be a credible bargaining strategy.

General hypotheses

Supranationalism explains European integration as a progressive, self-reinforcing process of institutionalization. Integration may initially correspond to intergovernmentalist expectations of a formal agreement negotiated among interdependent states, and shaped by their preferences and power. Once supranational organizations and rules are in place, however, integration produces unintended and unanticipated consequences, and escapes the exclusive control of the states. Several mechanisms triggered by initial integration and described by supranationalist approaches explain the dynamic.

- More transnational interactions create demand for more supranational regulation.

- (Transnational) societal actors turn to supranational organizations to obtain support for this demand (political spillover).
- Supranational organizations use their competences to support societal actors, strengthen supranational rules, and expand their own powers (institutional spillover).
- The externalities of integration in one policy area create demand for integration in other policy areas (functional spillover).
- The externalities of integration among a limited group of countries create demand for integration in other countries (geographical spillover).
- The short time horizons of governments and the incompleteness of treaty contracts strengthen the bargaining power and discretion of supranational actors.
- Prohibitive consensus requirements for treaty change and prohibitive exit costs stabilize the integration gains of transnational and supranational actors, and prevent the rollback of vertical or horizontal integration.

The general hypotheses of supranationalism, then, refer to the factors that trigger and sustain the self-reinforcing process of integration.

Integration is likely to progress if it increases transnational societal actors' expected utility. Firms, interest groups, and civil society organizations demand more vertical integration if supranational rules and competences promise higher profits and better regulation. When based in a non-member country, they advocate joining the EU.

Integration is likely to progress if supranational actors possess the capacity to further their own institutional interests and the interests of transnational actors. This capacity consists in filling the gaps in intergovernmental treaties, interpreting and elaborating the rules, and mobilizing and organizing transnational societal groups.

To the extent that successive rounds of integration strengthen the utility of transnational actors and the capacity of supranational actors (thanks to spillover and institutionalization dynamics), the process becomes self-sustaining. Governments are increasingly constrained: whereas the opportunities to stop integration or devolve competences to the national level become rarer, the pressure to strengthen and expand integration mounts. In addition, *the framework of substantial regulations and the rules of integration correspond increasingly to the constellation of transnational interests and supranational rule-making and rule-interpreting activity,* and less to the initial intergovernmental bargain.

Supranationalism and Differentiated Integration

What conjectures can we derive from supranationalism to account for patterns of differentiated integration? Following up on our discussion above, differentiation can be said to be the result of the same two major forces that also drive progress in integration. First, differentiation may be caused by variation in the intensity of transnational exchange between different sectors and countries. Second, it may be affected by the capacity and preferences of supranational actors to promote their policy and institutional interests by furthering the integration process.

We start from the assumption that both transnational and supranational actors tend to be interested in unified, rather than differentiated, integration.

Supranational actors have an institutional interest in achieving high levels of centralization across the board of policies in order to maximize their own turf and competences. They also tend to believe that supranational regulation is more efficient than are national regulations. For these reasons, they work towards minimizing the vertical differentiation inherent in a gradual integration process in favour of high vertical integration in all policy areas.

Supranational actors also have an institutional interest in avoiding horizontal differentiation. Horizontal differentiation makes European governance more complicated. Decision-making and monitoring become more cumbersome. Internal differentiation comes with exemptions and derogations that need to be managed by the supranational organizations, and sometimes requires additional organizational set-ups. For instance, the eurozone countries often meet separately; but there is a need to consult and discuss financial and monetary issues with the non-eurozone countries too. External differentiation also goes hand in hand with a proliferation of association councils and bilateral committees, and does not allow for centralized enforcement. Supranational actors should welcome the fact that horizontal differentiation allows member states to move ahead with supranational integration despite the opposition of others, and expands supranational rules to encompass countries that are otherwise unwilling or unable to join the EU. But they are unlikely to accept differentiation as a permanent condition, and will work towards overcoming opt-outs and towards the membership of associated countries.

Transnational actors can be expected to be comfortable with vertical differentiation but less so with horizontal differentiation. They often have a policy-specific agenda and organization, and strive for the level of centralization that corresponds to the level of transnational interactions in their area and that suits their policy-specific interests. But for each policy sector, they will want to ensure that all states participate. For instance, transnational business associations seek to create a level playing field for their members across the EU. The same is true for transnational trade unions trying to prevent a race to the bottom as a consequence of 'social dumping'. Transnational civil society organizations, such as environmental or women's rights associations, pursue the system-wide improvement of standards.

By contrast, initiatives for horizontal differentiation are usually rooted in the special interests or deviant preferences of national governments or societal actors. It then depends on the strength and capacity of transnational and supranational actors whether they can counteract these initiatives and push for more unified integration.

Intensity of transnational exchange

One core proposition of supranationalism posits that the intensity of transnational exchange is a good predictor for explaining patterns of supranational dispute resolution and rule-making (Stone Sweet and Brunell 1998). According to supranationalists, variation in transnational exchange should be correlated strongly with variation in the demand for supranational rules. Stone Sweet and Sandholtz hypothesize that in those policy sectors

> where the intensity and value of cross-national transactions are relatively low, the demand for EC level co-ordination of rules and dispute resolution will be correspondingly low. Conversely, in domains where the number and value of cross-border transactions are rising, there will be increasing demand on the part of the transactors for EC level rules and dispute resolution mechanisms. (Stone Sweet and Sandholtz 1997: 308)

We would therefore hypothesize that integration is more likely in policy areas characterized by high levels of transnational exchange. This implies that integration in economic policy sectors should advance more rapidly than in those areas with only few societal or transnational transactions to generate a demand for supranational rules, such as in the area of security and defence policy (Fligstein 2008: 99–102 for a qualification of this argument).

This hypothesis can also be cast in temporally dynamic terms. The fact that integration in the EC-6, and later in the EC-12, proceeded more rapidly in the area of the free movement of goods than in other policy fields can be explained by patterns of transnational exchange, which were initially more pronounced in the area of free movement than in other policy sectors. This logic also applies to non-EU member states: the higher the levels of transnational exchange between EU countries and 'outsiders', the stronger the demand on behalf of transnational social actors from EU and non-EU countries to partake in integration. Transnational societal demand for integration should thus be lowest in countries where the scope of transnational exchanges linking the EU and non-EU countries is small.

In *The Uniting of Europe*, Haas (1958) briefly touched upon this phenomenon: under what conditions would supranationalists expect the occurrence of 'geographical spillover' (Haas 1958: 314), i.e. the expansion of sector integration to non-EU countries? According to Haas, trading patterns play an important role: the more interdependent the economies and the higher the levels of cross-border exchanges between EU 'insiders' and 'outsiders', the higher the demand for integration should be – voiced by political and economic elites in general, and traders and actors engaged in transnational economic exchanges in particular.

Patterns of differentiation along the horizontal dimension encompass, for instance, full membership in the EU or – below the threshold of full membership – association agreements offering selective integration between the EU and a third country (external differentiation). In the context of an association agreement, a third country may, for instance, be granted tariff-free access to EU markets. Supranationalists would expect 'geographical spillover' when the scope and density of cross-border exchanges is high – and the higher the scope and density of exchange, the higher the likelihood that demands for full membership will be voiced. However, 'geographical spillover' may not merely be restricted to the economic realm: the externalities of market-making policies, which may pertain to issues such as environmental protection, but also to questions about controlling and managing immigration, border controls, and ensuring internal security (all of which become prevalent in an economic community without internal borders), trigger demand for managing these externalities with third countries.

The density and scope of transnational exchange should also have a demonstrable effect on the demand for supranational rules or the abolition of domestic rules acting, for instance, as barriers to cross-border economic exchange. This should be reflected, inter alia, in the absolute number of cases brought before national courts to enforce EU law, as well as in the scope and density of supranational rule-making (secondary legislation) in a policy area characterized by high levels of transnational exchange. This latter point is interesting since it points at a particular dynamic or pattern of differentiated integration, that between 'negative' and 'positive' integration. While negative integration refers to the abolition of national rules, which serve as obstacles to cross-border exchange, positive integration is the process whereby supranational rules are established to replace national rules in a particular area of policy.

As negative integration progresses, new obstacles to cross-border transactions – such as domestic laws, regulations and administrative rules to protect the environment, consumers, workers' health, and so on – will be exposed and targeted by social actors. These 'newly exposed strata of national regulatory systems' are likely to be targeted by traders 'in subsequent rounds of litigation' (Stone Sweet 2004: 74). Over the course of time, new groups of private actors not primarily engaged in cross-border trade but, instead, supporting an environmentalist agenda or non-discriminatory practices in the workplace, have pleaded rights under EU law. As a result, the ECJ has 'steadily developed a rights-oriented interpretation of the Treaty (and of relevant secondary legislation)' (Stone Sweet 2004: 148) thereby encroaching into new policy domains. Thus, indirect obstacles to trade, such as social provisions, as well as non-trade related issues, would become the (new) target of private actors. Thereby, the application of EU law spurred positive integration, i.e. the construction of EU-wide legal regimes in policy domains, such as social policy, environmental policy and even taxation, where policy outcomes are predominantly under the Council's (and also the EP's) control.

We can thus hypothesize that integration is most likely to proceed initially in the domain of market-making policies, but tends to spill over into the market-correcting domain as the EU's legal system grows denser and the Court becomes more activist, taking up the demand for supranational rule-making from transnational societal actors. This latter point is important, since market exchange and transnational demand do not suffice to bring about integration. As Philippe Schmitter has aptly remarked, in and of itself interdependence 'based on high rates of transactions is impotent' (Schmitter 1969: 164). We need to turn to the preferences and capacity of supranational actors in responding to, and even promoting, the demands of transnational societal actors.

Capacity and preferences of supranational actors

Recall our general supranationalist hypothesis that integration is most likely to be brought about when the level of transnational exchanges is high, the preferences of supranational actors are in sync with the demand of transnational actors, and the capacity of supranational actors is sufficient to advance the integration project. While we have addressed the scope and intensity of transnational exchanges in the previous section, we will now turn to the preferences and capacity of supranational actors. This discussion has already been touched upon in our discussion of *institutional* spillover. When and under what conditions do supranational actors, such as the Commission, the ECJ and the EP, act upon the demand of transnational society to expand the reach of supranational rules? Most treatises of the partial autonomy of supranational actors in the integration process rest (implicitly or explicitly) on the principal–agent analogy. The capacity of supranational agents to shift policy outcomes in directions that run counter to their principals' preferences is tied to the level of discretion that these agents can exercise. The more loosely *ex ante* and *ex post* control mechanisms are designed, the higher is the level of discretion that supranational actors can enjoy. As a result, 'they will try to expand the gaps in member-state government control, and they will use any accumulated political resources to resist efforts to curtail their authority' (Pierson 1998: 35).

What are the implications of this argument for our analysis of differentiated integration? We would expect that supranational actors less constrained by control mechanisms should be able to exercise higher degrees of discretion than supranational actors who are tightly controlled. Based on this reasoning, we would also expect integration to have a self-reinforcing effect. Looking at vertical integration, we would expect that in those policy areas where supranational actors, such as the Commission, already possess relatively high degrees of discretion (e.g. in competition policy), the capacity of supranational actors to shift policy outcomes beyond the principals' intentions should be higher than in policy areas where their discretion is smaller (e.g. in economic policy-making) or virtually non-existent (as in security and defence matters).

We also expect the processes of spillover and institutionalization to work against differentiation over time. First, if a policy sector is integrated earlier or at a higher level than others, the mechanisms of spillover create functional pressures or political steps to integrate neighbouring sectors (at a higher level) as well. Second, if a member state obtains an opt out, or is excluded from a policy sector, the respective government or relevant interest groups may find themselves disadvantaged or marginalized, and strive to become fully integrated. Alternatively, institutionalization at the supranational level stemming from court decisions, organizational development, and informal development provide *de facto* unification while differentiation continues *de jure*. For any given step of differentiation, supranationalism therefore leads us to expect an increase in unification as time passes.

Conjectures

As demonstrated in the previous sections, the main factors driving differentiated integration in supranationalist integration theory are the scope and intensity of transnational exchanges, as well as the preferences and capacity of supranational actors. At the level of *policies*, conjectures respond to the question as to why some sectors are more integrated, or have been integrated earlier, than others.

Conjecture 1

The *vertical and horizontal integration* of a policy sector increases with:

(i)   the scope and intensity of transnational exchanges; and
(ii) the capacity and discretion of supranational actors to advance integration in a given policy area.

As a corollary, the integration of a particular policy sector precedes the integration of another sector if:

(i)   the scope and intensity of transnational exchanges with regard to the former are critically higher in the former than in the latter; and if
(ii) the preferences, capacity, and discretion of supranational actors are such that it is more difficult to advance supranational rule-making in the latter than in the former.

Vertical differentiation. The extent of vertical differentiation in European integration increases with differences across policies in:

(i)   the scope and intensity of transnational exchanges; and
(ii) the capacity of supranational actors.

Horizontal differentiation. Policies that are less horizontally differentiated are characterized by:

(i)   more geographically extended and intense transnational exchanges; and
(ii) a higher capacity of supranational actors.

Conversely, differentiation decreases as transnational exchange and supranational actor capacity increase. Because supranationalism generally assumes these two conditions to obtain, it follows that any differentiation that occurs in the course of European integration will decrease over time. Spillover and institutionalization effects not only work towards more integration, but also towards more unified integration.

Conjecture 2

By contrast, conjectures at the level of *countries* seek to explain why some states are less integrated, or have joined the EU and its policies later than others.

The likelihood that a state participates in the integration of a particular policy sector increases with:

(i)   the scope and intensity of transnational exchange with the other participating states; and
(ii) the preferences and capacity of supranational actors to press for the expansion of supranational rules.

As a corollary, again, the integration of one country precedes the integration of another:

(i)   if the scope and intensity of transnational exchanges of this country with the other integrated countries are critically higher in the former; and
(ii) if the preferences and capacity of supranational actors are such that it is more difficult to press for the integration of the latter than the former.

In other words, less interdependent and stronger countries are more likely to reject or opt out from integration.

Chapter 4

Constructivism

A New Emphasis on Ideas

Constructivism is a comparatively recent addition to the portfolio of theoretical approaches to European integration. A 1999 special issue of the *Journal of European Public Policy* signalled that something like a 'constructivist school' was forming in EU studies (Christiansen *et al.* 2001). As in the case of intergovernmentalism and supranationalism, the theory was imported from IR, where constructivism had established itself a few years earlier as the counterpart to the rationalist mainstream. Indeed, most of the early proponents of constructivism in EU studies had their academic roots in IR. Since the turn of the millennium, constructivism has firmly established itself as an approach to studying the EU but has not yet consolidated as a theory of European integration on the same level as liberal intergovernmentalism or neofunctionalism.

Simply put, constructivism claims that social ideas and discourses matter for European integration. This is not to say that ideas had not featured in theorizing on the EU before, but they were prominent mainly in early theoretical approaches. Federalism relied heavily on 'ideas of Europe' and value-based commitments as a motivation and orientation for European integration movements (Burgess 1989; Lipgens 1982). Karl Deutsch's 'transactionalism' defined an emerging 'sense of community', i.e. a transformation of identities, as the essence of integration (Deutsch 1957: 5). Neofunctionalism envisaged that European integration would lead to the socialization of actors involved in the integrated policy-making process, and ultimately result in a shift of citizens' loyalties and identities from the nation-state to the supranational community (Haas 1968: 16). Even traditional intergovernmentalism had a place for ideas such as the diversity of national traditions and the dominance of national identities – albeit as a limiting factor in European integration (Hoffman 1966). By contrast, more recent theories of European integration were based on an explicitly 'rationalist' foundation (see Chapters 2 and 3). Liberal intergovernmentalism accords ideas only a minor role in the formation of preferences for integration and conceives them predominantly as a residual explanatory factor in situations of uncertain or negligible material consequences. The supranational institutionalist successor theories to neo-functionalism started from rationalist micro-foundations as well. The arrival of constructivism in EU studies thus redirected the theoretical attention to the ideational underpinnings, driving forces, constraints, and outcomes of European integration.

Table 4.1 presents the main building blocks of constructivist theorizing on European integration. As in the previous chapters, we start at the most abstract level with general assumptions and hypotheses of sociological institutionalism in IR. On this basis, we outline building blocks of a constructivist theory of European integration, which we will finally elaborate to explain differentiated integration.

Sociological Institutionalism

General assumptions: ideas and appropriateness

Constructivist assumptions are fundamental to sociological institutionalism in International Relations. The label 'sociological institutionalism' covers approaches to the study of international institutions that deviate on two accounts from rationalist institutionalism, as well as historical institutionalism – one relating to structure, the other to agency. First, sociological institutionalism assumes the primacy of ideational rather than material structures. Second, rather than behaving instrumentally or strategically, actors follow the 'logic of appropriateness' (March and Olsen: 160) or the 'logic of arguing' (Risse 2000).

According to constructivism, the most relevant structures in IR are social constructions or, simply put, ideas. These ideas are social insofar as they not only shape the thinking and actions of individuals, but also structure the cognitions of entire social groups. The literature distinguishes instrumental and principled ideas. Instrumental ideas (or knowledge) relate to shared understandings of cause-effect relationship and problem-solving, e.g. about the causes of environmental degradation or the best ways to encourage international trade. Principled ideas comprise values and norms. Political values describe the desired properties and purposes of political order, e.g. freedom, equality, or economic growth. Norms are collective standards of appropriate behaviour. They consist of 'dos' and 'don'ts' that describe the socially desired behaviour of individuals and organizations, and the appropriate means by which to achieve the purposes of political order.

Identities are another important type of idea. An identity expresses who we are, who belongs to us and what unifies us. Typically, an identity also conveys what distinguishes us from others, the 'in-group' from the 'out-group'. The identity of a group can be based on instrumental

Table 4.1   *Building blocks of constructivism*

General assumptions	Sociological institutionalism in IR Primacy of ideas Logic of appropriateness and arguing		
Explanatory theory	Community theory of institutions	Argumentation theory	Socialization theory
Factors explaining integration	Ideational consensus	Legitimacy of arguments and institutional settings	Legitimacy, exposure

and principled ideas. In this case, the group defines and distinguishes itself by its knowledge, values, and norms. Such identities are, in principle, universal. Any individual can adopt an identity and belong to a group by adopting the group's instrumental and principled ideas. As in the case of ethnic identity, however, identities may also be based on race, kin, homeland, or native language. Such identities are also socially constructed, but refer to properties that are difficult – or even impossible – for individuals or groups to change or adopt voluntarily.

A culture consists of the entirety of a group's ideas. To the extent that a group defines itself by its culture, it is a community. The members of a community possess a positive collective identity – they identify themselves as part of the group and with each other – and share values, norms, knowledge, and other common ideas.

Ideas shape social preferences, interactions, and outcomes, and they do so in ways that cannot be reduced to material structures and interests. The focus on ideas distinguishes constructivism from both intergovernmentalism, which gives primacy to the material structure of interdependence, and supranationalism, which additionally brings institutional and organizational structure into play. Constructivism does not deny the relevance of material and organizational structures. But from the constructivist perspective, ideas shape how actors interpret interdependence and which solutions they choose to deal with it. In addition, they may enable or prescribe individuals' actions and outcomes that run against actors' cost-benefit calculations or power constellations, and they may exclude or prohibit behaviour that would seem instrumental on the basis of given existing material structures. Finally, constructivism assumes organizations and their behaviour to be motivated and constrained by organizational culture (knowledge, values, norms, and identities).

The 'logic of appropriateness' is the logic of action that corresponds to the primacy of intersubjective structures. According to this logic, actors do not judge alternative courses of action by the consequences for the actors' utility, but by their conformity to values, norms, and identities, or to the actors' social obligations. Even if the ideas are unclear or contested, and thus do not prescribe a single appropriate behaviour, actors do not revert to instrumental behaviour and to maximizing their self-interest. Rather, they follow the 'logic of arguing', i.e. they enter into a discourse in which they exchange arguments in a search for the valid idea and the appropriate course of action.

Whereas rational institutionalism assumes governmental preferences to be exogenously given, sociological institutionalism treats them as endogenous, in principle. That is, the identities, ideas, and interests of states can be modified or changed in the process of international negotiations and as a result of participating in international institutions. This transformation of identities and interests can be a result of argumentation and socialization.

Explanatory theories: community institutions, argumentation, and socialization

Sociological institutionalism offers three substantive theories that specify how ideas affect international negotiations and institutions. The ideational or community theory of institutions specifies under which conditions international institutions are formed, how they work, and what they do. It is equivalent to the functional and club theory of institutions in rationalist institutionalism. Argumentation theory explains the outcome of international negotiations in which ideas are contested. It is the constructivist counterpart of bargaining theory. Finally, the theory of international socialization tells us how international institutions shape and transform the ideas of international actors. Its purpose is similar to the path dependence mechanism in historical institutionalism. Sociological institutionalism thus seeks to explain two cause-effect relationships: the ideational causes of international institutions and their ideational effects.

Community theory of institutions. According to sociological institutionalism, international organizations are 'community representatives' (Abbott and Snidal 1998: 24). The origins, goals, and procedures of international institutions are shaped by the standards of legitimacy and appropriateness of the international community they represent (and which constitutes their cultural and institutional environment) – rather than by the utilitarian demand for efficient problem-solving (see e.g. Barnett and Finnemore 1999: 703; Katzenstein 1997: 12; Weber 1994: 4–5, 32). Different international communities with different collective identities, values, norms, and instrumental ideas establish international institutions with different purposes and different organizational cultures and structures. Accordingly, an organization of democratic states will have other goals and rules than an organization of autocratic states, and an organization of Latin American countries differs from an organization of African countries.

First, international institutions depend on the strength of international community. The establishment of international institutions requires shared ideas, and their strength and stability increases with a common culture. Second, the culture and structure of international organizations depends on the ideas and identity of the underlying international community. What international organizations do, how they do it, and how they make and implement decisions is shaped by the instrumental and principled beliefs, as well as the values and norms, of the community. Third, participation in international institutions is patterned by shared ideas. The borders of international organizations are congruent with the borders of international communities. The design and membership of international institutions thus do not follow considerations of efficiency but, rather, community-based standards of legitimacy.

Argumentation theory. Put simply, an argument is a claim justified by a principle (a basic idea). Arguing is a negotiation mode based on the use of arguments – in contrast to the use of threats and promises in the bargaining mode. The theory of argumentation explains, among other things, under which conditions arguments are effective (Schimmelfennig 2003: 208–13). First, actors enter into arguing mode when claims are contested. If actors agree on the ideas and the behaviour that follows from them, there is no point in arguing. Second, the better argument prevails. The better argument is the one that provides a superior justification for the claim. The superior justification is either based on the better (correct or more legitimate) conclusion from a shared principle or – if the principle is contested – by the better (correct or more legitimate) higher-order idea. The actors with the better arguments thus obtain argumentative power and are able to define the consensus on the basis of their claims. They influence or shape the goals of the institution, the rules according to which it works, the collective decisions, and the distribution of gains and losses. If, however, the participants in a debate do not agree on either the principle of justification or any higher-order idea that can adjudicate between controversial claims, arguing does not lead to a consensual outcome.

In addition, the likelihood of argumentative persuasion depends on the institutional setting in which arguing takes place. In general, these are settings that facilitate or even normatively proscribe – but certainly do not punish – sincere argumentation and the openness of debates. Institutional settings that blur role identities, privilege authority based on expertise and/or moral competence, and oblige chairs to be neutral have been credited with the propensity to favour argumentative persuasion, whereas the effect of publicity is ambiguous (see e.g. Risse and Kleine 2010). At any rate, and in contrast to explanations of rational institutionalism, the substantive outcomes of international negotiations and the activities of international organizations do not necessarily reflect constellations of material preferences and bargaining power. Rather, they mirror constellations of ideas and the power of the better argument.

Socialization theory. International organizations are not only community representatives, but also community-building agencies. According to sociological institutionalism, they are able 'to impose definitions of member characteristics and purposes upon the governments of [their] member states' (McNeely 1995: 33). They 'define international tasks [and] new categories of actors ..., create new interests for actors ..., and transfer models of political organizations around the world' (Barnett and Finnemore 1999: 699). In that way, they do not simply regulate state behaviour but constitute state identities and interests. How and under which conditions they are able to induct actors to the community culture is the subject of theories of international socialization.

Constructivists have established a widely accepted catalogue of conditions under which international socialization is likely to be effective (Checkel 2001: 562–3; Johnson 2001: 498–9; Risse 2000: 19).

- Actors face novel situations characterized by high uncertainty. This makes them susceptible to learning new ideas, whereas their old ideas appear inadequate. = Glob ? Rise of US & China ?
- The organization possesses the authority to act on behalf of a community with which a particular actor identifies (or to which an actor aspires to belong). Actors that do not identify themselves positively with the community, or do not accept the authority of the community organization, are less likely to accept the community's constitutive ideas or the organization's prescriptions. Democracies.
- Actors are exposed intensely and consistently to the community ideas. The more closely and frequently actors participate in and interact with the community organization, and the more consistent the messages that they receive from it, the more effective international socialization is likely to be. dev° of institutional meeting
- Socialization concerns norms and rules that enjoy high legitimacy in the community. Role of Law
- Socialization takes place in an environment that encourages deliberation and is characterized by the absence of external and political constraints. Put differently, arguing is more conducive to socialization than bargaining.
- The domestic or societal resonance of community ideas is high. If community ideas appeal to, or can be demonstrated to build on, existing domestic ideas, they are accepted more easily.
- Socialization agencies and processes that fulfil these conditions are more likely to shape and transform the ideas to which international actors adhere.

Constructivism and European Integration

From the constructivist perspective, European integration is, at its core, a process of community-building. Over time, community-building and (institutional) integration mutually influence and potentially reinforce each other. Initially, strong communities with shared ideas and a positive collective identity are conducive to growth in integration. In turn, integrated institutions that provide for dense interactions and possess high legitimacy deepen the community through socialization processes. The constructivist research programme in European integration studies has three distinct foci that can be seen in a temporal sequence – roughly equivalent to the three-step explanation of integration in liberal intergovernmentalism. The first focus is on the effects of ideas on integration preferences. The second asks how the intersubjective context of negotiations and decision-making affect integration outcomes. Finally, constructivists are interested in the effects of European integration and institutions on community-building. The three foci correspond roughly to the three explanatory approaches. The community theory of institutions explains integration by ideational preferences, the theory of argumentation explains the outcome of negotiations, and socialization theory explains the effect of community institutions on actor beliefs and preferences.

The main assumption of the first research focus is that institutional integration depends on the strength of transnational community: the stronger the collective, 'European' identity and the larger the pool of common or compatible ideas, the more institutional integration we will see. By contrast, weak European and strong national identities generate resistance to institutional integration and, without shared normative and causal beliefs, common institutions and integrated policies are hard to agree on. This research focus follows the tradition of Karl Deutsch, who stipulated compatible social values (together with mutual responsiveness) as essential conditions of functioning international communities (Deutsch 1957: 66).

By contrast, the other two perspectives start from the assumption that institutional integration promotes community-building and elaborate neofunctionalist expectations of upgrading the common interest, actor socialization, and shifting identities and loyalties (Lindberg and Scheingold 1970: 117–20). Integrated policy-making generates intense and frequent contacts and cooperation, and takes place in a distinct environment structured by community norms. This environment facilitates integration-friendly decisions and promotes social learning processes that have the potential to transform identities, restructure discourses, and lead to common meanings and beliefs.

Ideas and integration preferences

The constructivist account of integration starts with ideas. In a first step, ideas shape the integration preferences of individual actors. In a second step, the constellations of ideas across relevant actors determine the chances for integration to occur. The most general hypothesis stipulates that the likelihood of integration increases with the agreement of pro-integration, 'European' ideas among the relevant actors. This hypothesis triggers further, more concrete questions: Which ideas matter? What is the meaning of 'Europe' or 'European'? How much agreement is needed? Who are the relevant actors?

All types of ideas are potentially relevant for community formation.

- The integration of policy sectors requires that the actors share instrumental ideas regarding the best or appropriate way to achieve policy goals – including the belief that the policy is best pursued through regional integration. From a constructivist perspective, the Common\Agricultural Policy is based, among other matters, on the belief that a secure supply of food in Europe requires the protection and subsidization of farmers by the Community. The 'meaning of Europe' at the instrumental or policy level consists in specific ideas on 'European governance', which are distinct both from national policy-making and global governance beyond Europe.
- *Principled ideas* shape both the policy goals and the constitution of the EU. For constructivists, European integration is based on, and committed to, promoting specific values and norms. To learn about these principled ideas and see what 'Europe' means, one can turn to the treaties. Liberty, democracy, respect for human rights, fundamental freedoms, and the rule of law, solidarity, national diversity, and economic and social progress are listed in the Preamble to the Treaty on European Union (TEU). These and other principles inform decisions on integration, as well as EU policy. According to the concept of 'normative power Europe' (Manners 2002), for instance, liberty, democracy, human rights, fundamental freedoms, and the rule of law provide the 'normative basis' for the EU's role in the world and its foreign policy.
- Finally, *identities* matter greatly for constructivist integration theory. Identities can be ethnic or civic. An ethnic conception of identity would conceive of European identity in terms of a sense of belonging and allegiance to the imagined community of Europeans as defined by a common culture or history. The second, civic conception of a European identity is based on the values and norms of European integration. In this view, 'Europeanness' is defined by adherence to such principles as liberal democracy, national diversity, multilateralism, and supranational integration. We can also

distinguish these two conceptions of 'Europe' as 'thick' and 'thin' European identities. Whereas a thick European identity resembles national identities as being based on group identification, a thin European identity consists of abstract transnational values and norms.

How much agreement is needed? At least at the beginning of the integration process, the ideas that shape integration preferences mostly stem from the national political and cultural environment. National policy paradigms regarding economic and other policies, national constitutional values and norms, and national identities and images of Europe inform preferences on the desirability, form, and substance of European integration. Constructivists assert that these ideas need not necessarily be harmonized, but must at least be compatible in order to allow for integration. For instance, empirical research shows that exclusive national identities weaken support for the EU (Hooghe and Marks 2005). By contrast, having a national identity is not detrimental to support for European integration, if people feel at least somewhat 'European', too. In addition, Ole Waever argues that the different visions of Europe he finds embedded in national identity discourses do not need to be replaced by a harmonized European vision. For stable integration, it is sufficient if these visions are compatible and include the European project as a part of national identity (Waever 2009).

Constructivism, as such, does not take any particular stance regarding the relevant actors in European integration. Ideas can operate at the level of governments, parties, associations, citizens, and supranational organizations. To some extent, whose ideas matter has to do with opportunities and constraints in the decision-making process – just as liberal intergovernmentalism relies on institutions and power constellations to determine whose interests become the national interest. Most fundamentally, there is an elite-mass or class divide on European integration. Educated and well-to-do people are more likely to see themselves as Europeans (Fligstein 2008: 145), and mainstream parties are generally in broad support of European integration. Conversely, exclusive national identities and the Euro-scepticism that they engender are most likely to be found outside the political mainstream. Consequently, progress in integration depends on the extent to which mainstream elites remain in control of the national preference formation process, or their opponents are able to mobilize identity-based dissent.

In their 'postfunctional theory of European integration', Liesbet Hooghe and Gary Marks (2008) argue that the intergovernmentalist and supranationalist focus on interest groups and their economic preferences was justified in the first three decades of the Community, when European integration had a narrowly economic focus and a limited impact on people's everyday lives, and could therefore operate in the context of a permissive popular consensus. In the 1990s, however, the Treaty of Maastricht introduced monetary union and expanded the integration agenda to non-economic issues; ten years later, the project of a European constitution further emphasized fundamental questions of identity and legitimacy. As a consequence, European integration became a salient issue of mass-level electoral and party politics in the member states. The permissive consensus gave way to a 'constraining dissensus'. This development put mainstream parties on the defensive because they could not embrace a Euro-sceptic agenda without producing internal divisions and risking their credibility (given that they had supported integration in the past). Leftist parties were also ideologically uneasy with the issue of national identity. By contrast, the salience of national identity offered populist or conservative right-wing parties an opportunity to mobilize and gain voters. In sum, identity has the highest potential to shape national preferences in those countries that have the highest percentage of voters with exclusively national identities. The likelihood that this potential is realized and constrains integration depends on the strength of right-wing populist parties and on institutional rules (such as mandatory referendums and other high thresholds for constitutional change) that accord these parties veto power (Hooghe and Marks 2008: 18).

Negotiations in a community environment

Constructivist integration theory emphasizes the diversity of national identities, images of Europe, integration discourses, institutional traditions, and policy paradigms. At least in the initial phases of integration, when European institutions are still young and weak, long-standing and well-established national ideas and discourses are likely to dominate. This state of affairs poses a problem for the constructivist explanation of progress in integration. After all, it starts with the assumption that integration depends on transnational community. The national constitution of ideational integration preferences will only be unproblematic under two conditions: first, that national ideas and preferences are similar, or at least compatible; or second, that integration remains limited to 'technical' issues without notable identity or value connotations, which are unlikely to be politicized. In addition, however, constructivism proposes mechanisms of argumentation and appropriate behaviour in negotiations on European integration that facilitate consensus in the face of diverse and value-laden preferences.

From the rationalist perspective, integration outcomes result from constellations of interests and power. If national interests diverge, states with superior bargaining power are able to shape integration according to their interests. By contrast, constructivists claim that actors with conflicting preferences engage in a process of arguing in which the 'better' argument prevails. The quality of an argument is mainly determined by its relative legitimacy in a given community environment. A more legitimate argument is, for instance, based on a more fundamental, time-honoured, consensual, or formalized community idea than another argument. In the context of European integration, preferences and arguments based on treaty rules, basic principles of the EU, uncontested identities, values and norms, or long-standing practice will thus have higher legitimacy than preferences and arguments referring to secondary law, technical rules, contested ideas, and recent practice.

The most far-reaching outcome of arguing is *persuasion*: actors with weaker arguments are convinced by the better arguments and change their integration preferences. In the end, consensus reigns. However, actors do not necessarily change their preferences. Rather, actors whose preferences are not (or are less) in line with the community identity, norms, and values are subjected to negative *social influence* such as shaming and shunning, ostracism and opprobrium (Johnston 2001). To avoid these sanctions and to restore their reputation as a community member, these actors conform to the legitimate arguments and behaviour without changing their convictions (Schimmelfennig 2001; Thomas 2009).

Studies of enlargement provide ample evidence for ideational effects on negotiations and their outcomes. Already in the early 1960s, when the big member states favoured giving Franco's Spain a membership perspective, the Parliamentary Assembly of the EEC invoked the liberal-democratic (and anti-fascist) identity of the Community to mobilize successfully against association (Thomas 2006). In the early 1990s, the same liberal-democratic identity worked in favour of Eastern enlargement. When a powerful majority of self-interested member states were reticent to give the Central and Eastern European countries (CEECs) a firm membership perspective, the CEECs' governments and their supporters in the EC framed enlargement as an identity issue, referred to the pan-European and liberal-democratic enlargement norms of the EC and reminded the opponents of past promises made to the East (Schimmelfennig 2001). This 'rhetorical entrapment' compelled the reluctant member states to agree to enlargement (without harmonizing their enlargement preferences). The same mechanism has been at work in EU–Turkey relations (Schimmelfennig 2009).

From the constructivist perspective, the constitutionalization of the EU has likewise been a result of arguing dynamics (Rittberger and Schimmelfennig 2006; Schimmelfennig 2010). Integration systematically undermines traditional channels of parliamentary representation and accountability by pooling sovereignty and delegating it to supranational institutions for reasons of efficiency. For the same efficiency reasons, governments are generally not interested in empowering the EP or other supranational institutions. In addition, their ideas about what constitutes a legitimate constitution for Europe diverge (Rittberger 2005). In this situation, actors with a preference for democratizing the EU scandalized the democracy deficit, invoked the uncontested principle of parliamentarianism, and successfully put normative pressure on reticent member state governments in order to strengthen the competences of the EP.

Finally, even if arguing fails because standards of legitimacy are too weak or too controversial to adjudicate between claims, negotiations do not necessarily resort to hard, strategic bargaining. Rather, constructivist analyses point to informal norms of deliberation, compromise, and consensus that govern intergovernmental negotiations and decision-making in the EU (Joerges and Neyer 1997; Lewis 2003a, 2003b). Jeffrey Lewis (2010) argues that the insulation from domestic politics in in-camera settings, a high intensity of interactions, a wide scope of issues under negotiation, and a dense set of formal and informal norms facilitate cooperative, accommodative behaviour – and he finds these conditions in the Council and its committee system. Thomas Risse and Mareike Kleine (2010) compare negotiations on the same issue in an Intergovernmental Conference and in the Convention that drafted the Constitutional Treaty. They find that the less rigid roles, the transparent debate, and the expert-based leadership during the Convention facilitated arguing and persuasion. Constructivists thus see a stark contrast between negotiations and decision-making in domestic, mass-level politics, which are likely to mobilize exclusive national identities and limit or slow down integration, and in international, elitist forums, where community standards of legitimate policy and appropriate behaviour are likely to dominate and facilitate further integration. In both arenas, integration is shaped fundamentally by ideas – but by extremely different ones.

Integration and socialization

In European integration, socialization processes are considered to take place at three different levels: the socialization of states or governments inside and outside the EU; the socialization of individual officials participating in integrated policy-making; and the socialization of citizens. The general causal factors of socialization listed can be grouped under two main conditions: exposure and legitimacy. First, European socialization is more likely to be successful if actors are frequently and intensively exposed to the outcomes of European integration, EU institutions, and European ideas. Exposure is facilitated if the actors are willing to engage in contact with the EU and open to adopting new ideas. Second, European socialization requires that actors find these ideas legitimate. This is more likely to be the case if actors identify with 'Europe', European ideas resonate with prior individual or national ideas, and socialization takes place in a deliberative setting.

We speak of 'state socialization' when countries incorporate EU policy ideas, values, and norms into their state institutions or policy rules. The socialization of governments means that governments, as corporate actors, come to share EU ideas and identities, and include them in their policy programmes and behavioural repertoires. State and government socialization operate at a collective, institutional level; they do not necessarily imply that individual members of government or state officials change their individual beliefs and attitudes. States or governments are more likely to be socialized and change their ideas in line with EU policy and normative ideas under the following conditions:

- states are new (e.g. newly independent), unconsolidated, or in a process of restructuring, which makes them more open to (and interested in) external ideas;
- state structures and institutions are conducive to supranational integration or multi-level governance (e.g. in federal states or states with international law-friendly constitutions);
- states have policy rules that resonate with EU rules;
- governments do not run on a nationalist or anti-integration platform, or do not include coalition partners that do so;
- states and governments are in frequent and close contact with the EU.

Although it is often assumed that long-standing member states are more likely to be socialized to EU policy ideas, values, and norms, these conditions make clear that this need not be the case. Whereas old member states have been exposed to integration for longer, novelty and uncertainty work in favour of new member socialization. Finally, identification, legitimacy, and resonance may vary independently of how long a state has been an EU member. Old member states with strong national identities, centralized and unitary state structures, and protectionist policy rules may be more resistant to European socialization than new member states with integration-friendly institutional and policy legacies.

These conditions also hold for non-member states. Factors such as novelty and uncertainty in the international system, identification with the EU community of values and norms, perceived legitimacy of the EU and its rules, resonance of EU norms and rules with domestic ones, and exposure to the EU explain the propensity of non-member states to seek membership and to adopt EU rules, as well as the willingness of member states to support their accession. Constructivism thus explains enlargement (and horizontal integration in general) as a result of successful socialization.

At the individual level of socialization, we can distinguish individuals who are directly involved in European institutions and policy-making processes from ordinary citizens. The first group consists of officials who either work for the EU or are sent to Brussels by their governments, but may also include lobbyists and journalists. Studies of officials hypothesize that socialization depends on factors such as the length of stay, the intensity of contact, previous experience, age, and prior attitudes. Officials who are employed by the EU full-time, began work for or with the EU at a young age, and were favourably disposed toward 'Europe' are more likely to adopt and internalize pro-European ideas than those who are only seconded by their governments late in their career and for a short time – and those who come to Brussels with strong national identities and beliefs in state sovereignty. Empirical studies emphasize the key role of prior beliefs and attitudes acquired at the national level, and domestic recruitment and selection patterns, and point to the limited relevance of exposure (Beyers 2005; Hooghe 2005). However, the fact that pro-European officials are more likely to participate in EU politics facilitates European policy-making, even in the absence of strong exposure effects.

Regarding the European socialization of ordinary people, constructivist analyses stipulate similar conditions. Direct experience of European integration – such as paying with the euro or crossing Schengen borders – should strengthen European identity. Young age, knowledge of foreign European languages, and travel experiences also have a positive influence on opportunities to interact with other Europeans and to build pro-European attitudes (Fligstein 2008).

Constructivist integration theory is open to the possibility that integration and socialization create a self-reinforcing process. As integration increases, so will the exposure of governments, officials, and ordinary people. To the extent that exposure is perceived as beneficial, these actors will adopt a pro-European identity and European policy ideas. This will then translate into pro-integration preferences and enable further integration. The 'virtuous circle' is not a foregone conclusion, however. Whether exposure results in positive socialization depends on prior attitudes and the nature of the exposure. Nationalist governments and individuals are likely to feel culturally threatened by increasing integration. EU policies that do not resonate with domestic values and policy beliefs produce ideas-based resistance toward integration, too. In addition, coercive, heavy-handed, or redistributive EU policies could trigger opposition. 'Too much' integration may therefore lead to ideationally motivated backlash.

General hypotheses

According to constructivism, integration is shaped by the nature and distribution of ideas – and by their development and transformation over time. Integration fundamentally depends on the extent of ideational consensus among the actors participating in the integration process. The more compatible or common the relevant identities, norms, values, and policy beliefs, the more likely integration can be achieved. This effect is reinforced or supported by the institutionalization of common norms, values, and policy ideas in the EU, and by argumentative settings at the supranational level. Successful integration contributes to the further institutionalization of ideas in the EU and generates socialization processes, which potentially increase the commonality or compatibility of ideas among the participating actors – in particular, if the integration outcome increases exposure and enjoys high legitimacy. Both institutionalization and socialization increase the likelihood of future integration.

Supranationalism and constructivism thus share the view – rejected by intergovernmentalism – that institutions have an independent and integration-friendly effect on the preferences and behaviour of actors. According to supranationalism, however, supranational institutions support integration mainly by altering the cost-benefit calculations of state actors, whereas they change actors' ideas in the constructivist account. On this basis, we can formulate three general constructivist hypotheses about integration.

Integration increases with the commonality of (pro-integration) ideas. The more that the relevant actors in European integration share ideas of 'Europe', the more likely it is that they can agree on further vertical and horizontal integration. The relevant actors are those that have a say in the making of integration decisions. In order to work in favour of integration, these ideas obviously have to support integration, or at least should not be anti-integrationist. If, for instance, all actors shared the idea of the primacy of national sovereignty, integration would not obtain despite a strong value consensus. Moreover, the ideas need to fit the scope of the envisaged integration step. Whereas a shared pro-European identity facilitates integration in general, agreement on policy ideas may promote further integration in the specific policy-area. Whereas further horizontal integration requires an expansion of ideational community to other countries, vertical integration requires shared ideas about the appropriate level of national sovereignty, the appropriate division of competences between the national and the supranational levels, and legitimate decision-making rules beyond the nation-state.

The substantive terms of integration are shaped by common ideas. European policies mirror policy ideas that are widely accepted as legitimate and that resonate well with national policy ideas among the member states. The constitution of the EU reflects European constitutional norms.

Integration is facilitated by the supranational institutionalization of ideas and decision-making in argumentative supranational settings. There are two reasons for this. First, ideas (norms, values, and policy beliefs) that have been institutionalized at the European level (in treaties, in declarations, or in political practice) enjoy high legitimacy and help form a consensus around contested integration proposals. Second, it is easier to build support for integration among elites (who tend to be more integration-friendly than ordinary citizens) at the supranational level, where decision-making is partly removed from the conflicts of domestic politics, and in committees that privilege the reasoned search for consensus. At the other extreme, domestic mobilization of national identity and decision-making involving referendums are most likely to block further integration.

Constructivism and Differentiated Integration

The constructivist explanation of differentiated integration is structurally similar to intergovernmentalism but based on legitimacy rather than efficiency considerations. Whereas intergovernmentalism stresses unequal interdependence as the main source of differentiation, constructivism emphasizes imperfect ideational consensus. The 'heterogeneity of preferences' in intergovernmentalism corresponds to 'ideational heterogeneity' in constructivism. Politicization is considered a relevant factor for differentiation in both theories. For intergovernmentalism, however, politicization results from threats to autonomy and security, whereas constructivism explains politicization by threats to national identity or fundamental national values and norms. Finally, domestic ratification constraints play a role in both intergovernmentalist and constructivist explanations of differentiated integration.

Conditions

The factors that influence differentiation in European integration in the constructivist perspective follow from the general hypotheses outlined above. The extent of consensus is the fundamental factor and depends on the sector-specific ideational consensus – as well as on domestic ratification constraints. In addition, argumentation and socialization effects matter.

Legitimacy of constitutional ideas. The extent of differentiation depends on legitimate constitutional ideas. If there were an ideational consensus that the level of integration has to be the same across all policy sectors, we would not see vertically differentiated integration, and if it were legitimate that all member states should be subject to the same rules and that non-member states ought not to participate in EU policies, we should not observe horizontal differentiation. By contrast, if the dominant constitutional ideas about European integration allowed for, or even proscribed, vertical or horizontal differentiation, we should observe it more frequently. For instance, the actors may believe that trade policy ought to be more integrated than defence policy, or that member states should be allowed to select autonomously in which integrated policies to participate.

Ideational contestation. In general, ideational contestation produces integration failure, or low levels of integration. If it varies across policies, however, it is another source of differentiation. Policies with a strong ideational consensus are likely to be more integrated – and integrated earlier – than those in which policy ideas are contested. The difference in the extent and timing of integration in trade and defence could therefore alternatively be attributed to the early existence of shared policy ideas in trade and to contested policy ideas in defence. The larger the difference in ideational consensus across sectors, the more differentiated integration will be.

Politicization. From the constructivist perspective, politicization is related to identity. Policies differ with regard to how relevant they are considered to be for collective identity or fundamental values and norms. Some issues are 'identity issues'. They are important for identity construction and are based on fundamental community values and norms. Other issues are 'technical'. This is a matter of social construction and does not follow from objective properties of the issues. The national currency may be regarded as a technical means of payment in one country, and a symbol of national independence and achievement in another.

Technical issues are likely to be more integrated than identity issues. International ideational consensus is less relevant for such issues and not required for agreement. Even if there is ideational contestation, states and other actors are more likely to compromise on technical rather than identity issues. Technical issues can be left to elites and dealt with at the supranational level. In addition, the ideational relevance of an issue influences horizontal differentiation. First, in cases of ideational disagreement, states are less willing to compromise if they perceive the issue as an identity issue. They prefer to opt out from integration than to make concessions or play along if a policy violates fundamental values and norms that are essential for their identity. Second, such policies are also likely to boost Euro-sceptic parties and mobilize domestic opposition to European integration. Even if governments were willing to compromise, they may be forced to opt out as a result of domestic pressures.

Domestic ratification constraints. The higher domestic ratification constraints, the more likely domestic opposition on identity issues is to inhibit integration and produce opt-outs,. In other words, if two countries exhibit the same degree of ideational opposition to integration, the one with higher domestic ratification constraints (such as a mandatory referendum) will more probably opt out from integration than the one with lighter ratification constraints (such as a simple parliamentary majority).

Integration norms. Differentiation is potentially inhibited by integration norms. The most general is enshrined in the general principle of 'ever closer union', which entails two norms that are relevant in the context of differentiated integration: the unity norm and the integration norm. The unity norm demands that the member states preserve the unity of the EU and EU law. The integration norm obliges the member states to integrate further. Both norms work together in discouraging differentiated integration if it destroys the unity of the EU without promoting integration. They are compatible with vertical differentiation if issue-areas are integrated more strongly and more quickly than others, and if new integrated policies start at a lower level of vertical integration than older ones. The premise is that the less integrated areas will catch up in due course. By contrast, regressive vertical differentiation resulting from a reduction in integration would run counter to these norms. Horizontal differentiation is also permissible if it permits one group of countries to move ahead with integration, rather than being blocked at a low level of uniform integration – especially if it allows and encourages the laggards to join later.

Institutionalization of ideas and argumentative setting. If an issue is perceived as a technical issue, its integration potential benefits from avoiding domestic identity politics and identity-based mobilization. Negotiations in a community environment further increase the chances that integration can be achieved and differentiation can be circumvented – even if there is no ideational consensus in the first place. Agreement on further and unified integration is most likely to obtain if the ideas on which a policy is based are in line with fundamental values and norms, and well-established instrumental beliefs of the community, and if these values, norms, and beliefs have been institutionalized in EU rules and practice. Under these conditions, they possess high legitimacy and exercise a consensus and compliance pull on the actors. The norms of arguing and consensus operating in the supranational negotiating forums of the EU reinforce this effect. It needs to be stressed, however, that this only holds for technical issues. Issues of national identity cannot be insulated from domestic politics.

Socialization. Socialization may reduce differentiated integration if the conditions are right. Assume that, initially, the integration of a policy is low or differentiated because of high ideational contestation and national identity relevance. Exposure to the new policy – and the

European institutions executing it – may then soften the initial opposition and help in building a consensus that makes stronger integration possible and persuades member states to give up their opt-outs. As time elapses, the new policy is likely to gain legitimacy. In addition, officials and citizens of the opt-out countries may feel marginalized and seek to reconnect fully with the community. Thus, all else being equal, both institutionalization and socialization can be expected to reduce differentiation over time.

Conjectures

On the basis of these considerations, we can now formulate general conjectures about (differentiated) integration. The main conditions are consensus, legitimacy, and politicization. Consensus refers to the commonality of integration-friendly ideas across countries, legitimacy to the institutionalization of such ideas in the EU, and politicization to the social construction of a policy as technical and apolitical or identity-relevant.

Conjecture 1

The *vertical and horizontal integration* of a policy increases with:

(i)   consensus; and
(ii)   legitimacy;

and decreases with:

(iii) politicization.

As a corollary, policies are integrated earlier and faster if:

(i)   they exhibit higher consensus;
(ii)   integration is more legitimate; and
(iii) they are regarded as technical policies.

We can further derive two expectations from this conjecture that relate to vertical and horizontal differentiation.

Vertical differentiation. The extent of vertical differentiation in European integration increases with the difference in:

(i)   consensus;
(ii)   legitimacy; and
(iii) politicization across policy areas.

Horizontal differentiation. The extent of horizontal differentiation in an integrated policy is likely to be higher if:

(i) the policy and its integration are contested;
(ii) integration is less legitimate; and
(iii) the policy is more politicized.

Conjecture 2

This conjecture explains the extent of *integration* for individual states. The likelihood that a state participates in the integration of a particular policy increases with:

(i) the weakness of exclusive national identities in the country;
(ii) the proximity of its values, norms, and policy ideas to the other participating states; and
(iii) the domestic legitimacy of European integration;

and decreases as:

(iv) the policy is politicized domestically; and
(v) domestic ratification constraints increase.

As a corollary, countries are more likely to participate in European integration later or more selectively, and to seek opt-outs from further integration when they have:

(i) more exclusively national identities;
(ii) outlier idea;
(iii) contested domestic legitimacy of European integration;
(iv) more strongly politicized perceptions of European integration; and
(v) higher ratification constraints.

In the constructivist perspective, a decrease in differentiated integration requires that:

(i) national identities become less exclusively national;
(ii) national ideas converge;
(iii) European integration is depoliticized; and
(iv) domestic ratification is facilitated.

Even though constructivism assumes that socialization can further these developments in principle, it gives less reason to be optimistic about the prospects of making European integration more unified than supranationalism. Deeply-rooted national identities and ideas, together with the politicization effects of deepening European integration and the increase in referendums on the EU, may well indicate that differentiation is likely to spread and stabilize.

PART II

POLICIES

In Part II of the book, we show how the theories of integration can be used to analyze and explain integration and differentiation in major policy areas of the European Union. In this introduction, we summarize our theoretical expectations, explicate our approach to theory application, and describe our selection of policies.

Table PII.1 summarizes and juxtaposes the conjectures on integration and differentiation stipulated by intergovernmentalism, supranationalism, and constructivism. From an intergovernmentalist perspective, the demand for vertical integration increases with international interdependence and, in particular, with the compliance problems that international cooperation creates. It is further facilitated by compatible national preferences and relatively low autonomy costs of integration. Supranationalism stipulates that intense transnational interactions and strong supranational actors further vertical integration. By contrast, constructivism expects vertical integration to be more likely if it benefits from high international legitimacy, a strong ideational consensus among the participating states, and low relevance for national identities.

Correspondingly, constructivists expect horizontal integration to be the more extended, the more widespread the legitimacy of integration, the ideational consensus, and the perception of integration as a technical issue is in the European system of states. Supranationalists expect horizontal integration to be correlated with the geographical scope of relevant transnational interactions and with the capacity of supranational actors. From an intergovernmentalist point of view, integrated European policies have the more participants, the more critical interdependence, compatible preferences, and low autonomy costs are shared among European countries.

Differentiation obtains if these factors are distributed unevenly across policies and countries. If interdependence, preference compatibility, compliance problems, and autonomy costs are significantly higher in one policy than another, intergovernmentalists expect vertical differentiation – under the condition that transaction costs and negative externalities across policies remain low. Correspondingly, horizontal differentiation is more likely to occur if a policy area is characterized by uneven international interdependence, national preferences, and

106

Table PII.1 *Conjectures compared*

Conditions of:	Intergovernmentalism	Supranationalism	Constructivism
Vertical integration	– Strong interdependence – Compatible preferences – Problematic compliance – Low autonomy costs	– Strong transnational interactions – Strong supranational actors	– High legitimacy – Strong consensus – Low politicization
Horizontal integration	– Extended interdependence – Compatible preferences – Low autonomy costs	– Extended transnational interactions – Strong supranational actors	– Widespread legitimacy – Extended consensus – Low politicization
Vertical differentiation	– Different interdependence, preference compatibility, compliance problems, and autonomy costs across policies – Low inter-policy externalities and transaction costs	– Different transnational interactions and capacity of supranational actors across policies	– Different legitimacy, consensus, and politicization across policies
Horizontal differentiation	– Heterogeneous international dependence, preferences, and autonomy costs across countries – Low intra-policy externalities and transaction costs	– Heterogeneous transnational interactions across countries – Weak supranational actors	– Contested ideas and legitimacy – Different politicization across countries
State participation	– High international dependence – Mainstream preferences – Low compliance costs – Low autonomy costs – Small state – Weak ratification constraints	– Strong transnational interactions – Strong supranational actors	– Weak exclusive national identities – Mainstream ideas – High legitimacy of European integration – Low politicization – Weak ratification constraints

autonomy costs – again, under the condition that differentiation does not create prohibitive transaction costs and free-riding opportunities. For supranationalists, differentiation results from the uneven intensity of transnational exchange across policies (vertical differentiation) or the uneven participation of countries in transnational exchange (horizontal differentiation). Vertical differentiation is also more likely to occur if supranational organizations have higher capacity in one policy area than in another. Assuming that supranational organizations have an interest in unified integration, horizontal differentiation is more likely to obtain if supranational organizations are too weak to achieve this goal. From the constructivist perspective, we will see vertical differentiation if integration is more legitimate, less contested, and less relevant to national identities than another view. Horizontal differentiation is the result of difference and contestation across countries regarding the legitimacy, the policy ideas, and the identity-relevance of integration in one policy area.

The last row in Table PII.1 lists the theory-specific conditions under which one state is more likely to seek or accept integration than another. Intergovernmentalism regards small and highly dependent states with low autonomy and compliance costs and weak ratification constraints as the most integration-friendly countries. For supranationalism, states with dense and intense transnational exchanges and strong dependence on supranational organizations are most likely to integrate and less likely to opt-out from, or remain outside, policy integration. Constructivism, finally, expects states with exclusive national identities, outlier ideas, high domestic politicization and weak domestic legitimacy of European integration, and high domestic ratification constraints to be the most likely non-member or opt-out countries.

We use the integration theories and the conjectures we derive from them for three purposes in the subsequent chapters: to illustrate how they can be applied to empirical cases, to learn something about European integration, and to learn something about the theories. Most basically, we show how the abstract concepts and the general assumptions and conjectures of the theories can be translated into concrete, case-specific expectations, and applied to real events in European integration.

Additionally, we use the theories in order to learn something about integration and differentiation in a variety of policy areas. Theories 'organize reality'. They distinguish what is relevant from what is irrelevant, help us select and sort information, and provide us with the general concepts to describe and classify what we observe. They also tell us why and how the phenomena and events that we observe and describe have come about. They direct us to the causes and conditions of our observations. In sum, theories help us 'make sense' of what we observe.

In line with this approach, we begin each policy chapter with the history of the policy in European integration. We describe the major events in the development of the policy, and the evolution of its integration and differentiation. These descriptions produce many questions: Why was the policy integrated? Why did it happen when it happened, and why not before? What explains the major changes in the integration of the policy and the level of integration that it has now? And why do some member states not participate in integration, whereas some non-member states do? We then apply each theory separately in order to see what we can learn from it in order to answer these questions. We start with an intergovernmentalist account, move on to a supranationalist account, and conclude with a constructivist account of policy integration. Each theory points us to different actors, factors, and processes, and it gives us different explanations of integration, some of which may be competing whereas others are complementary or overlapping. In the end, we hope to gain a fuller and more nuanced understanding of European integration than would be obtained from the application of a single theory.

Finally, the analysis of integration and differentiation also tells us something about the theories. The theory may account well for our observations, but the analysis may also reveal weaknesses. First, we may detect 'blank spots' in the theories – i.e. events, processes, and outcomes – on which they have little or nothing to say. Second, the expectations of the theory may be indeterminate: the theory does explain what happened, but it would also have explained a different course of events, or the opposite outcome. Finally, the expectations may be wrong: on the basis of the theory, we would have expected a different result, or the process of how the result came about does not fit with the theory's assumptions.

In line with this approach, we end each policy chapter with a balance sheet. First, we will offer an idea of the strengths and weakness of each theory in explaining integration in the particular policy area. Does it provide a plausible explanation of integration and differentiation overall? Or is it silent, indeterminate, or simply wrong on some aspects of the case? Second, we discuss the relative merits of each theory. Are their accounts equivalent, or does one theory provide a more convincing explanation of policy integration (or certain aspects of it) than the others? Finally, comparing how the theories fare across the policy chapters also gives us an idea of their systematic strengths and weaknesses. For instance, does one theory generally neglect or underestimate relevant actors and processes? Is one theory generally better at explaining vertical integration, horizontal integration, or horizontal differentiation than the others? These questions will be further explored in Chapter 9.

Our approach to the theory-guided analysis of European integration is pluralistic. We start from the assumption that European integration is unlikely to be fully explained by a single theory, and that each theory has something valuable to contribute to our understanding. Pluralism is not relativism, however. We do not assume that each theory explains each aspect of European integration equally well, and reject the idea that the empirical analysis of European integration cannot tell us anything about the relative merits of each theory. Whereas we do not expect to find a single, clear winner, we do expect to learn something about the relative strengths and weakness of each theory of integration.

For both purposes – learning about integration and learning about theory – it is important that we select the right policies for detailed study. Our selection was guided by relevance and variety. Our choice of market integration (Chapter 5) and monetary integration (Chapter 6) followed considerations of relevance. Market integration was the first, and has remained the fundamental policy area of European integration. At its core, European integration has been a process of economic policy integration – whatever the ultimate purposes that member states have attached to it. Monetary integration is the most ambitious and contested policy area of European integration. Since the onset of the financial and debt crisis of the Euro zone, monetary integration has clearly been at the centre of European integration, and EU leaders have linked the survival of the Euro emphatically to the survival of the EU as a whole.

By contrast, our choice of defence policy (Chapter 7) and the Area of Freedom, Security, and Justice (AFSJ) (Chapter 8), a policy area comprising home affairs and judicial policies, was guided by an attempt to increase variation. These policies were integrated at a later point than market and monetary policy, and they were initially integrated in separate 'pillars' of the EU – the second pillar for the Common Security and Defence Policy and the third pillar for Justice and Home Affairs. Defence policy has remained at an intergovernmental level of centralization, whereas the AFSJ has seen a dynamic development of vertical integration since the early 1990s. And while defence policy is almost not horizontally differentiated at all, the AFSJ shows a peculiar pattern of both internal and external differentiation.

Our selected policies thus vary on several dimensions:

- *Timing of supranational integration.* European integration started with market integration in the 1950s. Monetary policy was integrated supranationally in the 1990s, and the AFSJ followed roughly a decade later. Defence policy is not yet supranationally integrated.
- *Level of vertical integration.* Monetary integration is one of the most supranationally centralized policies of the EU, whereas defence policy is one of the least centralized EU policies. Market integration and the AFSJ fall in between. By the same token, our case selection explores the full range of vertical differentiation.

- *Extent of horizontal integration.* The extent of horizontal integration of our selected policies ranges between 30 (the European Economic Area for the internal market) and 17 (the Euro zone for monetary policy). These two policies mark the maximum and minimum horizontal integration across the EU's policy areas.
- *Types of horizontal differentiation.* The internal market is the paradigmatic case of external differentiation without internal differentiation. The Euro zone exemplifies internal without external differentiation. The AFSJ has long combined external and internal differentiation, whereas defence policy has hardly any differentiation whatsoever.

In sum, the policy areas we analyze in Part II of the book are not only highly relevant for the EU; they also cover the full range of vertical and horizontal integration, and differentiation, and represent highly different points in time for the move towards supranational integration. Our policy selection thus allows us to examine whether the theories of integration are able to explain the full range of integration outcomes. (On a cautionary note, we point out that, for a conclusive theory test, we also have to make sure that there is significant variation in the values of the *explanatory factors* proposed by the theories, too. We assume that this is a case, although we cannot examine this requirement in detail here.)

In addition, each of our policy chapters benefits from internal variation. For each policy, we study variation over time. Chapter 5, on market integration, examines both the early market integration envisaged by the Treaties of Rome and the deepening of market integration agreed on in the Single European Act of 1986. Chapter 6, which deals with monetary integration, compares monetary policy before and after Maastricht, and also takes into account the changes made in response to the current crisis. Chapter 7 looks at the failure of the European Defence Community in the 1950s and the developments since the 1990s, and Chapter 8, on the AFSJ, follows the development of policy since the 1970s. Moreover, some policy areas are composed of policies with different levels of integration. For instance, Chapter 6, on the EMU, compares monetary and fiscal policy. These comparisons, over time and across policies, increase the analytical leverage of our case studies.

Chapter 5

The Single Market

In October 2010, the European Commission published a Communication with the telling title 'Towards a Single Market Act. For a highly competitive social market economy. 50 proposals for improving our work, business and exchanges with one another'. These proposals ranged from the introduction of an EU patent, the management of copyrights, energy efficiency, the coordination of national tax policies, the recognition of professional qualifications, to the creation of a single integrated mortgage market, aimed at stimulating growth in an era of globalization and digitalization. The Commission's communication highlights at least two important facts about the single market. First, the main ambition of the single market is to promote economic growth by increasing competition and by enabling a Europe-wide efficient allocation of resources. Second, and more important for the topic of this book, the creation of the single market remains an ongoing project. Since the signing of the Treaties of Rome in the 1950s, the Common Market, with its four freedoms, has been on the European agenda. And the reforms continue.

At the time of writing, the internal or single market importantly shapes the patterns of state–market relations in Europe, affecting citizens as consumers, producers, traders, or employees. Historically, three phases of market integration can be distinguished. The treaty establishing the European Economic Community (EEC) first created a Customs Union in which all quotas and tariff barriers between its member states were gradually abolished. The second phase is characterized by an emphasis on harmonization. 'Euronorms' were designed to establish common standards for all partners. The third phase is heralded in the 1970s with the Dassonville and Cassis de Dijon rulings of the European Court of Justice. Later taken up by the Commission and the member states in the Single European Act (SEA), these rulings promoted the principle of mutual recognition. According to this principle, a member state is required to accept – subject to certain exceptions – goods that have been produced in accordance with the rules of another member state. Given that the negotiation of harmonized standards proved to be a rather cumbersome and time-consuming process, this new principle promised to speed up market integration. Since this approach focuses on the abolishment of technical barriers to trade, it is often referred to as 'negative' or market-making integration (Scharpf

1999). In order to compensate those losing as a result of deregulation and market-making, the SEA has introduced and intensified 'positive', market-correcting measures by promoting economic and social cohesion across Europe. For example, environmental policy, consumer protection, public health, security in the workplace, or cohesion policies are typical market-correcting policies.

Market integration has been at the heart of European integration since the 1950s. Because it covers a wide range of policies, we here need to restrict our analysis to a few topics. We will concentrate on the establishment of the four freedoms: the freedom of people, goods, services, and capital. Besides the Treaties of Rome, the SEA will be analyzed as a major step towards a further deepening of the Common Market. The SEA is often considered a major milestone of the so-called *'relance européenne'* of the 1980s, the revival of the integration project. Because legal rulings first spurred the debate on negative integration, the issue of integration through law will also be discussed in this context.

In terms of horizontal integration, the single market is mostly characterized by a uniform application of rules. At the same time, discriminatory measures affecting new EU member states are examples of a temporary internal differentiation. For instance, in the first years after the 2004 and 2007 enlargement rounds the free movement of workers was restricted for citizens from the new Eastern European member states (cf. Schneider 2009). The single market, in addition, has some important repercussions in non-EU member states. An important example of external differentiation is the European Economic Area (EEA), which incorporates the European Free Trade Area (EFTA) countries of Iceland, Liechtenstein, and Norway in the internal market. The EEA allows a fine-grained testing of integration theories since it exposes a range of different trajectories of European states. In the EEA negotiations, three different pathways emerged: three members of the EFTA – Austria, Finland, and Sweden – chose full EU membership; Iceland, Liechtenstein, and Norway opted for the EEA; and Switzerland – whose voters had rejected the EEA in 1992 – entered into bilateral negotiations. Another interesting case for our theoretical discussion of horizontal integration is the UK, which initially rejected the EEC only to apply for membership a few years later.

The chapter next offers a brief historical overview of the single market. After describing vertical and horizontal integration in this sector, we survey what our theories have to offer, first, on the Rome treaties, then, on the SEA and, finally, on differentiated integration. We conclude by evaluating the strengths and shortcomings of the theoretical approaches.

The Development of the Single Market

The Treaties of Rome

The Treaties of Rome were signed in March 1957 by France, Germany, Italy, and the three Benelux countries (Belgium, the Netherlands, and Luxembourg). The Treaties of Rome consist of two key treaties: first, the treaty establishing the atomic energy community, Euratom, and, second – and, for the purposes of this chapter, more importantly – the treaty establishing the European Economic Community (EEC). Ratification of this treaty went comparatively smoothly in the member states of the European Coal and Steel Community (ECSC), and the Treaty came into force in January 1958. The Treaties of Rome are generally considered a major step in setting the integration process back on track after the ratification failure of the European Defence Community in 1954 (a matter that will be discussed in greater detail in Chapter 7).

The idea of revitalizing the community project had been taken up by the Messina conference of June 1955. In their resolution, the ministers of foreign affairs of the ECSC member states declared that 'the moment has come to go a step further towards the construction of Europe'. In their view, the first step should be taken in the economic field. In Messina, the six ministers of foreign affairs decided to create an intergovernmental committee to investigate further steps of integration. This committee, under the chairmanship of the Belgian Minister for Foreign Affairs, Paul-Henri Spaak, drafted a report on economic integration, presented to the foreign ministers in April 1956. The 'Brussels Report on the General Common Market' pleaded for the fusion of markets by the establishment of a Customs Union between the six member states of the ECSC, and the setting up of a common external tariff and commercial policy. Britain observed the deliberations of the Spaak committee cautiously at first; however, it later pulled back its observer when it realized that it was unwilling to pursue matters that would ultimately commit it to becoming a member of a customs union.

The foreign ministers of the six approved the Spaak Report in Venice in May 1956; it became the basis for the intergovernmental conference that prepared the Treaties of Rome. Central components of the EEC treaty were the setting up of a customs union that eliminated tariffs and quotas among the member states; the creation of a common external tariff on goods entering the Union; and the establishment of a common agricultural, transport, and competition policy (cf. also Lindberg 1963: 14–26). Article 2 of the EEC Treaty specifies that 'The Community shall have as its task, by establishing a common market and progressively approximating the economic policies of member states, to promote throughout the community a harmonious development of economic activities, a continuous and balanced expansion, an increase in stability, an accelerated raising of the standard of living and closer relations between the states belonging to it.' The EEC Treaty establishes the 'four freedoms'.

The customs union is accompanied by a common trade policy. This policy importantly distinguishes a customs union from a mere free-trade association. In order to assure free competition, the EEC treaty prohibits restrictive agreements and state aids (except for specific derogations provided for in the Treaty) which can affect trade between member states and whose objective is to prevent, restrict, or distort competition. Competition policy is a typical market-making measure and it is clearly 'anchored in the principles of free-market capitalism' (Wilks 2010: 134).

In terms of its institutional set-up, the EEC Treaty built on the institutional triangle established by the ECSC. Besides the Council, the Treaty foresaw a consultative assembly, which later became the European Parliament, and a Commission that was mandated to propose Community legislation (its executive tasks, however, were more limited than those of the ECSC's High Authority). In addition, the Treaty granted norm controlling powers to the ECJ. In 1958, decision-making in the Council demanded unanimity, but a shift towards qualified majority voting (QMV) was foreseen after a transition period for the 1960s. On our integration scale, the Common Market therefore can be coded as 'joint decision-making I' (see Table 1.4).

The establishment of the EEC did not receive uniform support in Europe. In response, Austria, Denmark, Norway, Portugal, Sweden, Switzerland, and the UK established the EFTA, which entered into force in May 1960 (Finland joined in 1961, Iceland in 1970, and Liechtenstein in 1991). The EFTA considered itself an intergovernmental organization and, in contrast to the EEC, it did not establish a common external customs tariff. Its basic goal was to promote free trade amongst its members. It continues to describe its roots on its homepage as an 'economic counterbalance to the more politically driven EEC'.

The Single European Act

The Treaties of Rome had scheduled the completion of the Common Market for 1968. And, within the customs union, the internal tariffs on manufacturing products had, indeed, been eliminated by that date. However, tariffs are just one – and, arguably, only the most obvious – barrier to trade. The period between the 1960s and the early 1980s has often been described as a period of stagnation, or even 'Eurosclerosis'. This characterization, however, neglects the role that the ECJ has played since the early 1960s in promoting integration. Famous legal doctrines – such as the supremacy of EC legislation over national legislation, the principle of the direct effect of EC legislation, and the principle of mutual recognition – have made a lasting impact on European integration, not only in the legal sphere, but also in the political. The principle of mutual recognition, formulated in the Dassonville (1974) and Cassis de Dijon (1979) rulings, has played a major role in shifting the EC's focus in market integration from harmonization towards mutual recognition. The principle of mutual recognition prevents a member state from discriminating against foreign goods that have been produced in accordance with the standards of another member state – unless they endanger public welfare (Craig and De Búrca 2008: 606).

The decisive step that transformed the common market into a single market on 1 January 1993 is the Single European Act (SEA). The negotiations about institutional reform had started in the early 1980s. In June 1983, the heads of state and government passed the 'Solemn Declaration of Stuttgart' based on a draft by the German and Italian Ministers of Foreign Affairs, Hans-Dietrich Genscher and Emilio Colombo. In the Declaration of Stuttgart, the heads of state and government underlined their will to promote a 'united Europe'. They confirmed their commitment to 'progress towards an ever closer union among the peoples and Member States of the European Community'. In addition, they identified 'serious economic problems' facing the member states and proposed more efficient decision-making, an upgrading of social policy in the Community, and a strengthening of European political cooperation.

The next important step after Stuttgart was the Fontainebleau summit of June 1984. During this summit, Prime Minister Margaret Thatcher received the long-requested rebate for the UK's contribution to the EC budget. By solving the 'BBQ' (British budgetary question), the heads of state or government were now able to turn towards institutional reforms. The Fontainebleau summit commissioned the Irish senator James Dooge to form an ad hoc committee to examine institutional reforms in the EC. The Dooge Committee was able to draw on both the Genscher–Colombo initiative and a 'Draft Treaty Establishing the European Union' the EP had proposed and adopted in February 1984. Following the presentation of the Dooge Report, the Milan European summit of June 1985 – against the explicit opposition of the UK, Greece, and Denmark – decided to convene an intergovernmental conference to begin the negotiations on the SEA.

At the same time, in preparation for the Milan European summit, the Commission under its new president, Jacques Delors, had published the White Paper 'Completing the Internal Market' (COM(85)310, 14 June 1985). Elaborated under the supervision of British Internal Market Commissioner Lord Arthur Cockfield, it identified about 280 legislative measures to be implemented by the end of 1992. Some of these measures aligned well with the liberal economic ideas of the British government – e.g. on matters concerning the liberalization of insurance services and public procurement. At the same time, Lord Cockfield was able to draw on ideas previously developed by the Thorn Commission (cf. Cameron 1992: 52). For instance, in 1981 Internal Market Commissioner Karl-Heinz Narjes had already proposed the removal of customs booths across Europe, level value-added taxes, and expedition of the movement of goods (Fligstein and Mara-Drita 1996). The White Paper proposed a set of detailed measures to remove physical, technical, and fiscal barriers to European trade. Physical barriers, for instance, refer to customs or border controls. Technical barriers, for example, concern product safety rules and public procurement policies. Fiscal barriers mainly constitute differences in tax rates and laws. The Commission's White Paper was an ambitious project. It concluded with the statement:

> Europe stands at the crossroads. Either we go ahead – with resolution and determination – or we drop back into mediocrity. ... Just as the Customs Union had to precede Economic Integration, so Economic Integration has to precede European Unity. What this White Paper proposes therefore is that the Community should now take a further step along the road so clearly delineated in the Treaties. To do less would be to fall short of the ambitions of the founders of the Community, incorporated in the Treaties; it would be to betray the trust invested in us and it would be to offer the peoples of Europe a narrower, less rewarding, less secure, less prosperous future than they could otherwise enjoy. That is the measure of the challenge which faces us. Let it never be said that we were incapable of rising to it.

The SEA was the first major reform of the EEC Treaty. It was signed in 1986 and entered into force in July 1987. The SEA combines market liberalization – including the movement of capital – with institutional reform. While the institutional side is geared towards rendering the decision-making process more efficient and more legitimate, the liberalization component aims to promote trade, competition, and economies of scale. It represents a clear commitment of the member states to the four freedoms, as highlighted by the new article 8a to the EEC Treaty: 'The internal market shall comprise an area without internal frontiers in which the free movement of goods, persons, services and capital is ensured in accordance with the provisions of this Treaty.' With the aim of removing physical, technical, and fiscal barriers to trade, as formulated in the Commission's White Paper 'Completing the Internal Market', the SEA announces a paradigmatic shift from harmonizing member states' national legislation towards liberalization based on the principle of mutual recognition. In terms of policies, the SEA promoted the development of European political cooperation (Title III of the

SEA; cf. also Chapter 7 of this book), and the inclusion of research and development (Title VI) and environmental matters (Title VII). Title V of the SEA introduces 'Economic and Social Cohesion' as an accompanying branch to the completion of the internal market, thereby complementing negative with positive integration.

In terms of institutional provisions, the SEA envisaged QMV in the Council and, hence, marked a significant departure from the informal 'Luxembourg compromise' (the 'gentlemen's agreement' which stipulated that, in matters a member state declared as vital to its national interest, negotiations had to be continued until agreement could be found amongst all member states). In addition, the SEA introduced the assent procedure that granted the EP the right to veto enlargements and international agreements, and the cooperation procedure, which was chiefly designed to pass legislation pertaining to the completion of the Internal Market. The SEA thus extended the range of QMV and declared that unanimity is no longer required for measures designed to establish the single market, with the exception of measures concerning taxation, the free movement of persons, and the rights and interests of employed persons. The shift from unanimity to QMV in matters pertaining to the Internal Market is often seen as the most important reform of the SEA (cf. Garrett 1992: 548). The cooperation procedure also strengthened the role of the EP by providing the Parliament with the opportunity to amend the Council's common position, or to reject it (SEA, Art. 7). If the EP has rejected the Council's common position, unanimity is required for the Council to act on a second reading (Crombez 1996; Tsebelis 1994). We thus find that the SEA moves single market issues from joint decision-making I towards joint decision-making II ('community method and pooling') on our vertical integration scale.

After the SEA

After the SEA, the next institutional changes to the legal foundations of the single market came into force with the Treaty of Maastricht, which most prominently introduced the co-decision procedure for market-related issues. Co-decision strengthens the EP's role as compared to the cooperation procedure; the EP, under co-decision, acts as co-legislator on an almost equal footing with the Council. Reformed at Amsterdam, the co-decision procedure was finally replaced by the 'ordinary legislative procedure' in the Treaty of Lisbon (Art. 294 TFEU). Also note that, according to Art. 238(3) TFEU, the Nice Treaty's long-contested qualified majority rule will be replaced by the 'dual majority' of 'at least 55% of the members of the Council representing the participating Member States, comprising at least 65% of the population of these States' by November 2014. Otherwise, the Treaty of Lisbon only made 'modest changes' to the single market programme (cf. Young 2010: 116) – for instance, by establishing provisions for a 'uniform protection of intellectual property rights throughout the Union and for the setting up of centralised Union-wide authorisation, coordination and supervision arrangements' (Art. 138 TFEU).

Moreover, even beyond the setting of primary law, market integration remains an ongoing process, as already illustrated above with reference to the Commission's 2010 communication 'Towards a Single Market Act'. In addition, in 2007 the Commission launched an initiative on 'A Single Market for 21st Century Europe' in which it pleaded for a 'smarter mix' of policy instruments, including an increased usage of soft law for the sake of better implementation and enforcement (Young 2010: 127). All these measures broadly relate to the Barroso commission's goal of promoting 'better regulation' in the single market. However, since these proposals do not relate to primary law we will not cover them in detail in this book.

Horizontal integration

The EEC set out with six member states. Over time, the single market has grown to include the 27 member states of the EU. In addition, Iceland, Liechtenstein and Norway participate in the single market through the EEA agreement. Switzerland is also hooked to the development of the single market through bilateral treaties and by adapting most market regulations on a case by case basis in order to ensure unobstructed access of Swiss products into the EC. As already highlighted in the introduction to this chapter, the single market is an instance of a mostly uniform application of EC legislation. Other than some temporary exceptions in the context of enlargement, all EU member states participate fully in the single market. At the same time, the EEA is an interesting example for external differentiation by allowing non-EU member states access to a particular EC regime.

The EEA agreement coincides with the single market programme. The ambitious plans towards the completion of the single market raised concerns of marginalization and of being left behind in the remaining member states of the EFTA. Already by 1984, the so-called 'Luxembourg process' had launched a sector-by-sector approach of establishing closer cooperation between the EC and the EFTA countries in new policy areas (cf. Gstöhl 1994). This process, however, was perceived to become increasingly complicated. As a consequence, European Commission President Jacques Delors proposed the establishment of a stronger institutionalized form of cooperation through the EEA in January 1989. The aim of this more encompassing approach was to guarantee the persistence of the four freedoms between the EC and the EFTA states. Talks on the EEA started in

Box 5.1   *Timeline: EC market integration*

1951	European Coal and Steel Community	1985	Messina Conference
1955	Messina Conference	1986	Southern Enlargement
1957	Treaties of Rome	1987	Single European Act
1973	Northern Enlargement	1993	Treaty of Maastricht
1974	Dassonville Ruling	1994	European Economic Area
1979	Cassis de Dijon Ruling	1995	European Free Trade Area Enlargement
1981	Greek Enlargement		
1983	Declaration of Stuttgart	2004	Eastern Enlargement I
1985	Commission White Paper 'Completing the Internal Market'	2007	Eastern Enlargement II

1989, and continued during 1990 and 1991. However, eventually, in 1994 only Iceland, Liechtenstein, and Norway became EEA member states. The Swiss people rejected membership in 1992; Austria, Finland, and Sweden had, in the meantime, opted for full EU membership (the Norwegian voters had voted against EU membership in November 1994). At the time of writing, Iceland, Liechtenstein, and Norway have to adopt the internal market relevant *acquis* quasi-automatically, with the exception of matters related to fisheries and agriculture. These three countries, also known as the EFTA EEA states, have almost no say over EU rules and only contribute weakly to 'decision-shaping' by formally participating in Commission-sponsored committees. Despite EFTA EEA states' limited capacity to impact on new pieces of legislation, new community legislation is dynamically incorporated into the EEA agreement – assuring a uniform application of internal market related rules in the EU and EEA. This also includes flanking policies of the internal market, such as research and development, environment, consumer protection, social policies, and policies directed towards achieving economic and social cohesion. Iceland, Liechtenstein, and Norway also agreed to contribute financially to support the reduction of the economic and social disparities inside the EU.

The case of Switzerland is more complicated. After the Swiss voters had rejected the EEA agreement in a referendum in 1992, the Swiss government negotiated a more flexible form of integration with the EU (cf. Lavenex 2009; Tovias 2006). In 1999 and 2004, Switzerland and the EU passed two packages of bilateral treaties (a third package is on the negotiation table at the time of writing). The so-called 'bilateral treaties' (or 'bilaterals') cover important internal market issues such as the free movement of persons, technical barriers to trade, public procurement, research policy, and road and air traffic. In contrast to the

EEA agreements, the bilateral agreements are neither dynamic (which means that changes in the single market are not automatically incorporated into the agreements), nor subject to judicial monitoring (cf. Lavenex 2009: 551). Accordingly, Switzerland is neither formally involved in decision-making on internal market issues, nor obliged to enact new pieces of EU legislation. At the same time, the Swiss legislator 'autonomously' copies large parts of EU legislation in order to secure smooth access to the internal market to Swiss economic actors.

Following successive rounds of enlargement, and including all EEA members, the single market comprises 30 states. Because market legislation is mostly uniformly applied inside the EU and attracts some outside states to participation, the single market is an important case displaying internal uniformity and external differentiation.

Conclusion of historical overview

The Common Market has been at the heart of the European integration project since the 1950s. The Treaties of Rome mark the starting point of the Common Market. In terms of vertical integration, the EEC Treaty established intergovernmental coordination between the EEC member states. This equates to a value of 3 on our scale of vertical integration introduced in Chapter 1 (see Figure 5.1). The 'Luxembourg compromise' of 1966 blocked the introduction of QMV, and more than two decades passed until the next major integration step, the SEA, was enacted in 1987. The SEA established QMV for acts relating to the single market and replaced the consultation procedure with the cooperation procedure. Therefore in 1987 the level of integration of the economic freedoms rises to 4.0 on our scale, representing 'joint decision-making II'. Another deepening of decision-making is introduced by the co-decision procedure of the Maastricht treaty and therefore the line for vertical integration reaches a level of 4.5 after 1993.

Horizontal integration of the single market starts at a lower level but increases gradually over time. At the time of writing, more than 80 per cent of all European states participate in the single market (this relates to a level of 4 out of 5 in Figure 5.1). Note that the drop of the line in the early 1990s and 2000s is an arithmetical artefact due to an increasing number of European states. So far, a story of 'ever-wider' Union holds for the single market.

All in all, the single market is a comparatively early and highly integrated policy area in the EU – in vertical as well as in horizontal terms. With the historical trajectory and the levels of vertical and horizontal integration in mind, we will now turn to the integration theories with the aim of inspecting how well they are able to explain the patterns of market integration in Europe. As we will see, the single market has received strong attention from integration theorists. In fact, because the single

Figure 5.1   *Vertical and horizontal integration of economic freedoms*

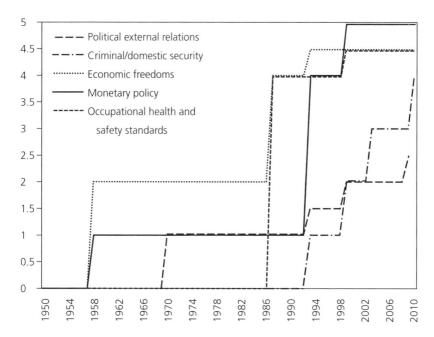

market has been so central to the European project, one could argue that every serious theory of European integration needs to be able to account for the dynamics of market integration. Also, the founding of the European Coal and Steel Community and the Common Market in the 1950s gave birth to theorizing about integration in the first place. The intellectual enthusiasm raised by these early steps of market integration resonates well in Lindberg's (1963: 4) statement that these developments in Europe allowed political scientists to 'observe the actual processes whereby political actors move beyond the nation-state as a basic framework for action, appearing finally to realize the oft-proclaimed 'fact' of the international interdependence of nations. Forces are at work in Western Europe that may alter the nature of international relations.'

In the following, we will take up our theoretical expectations derived from intergovernmentalism, supranationalism, and constructivism to address the following questions:

- First, how can we explain the degree and form of market integration over time? Why was the Common Market founded in the 1950s to be followed by the *relance européenne* only in the 1980s? Why has the single market been one of the most integrated policy areas in the history of the EU, and what explains the particular form market integration has taken in Europe?

- Second, what explains the horizontal patterns of market integration? Why does the single market display mostly uniform integration inside the EU while, at the same time, attracting outsiders (leading to external differentiation)?

We will begin with a review of intergovernmentalism, and then submit supranationalism and constructivism to empirical scrutiny. For each of these theories, we will start addressing vertical integration over time by investigating the EEC Treaty and then the SEA. We then take up the issue of horizontal integration and differentiation.

Intergovernmentalism

For many years, one important cleavage dominated the field of European integration research and separated theorists into two seemingly irreconcilable camps. Neofunctionalism and supranationalism opposed (liberal) intergovernmentalism. Whereas neofunctionalism and supranationalism underlined the dynamic and self-reinforcing character of regional integration in Europe driven by transnational exchange and supranational entrepreneurship, intergovernmentalists took a more static – and also statist – perspective by maintaining that the nation states remain in the driver's seat of integration. However, when reviewing the literature on the single market from the perspective at the time of writing, this tension appears somewhat exaggerated. When Haas (1958: 25) writes that '[i]ntegration is the result of specific decisions made by governments acting in conjunction with politically relevant, organized groups', it is hard to imagine Andrew Moravcsik disagreeing. But let us first more systematically formulate, and then investigate, expectations derived from intergovernmentalism regarding the integration of the single market.

- For intergovernmentalism state preferences and bargaining power determine integration. Governmental actors weigh the costs and benefits of integration. Only when the benefits outweigh the costs does integration become possible. For realist intergovernmentalists, the measure of costs and benefits is state autonomy and power. Accordingly, for realist intergovernmentalists geopolitical developments determine the scope and pace of integration. In particular, the devastating effects of World War II and the emergence of the Cold War led European states to closer cooperation. Cooperation will be limited to 'low politics' that do not substantively harm state sovereignty. For liberal intergovernmentalists, governmental actors strive to maximize societal support and therefore take societal demands closely into account when formulating their European policy positions. In contrast to realist intergovernmentalism, liberal intergovernmentalism therefore sees interdependence and converging preferences as driving forces of regional economic integration.

- From a realist intergovernmentalist perspective, horizontal integration and differentiation can best be explained by a variation of geopolitical conditions and imperatives. For liberal intergovernmentalists, uneven interdependence and varying costs of economic integration can account for the differentiated patterns of horizontal integration.

The beginnings of integration: post-World War II Europe, economic interdependence

For realist intergovernmentalists, Western Europe after World War II was in a state of turmoil. The war had devastated most parts of the continent. Hoffmann (1966: 872) speaks of the 'political collapse of Europe' and finds that 'Europe did not merely lose power and wealth: such losses can be repaired, as the aftermath of World War I had shown. Europe, previously the heart of the international system, the locus of the world organization, the fount of international law, fell under what de Gaulle has called "the two hegemonies".' The nuclear stalemate and the emerging bipolarity of the international system of states posed new challenges for European leaders. Not only was Europe harmed in material respects, it also suffered from the ideational shocks of the war. For Hoffmann, these are key conditions in explaining the readiness of the founding states to engage in an institutionalized economic cooperation in the form of the EEC. In his view, the national interest – defined as the 'national situation times the outlook of the foreign policy makers' (Hoffmann 1966: 869) – allowed integration in the economic realm.

Against the backdrop of the tensions between the two superpowers, the USA and the Soviet Union, the beginnings of European integration can be considered an instance of external balancing. Interestingly, the most prominent neofunctionalist, Ernst Haas (1958: 279), cites Chancellor Adenauer's adviser Walter Hallstein – later the Commission's first president, who declared at the opening of the Brussels Expert conference convoked after Messina: 'The Federal Government believes that we must take a decisive step now. This is much more a political than an economic necessity. A balance between East and West is only possible if there is European unity. We believe that the purely economic activities of GATT and OEEC must have a political counterpart.' Haas (1958: 298) also stresses the importance of the Suez Canal crises underlining the importance of European integration as a 'means of survival in a global setting of Soviet-American dominance and rising Asian and African nations'. It is surprising to find such geostrategic arguments in the neo-functionalist classic *The Uniting of Europe*, since the logic perfectly conforms to realist intergovernmentalist theory.

At the same time, for realist intergovernmentalists the transfer of competences remains selective to specific issues, and the process of partial integration is carefully conducted by interest-maximizing nation states. British historian Alan Milward (1994) speaks of the 'European rescue of the nation-state'. For Milward (1994: 18), '[i]ntegration was not the supersession of the nation-state by another form of governance as the nation-state became incapable, but was the creation of the European nation-states themselves for their own purposes, an act of national will.' Realist intergovernmentalists underline that a demise of independence is clearly limited to sectors of 'low politics'. For realists, there is no question that 'high politics' – defined as those sectors that substantively relate to national sovereignty – should remain unaffected by integration. Therefore, it comes as no surprise to realists that the establishment of the Common Market was more successful than the setting up of the European Defence Community (EDC).

Finally, a realist expectation that small states have a stronger interest in establishing institutionalized ties between states is partly confirmed by the role the smaller delegations played in the preparation of the Treaties of Rome. For instance, Dutch Foreign Minister Beyen is often argued to have importantly set the agenda before the Messina conference of 1955 (cf. Haas 1958: 269). The horizontal patterns of integration and the differences in demand for integration from different states in the 1950s can be explained from a realist perspective by the degree to which different nations were affected by the war and the emerging Cold War situation. But we will discuss this in greater detail below.

For liberal intergovernmentalism, economic concerns and incentives are the main driving forces of regional integration. For Moravcsik (1998), the issue of export promotion determines the preferences of the British, French, and German governments. Since, during the 1950s, British industry relied heavily on preferential access to colonial and Commonwealth markets, the UK was more hesitant with regard to establishing a customs union than France and Germany (cf. Moravcsik 1998: 135). At the same time, Moravcsik acknowledges that economic preferences alone cannot explain the establishment of the EEC and he grants individual politicians a decisive role. For him, Chancellor Adenauer's geopolitical orientation determined the German preference for the establishment of the EEC: if 'Erhard had ruled Germany, the likely result would have been an Anglo-German FTA with no agricultural component' (Moravcsik 1998: 137). Thus, Moravcsik borrows from the realist intergovernmentalist toolbox in order to explain the emergence of the EEC. While economic interests have primacy for the formulation of national preferences, they seem insufficient for explaining the particular choices taken in 1957. At the same time, from a liberal intergovernmentalist perspective, supranational actors such as the High Authority and Jean Monnet's Action Committee for the United States of Europe play only a negligible role in the process.

Integrative dynamics: growing interdependence and preference convergence before the SEA

The shift from unanimity to QMV, together with the empowerment of the EP enacted by the SEA, should constitute a puzzle for realist intergovernmentalists. QMV hollows out a state's autonomy, since it can be forced to implement policies that it does not support. Realist intergovernmentalists may counter that the integrative developments of the SEA are still primarily restricted to 'low politics', and are therefore less important. In addition, they would agree with the supranationalists' reading that, due to structural changes in the world economy, Europeans had strong incentives to make their economies more competitive. If the single market programme can contribute to this goal, the demise of the Luxemburg compromise may be a bitter pill that the nation states have to swallow.

Liberal intergovernmentalism only partly agrees with this traditionalist reading and, instead, puts forward a different set of causal mechanisms. In his analysis of the timing and content of the SEA, Moravcsik (1998) challenges the supranationalist view that the reform resulted primarily from an elite alliance between supranational actors such as the Delors Commission and the EP, and pan-European business interest groups. He finds that the role of Jacques Delors is often exaggerated in the literature: 'the breakthrough in the relaunching of the EC had already occurred before Delors became president of the Commission. The causality of the supranational explanation is thus reversed: the selection of a prestigious politician for the presidency was merely a symptom of mounting trilateral pressure for reform' (Moravcsik 1991: 46). Similarly, for Moravcsik it is important to note that, while the White Paper 'Completing the Single Market' was drafted by Lord Cockfield in the Commission, it had previously been mandated by the member states. This implies that the nation states, as principals, remained the masters of the integration process.

Geoffrey Garrett (1992: 538) finds that an 'ever-growing trade dependence of the European economies, combined with more than a decade of poor and declining economic performance ('Eurosclerosis'), greatly increased the benefits of completing the common market relative to the costs of participation', and – in line with supranationalist expectations – underlines that 'the power of large transnational firms increased significantly during the early 1980s. Given the strong preferences of these firms for free access to other markets and for reducing cross-border transactions costs, the greater influence of transnational business added further to the pressures for trade liberalization in Europe.' But, at the same time, he claims that these demands were 'significantly mediated by domestic political and institutional factors, such as electoral competition, government partisanship, ideology, and the organization of economic interests' (Garrett 1992: 541). Thus, the member state governments kept their hands on the project by representing the aggregated societal interests, but also infused their own political ideas into the European negotiations.

Moravcsik (1991) explains the deepening of the single market by pointing to the convergent economic positions of the large member state governments – the UK, Germany, and France (see also Cameron 1992: 56). There is hardly any doubt that a wider liberalization of commerce in the EC was fully in line with the ideological standing of the British Conservative government. Moravcsik (1991: 37) cites British Foreign Minister Geoffrey Howe who called for the removal of 'all – and I mean all, economic barriers' by 1990. Most observers agree that the Northern member states shared the 'common goal of increasing the competitiveness of European goods and services in global markets' (Garrett 1992: 535). The economically less competitive member states demanded compensatory measures for their agreeing to a liberalization agenda that was likely to imply heavy political costs. Against this backdrop, the declared goal of article 130 of the SEA – to promote economic and social cohesion, which later led to a substantive increase of structural funds – can be viewed as a side-payment to the Southern and less competitive member states. Their necessary support was thus 'bought'. This pattern matches the intergovernmentalist emphasis on interstate bargaining rather well.

Similarly, the enactment of institutional reforms – such as the extension of QMV against the explicit critique of some member states, notably the UK – can be explained by inter-state bargaining (cf. Moravcsik 1991: 36). France and Germany as the drivers of vertical integration were in a strong position, since they could credibly threaten the UK with exclusion from deeper market integration. At about the same time, they enacted the intergovernmental Schengen agreement together with the Benelux countries outside the EC institutional framework in order to circumvent British, Danish, and Greek opposition (cf. Chapter 8 on the AFSJ). The threat of establishing a two-tier Europe was thus used to 'discipline' more reluctant Europeans.

At the same time, the pro-European side, too, had to compromise. In line with intergovernmentalist expectations, during the negotiations of the SEA many progressive proposals were watered down. Truly ambitious reforms were ultimately limited to Internal Market issues and, even here, some more contentious issues (such as fiscal and social regulation) were excluded from the majority voting rule. For intergovernmentalists, the SEA thus represents a lowest common denominator outcome. In addition, the conflation of market liberalization and institutional reform is often described as a package deal. For instance, Parsons (2010: 711) argues that 'the SEA resulted from a deal between distinct liberalizing and Europeanist agendas' (see also Cameron 1992). This interpretation fits nicely into the liberal intergovernmentalist framework.

Differentiated integration

The patterns of integration in the single market conform in parts to intergovernmentalist expectations. For realist intergovernmentalists, the initial reluctance of the UK is in line with this country's 'special' position after World War II. The UK had not been defeated during World War II; additionally, after the war this country kept close ties with its former colonies through the Commonwealth, and maintained a pronounced transatlantic outlook. As Winston Churchill succinctly put it in the House of Commons on 11 May 1953, 'We are with Europe but not of it. We are linked but not comprised. We are associated but not absorbed.' However, why did the UK seek membership from the early 1960s yet finally join the EC in 1973? From a realist intergovernmentalist perspective, one could argue that the Suez crisis of 1956 revealed that Britain was no longer a great imperial power – in fact, Prime Minister Anthony Eden's successor, Harold Macmillan, strongly supported British accession to the EEC. But the fact that in the meantime, apart from Switzerland, Norway, and Liechtenstein, all Western European states have joined the community does not really support realist intergovernmentalist expectations concerning horizontal integration.

The case of the UK, in our view, fits better into the liberal intergovernmentalist framework. Andrew Moravcsik (1998: 123) argues that 'the British policy of apathy and opposition to the customs union was the rational one for a government that traded little with the continent, had high tariffs in place, and feared competition with German producers'. In particular, the close economic ties with former colonies and overseas countries initially dictated different priorities to the UK. Milward (1994: 426) supports this economic explanation for the initial British reluctance, but also underlines that the British administration had serious doubts about a successful establishment of the EEC. At the same time, outsiders such as the UK kept a jealous eye over the economic progress of the EEC and, indeed, as the Common Market promoted growth through the abolishment of tariffs and duties in Europe, Britain found that staying out of the system was becoming increasingly costly. When the importance of the Commonwealth declined, the UK applied for EEC membership. For Moravcsik (1998), the UK's position is therefore primarily driven by commercial interests. This view is shared by Ernst Haas (1958: 159), who argues that the UK had been reluctant regarding the ECSC for economic reasons. As to the EEC, he finds a growing support for the project in Britain: '[a] common market, implying the possibility of discrimination against British trade in search of increasing Continental rather than Commonwealth outlets, proved to be a potent centre of attraction' (Haas 1958: 161).

An interesting pattern of external differentiation is the establishment of the EEA. In fact, the relationship of Iceland, Liechtenstein, and Norway towards the EU is characterized by sector-specific homogeneity in a relationship that, overall, remains characterized by too much heterogeneity for full membership. This is in line with intergovernmentalist ideas. The EFTA states faced negative externalities from the single market project. Fearing discrimination in the single market, they took up the Commission's idea of negotiating a global agreement that would ensure access to the single market. As already briefly highlighted above, the establishment of the EEA agreement coincides – with a small time lag – with the *relance* of the European integration project through the single market programme. The ambitious plans towards completing the single market raised concerns of marginalization, and of being left behind, in the remaining member states of the EFTA. Since they were hesitant to go all the way towards full membership, they had a weak bargaining position that is illustrated by the rather costly outcomes for the EFTA EEA states Iceland, Liechtenstein, and Norway.

The price for participation in the internal market can, indeed, be considered high for those EEA states. One important cost is what is sometimes called the 'influence deficit'. While EEA countries have better access to the internal market, there is a loss of operational sovereignty: Iceland, Liechtenstein and Norway only have a very limited influence in EU decision-making, but new community legislation is dynamically incorporated into the agreements. They have access to internal market related agencies in the decision-shaping phase of the legislative process, but they do not participate in the Council structure and have no right to vote (Tovias 2006: 204). In addition, as Baldwin (1995: 30) has argued, the internal market grants the Commission important powers of surveillance for the enforcement of competition policy, state aids to industry, and national public procurement policies. But, since the EFTA states cannot control the Commission politically, the agreement for them demands 'regulation without representation'.

In addition, the EEA states agreed to contribute financially to strengthening cohesion in the single market through the so-called 'EEA grants'. While it can be argued that these states had previously profited from EU cohesion policies without contributing to them (positive externalities), their contributions can be considered a price those countries had to pay for receiving legal homogeneity and unrestricted access to the Internal Market. Interestingly, after the Swiss rejection of the EEA in 1992, the EC even demanded compensation for the Swiss dropout from the remaining EEA candidate states Iceland, Liechtenstein, and Norway. Note however, that Switzerland, too, has subsequently supported development programmes in Eastern Europe through an enlargement contribution, also known as the 'cohesion billion'. The EEA grants and the design of the Swiss contributions allow the EFTA states to select the specific programmes and recipients of their contributions. This, however, only seems cold comfort for the EFTA countries.

Overall, the bargaining dynamics and outcomes of the EEA agreement illustrate that, in line with intergovernmentalist expectations, the EU negotiated from a position of strength. For Gstöhl (1994: 356) there is 'no doubt that the bargaining leverage was on the Community's side. The EFTA countries needed an agreement more than the EC, and their expectations did not correspond to what the EC was either able or willing to deliver.' Ultimately, only few countries opted for the 'half-way' house between isolation and integration. According to Gstöhl (1994: 334), the 'unanticipated shape of the EEA is likely to have contributed to the EFTA countries' change of policy in favor of full EC membership' (see also Varwick and Windwehr 2007: 19). Fearing 'cherry-picking' in the single market, the EU demanded a high price for allowing selective integration.

Finally, liberal intergovernmentalists can explain the fact that the EFTA countries and Switzerland still object to full membership by pointing to idiosyncratic factors relating to those countries. For, instance, the Swiss *Sonderweg* can be explained by the institutional structure of a direct democracy in combination with an economy that relies heavily on the banking sector.

Internal differentiation in the area of the single market is rare, and uniform application of EU legislation is the rule. This observation seems in line with the theoretical expectations formulated by the literature on the EU as a regulatory state (Majone 1996), since a regulatory state primarily enhances efficiency. At the same time, despite compelling market logic, there often are disputes between the EU member states concerning single market issues. A recent dispute, for instance, erupted on the question of the establishment of an EU patent. This case is particularly interesting because it is, so far, one of the few examples in which the enhanced cooperation procedure has been used in practice (cf. Box 5.2). Enhanced cooperation had first been institutionalized in the Treaty of Amsterdam. It allows a subset of EU member states to cooperate more closely on matters covered by the Treaties, and to use the institutions and procedures of the EU (see Art. 20 TEU). Since the terms of cooperation do not bind the member states that do not participate in the enhanced cooperation, it introduces horizontal differentiation in the application of secondary law (cf. Stubb 2002). For us, it is interesting to see that the mechanisms of decision-making in primary and secondary law sometimes resemble one another. For instance, Box 5.2 illustrates that horizontal differentiation can be considered problematic by some states in the single market.

Box 5.2   *Enhanced cooperation in practice: EU patent*

In April 2011, the European Commission issued a proposal for a regulation that implemented enhanced cooperation for the creation of a European Union (EU) patent. The decision to choose the road of enhanced cooperation followed a long dispute within the EU's legislative machinery. The Commission had already published a Communication on 'enhancing the patent system in Europe' in 2007. In this communication, the Commission underlined that European patents are about nine times more expensive than Japanese and US patents, which would impose unnecessary costs on European economies. At the end of 2009, the Council has reached a general agreement about the usefulness of such a system; however, the translation arrangements for the EU patent were not covered in its conclusions. In 2010, it became evident that the member states were unable to reach unanimity on the translation arrangements. In particular, Spain and Italy objected to an EU patent restricted to English, French, and German. It therefore seemed unlikely that a uniform patent system would be established in the EU. In response, several member states expressed their desire to establish enhanced cooperation in this area. On 15 February 2011, the European Parliament consented to proceeding with enhanced cooperation. The procedure was then formally authorized by the Council in March 2011.

Italy and Spain – the opponents of an EU patent – lodged a complaint before the European Court of Justice against enhanced cooperation on the EU patent. Spain's EU affairs minister, Diego Lopez Gariddo, explained that the Spanish government 'insists that the reinforced cooperation mechanism was used to impose a solution which excludes Spain with a mechanism which, paradoxically, was thought up to facilitate the integration of the Member States.' In a statement, the Italian Ministry of Foreign Affairs declared: 'The use of enhanced co-operation within the patent sector is contrary to the spirit of the single market, because it tends to create division and distortion within the market, and will thus prejudice Italian businesses.' Internal Market Commissioner Michel Barnier replied that he was 'confident, that the enhanced cooperation procedure presented by the Commission is not discriminatory. We are assured that Spanish and Italian business will suffer no discrimination. ... I hope that in time Italy and Spain will join in the enhanced co-operation: that would be in the general European interest.'

Sources: Citations from www.euractive.com; for further information see http://www.consilium.europa.eu/ueDocs/cms_Data/docs/pressData/en/intm/119665.pdf

Supranationalism

For supranationalism, transnational exchanges are a necessary condition for the emergence of regional integration. With denser transnational exchanges, there is assumed to be a greater demand from (transnational) societal actors for closer policy coordination between nation states. Following the establishment of supranational institutions, societal and supranational actors can work together to promote further integration. The following expectations on the emergence and the development of the single market can be generated from supranationalism:

- The decision to establish the EEC in the late 1950s is primarily motivated by economic concerns. Transnational exchanges can best explain the EEC Treaty. When surveying the process leading to the establishment of the EEC, we should observe that transnational interest groups play an important role. In addition, the organs of the ECSC should actively support the establishment of the Common Market. Once the Common Market has been set up, supranationalism expects an increase of transnational exchanges inside the EEC. This, in turn, should spur demand for further integration among transnational actors. The supranational actors of the EEC should also be able positively to shape the integration agenda.
- Successful integration of the Common Market leads to spillover effects to other policy sectors, and incites demand for integration from neighbouring and initially recalcitrant states. Supranationalism thus predicts a deepening and widening of the Common Market over time.

The beginnings of integration: transnational exchanges and the EEC Treaty

Interestingly, neither of the neofunctionalist classics, the *Uniting of Europe* (Haas 1958), Lindberg's (1963) *The Political Dynamics of European Economic Integration*, or Lindberg and Scheingold's (1970) *Europe's Would-be Polity* provides an in-depth analysis of the founding of the Common Market. The *Uniting of Europe* analyzes 'political, social, and economic forces 1950–1957', and thus focuses on explaining and describing the ECSC. Since the book was published in 1958, Ernst Haas's work is constructed against the backdrop of Euratom and the EEC, but the ECSC remains at the centre of his analysis. Lindberg (1963) focuses on the political consequences of integration. How does integration impact on decision-making patterns in the Europe of the six? Further elaborating on this topic, Lindberg and Scheingold (1970) analyze the patterns of change in the European

Community. Similarly, the supranationalists of the 1990s are more concerned with developments of the single market over time than with its beginnings.

Why did market integration begin in the 1950s? Explaining the timing of political decisions and events is a challenging task for social science theories. In fact, dense transnational exchanges between European states had already been present long before the outbreak of World War II. This suggests that this variable alone is not sufficient to explain the foundations of the EEC. This is also accepted by Haas (1968: xix), who argues that a purely functional argument is insufficient to explain integration in the 1950s: 'Politicians were important in the process. Economic reasoning alone was not sufficient. ... Politics remained imbedded in the functional logic.' For Haas (1958: 524), state support remains a necessary condition for integration: 'when the governments, for identical or converging reasons, are determined *not* to find a federal solution to their problems ... High Authority initiative will be neither solicited nor respected.' At the same time, it is noteworthy that integration, indeed, occurred in a sector where a high level of transnational exchanges was present. As we will highlight in Chapter 7, on defence policy, the EDC failed to be ratified by the French National Assembly in 1954, whereas the Common Market turned out to be an instance of successful integration only three years after the EDC was buried. When comparing these two sectors, one could, in line with supranationalism, argue that there was more transnational demand for integration in the economic than in the external security domain.

In addition, from a supranationalist perspective, previous integration of the coal and steel sectors should have paved the way for a further economic integration. Although the High Authority's competence was initially limited to issues relating to the ECSC, it made use of its visibility more generally to promote a pro-European agenda. Giving a voice to societal demands for integration, the High Authority accelerated spillover processes towards a 'general economic unity' (Hass 1958: 109). For instance, High Authority President Jean Monnet's proposal of an extension of the powers of the ECSC to all sources of energy found wide support amongst the participants at the Messina conference (cf. Haas 1958: 107). Representatives from the High Authority and the ECSC Council of ministers were present at the EEC negotiations and – according to Haas – they were able to shape the outcomes by drawing on their expertise: '[f]our years of experience with sector integration were thus brought to bear on future plans and the conclusions of ECSC personnel found a wide hearing in the proposal before the six governments' (Hass 1958: 108). Jean Monnet's Action Committee is often argued to have provided important stimuli for the Euratom treaty. The continuity from the ECSC to the EEC is thus not surprising from a supranationalist point of view. Haas (1958: 301) detects a 'direct causal connection between the negotiation of the Euratom and the General Common Market treaties and the crisis over the extension of ECSC powers'.

For neofunctionalism, the EEC was only a starting point for further political integration (cf. Lindberg 1963: 7). Integration was conceived as an incremental process but, to the surprise of the early neofunctionalists, the next important steps of vertical integration were only taken more than 25 years after the entry into force of the Treaties of Rome through the SEA.

Explaining the single market programme: transnational exchanges, institutionalization, and spillover

After a period of conceived 'Eurosclerosis' in the 1970s, the SEA is often considered a major step in putting European integration back on track. At the same time, it revived a theoretical interest in European integration. Had integration theories been identified as 'obsolescent' by Ernst Haas in 1976, the SEA revived the debate between neofunctionalists and intergovernmentalists; this time with supranationalists and liberal intergovernmentalists opposing each other. For supranationalists, the development of the SEA confirmed some important expectations of neofunctionalism. Supranationalists identified an alliance between economic transnational interest groups and the supranational actors as the central driving force behind the *relance européenne* in the early 1980s.

Sandholtz and Zysman (1989: 96) underline that both international economic factors and the capacities of supranational actors – most notably the Commission – paved the paths towards further integration. Changes in the international economic structure – the stagnating economies in Europe and in the USA, and the rise of the Japanese economy – were a necessary but not a sufficient condition for '1992', i.e. the single market programme:

> Other conditions were equally necessary and, in combination, sufficient. First 1992 emerged because the institutions of the European Communities, especially the Commission, were able to exercise effective policy leadership ... In addition, a transnational industry coalition also perceived the need for European level action. The Commission, aided by business, was able to mobilize a coalition of governmental elites that favored the overall objective of market unification.

In addition, as these authors acknowledge, favourable domestic conditions facilitated the enactment of the single market programme. A decisive moment was French President François Mitterrand's 1983 decision to move towards a more liberal shift of French policy in order to avoid a withdrawal of the franc from the European Monetary System. Government shifts in Germany and the UK additionally allowed the enactment of more market-oriented solutions. As Sandholtz and Zysman (1989: 113) metaphorically put it, this was 'the domestic political soil into which the Commission's initiatives fell'.

The explanation thus consists of three steps that mirror the historical developments. First, structural change in the global economy leads to a societal demand for integration (cf. Fligstein and Mara-Drita 1996). Moreover, transnational exchanges had made the persistence of disparate national rules increasingly costly: 'intra-EC trade and investment have grown steadily since the founding of the EEC, creating the need for greater degrees of supranational governance in issue areas closely linked to expanding the common market. Naturally, the EC rules for the single market have in turn encouraged increases in the trans-border transactions they were meant to facilitate' (Stone Sweet and Sandholtz 1997: 308). In the case of the single market programme, as a reaction to US decline and the rising economic importance of Japan, European business – represented, for example, by the European Roundtable of Industrialists – demanded more European support for research and technology development. The demand for liberalization – also driven by an increasing amount of intra-European mergers and alliances – is, second, taken up by an entrepreneurial Commission. An alliance of societal and supranational actors thus managed to set the agenda, for instance, by publishing the 1985 White Paper 'Completing the Single Market'. The Commission also displayed leadership when Common Market Commissioner Etienne Davignon built an alliance between 12 major electronics companies in the EC to promote the information technology sector, which culminated in the creation of the European Strategic Programme for Research and Development in Information Technology (ESPRIT). Finally, elite bargains among governments made the reforms possible. Market-oriented governments supported the Commission and established the goal of '1992'. Thus, the support of governments is a necessary condition in Sandholtz and Zysman's account; however, it cannot explain by itself why integration came about.

Sandholtz and Zysman (1989) also find that national parliaments, political parties, and trade unions at that time had not become centrally involved in the integration process and thereby qualify central intergovernmentalist expectations and claims. Since business is identified as a driving force behind the removal of non-tariff barriers to trade, supranationalists are not surprised about the 'decisively neoliberal (pro-market) character' (Stone Sweet and Sandholtz 1997) of '1992'. The substantive policy outcomes are thus in line with their theoretical expectations.

In addition, supranationalists have drawn our attention to the important role of the European Court of Justice for promoting integration. Stone Sweet and Brunell (1998: 65) have demonstrated forcefully that transnational exchanges create a demand for dispute resolution; and by 'revealing important collective action problems that beg for normative solutions (transnational rules)' push for modes of supranational governance. According to Burley and Mattli (1993), a triangle of private litigants, national judges and the ECJ – aided by the preliminary ruling system – has spurred integration to an extent exceeding that which member states had initially envisaged. Integration, moreover, is characterized by positive feedback: the dismantling of national rules preventing the free flow of goods and services fuels more transnational activity – in particular, trade – which, in turn, increases the potential for further disputes over those domestic rules, which are considered to inhibit free trade. Institutionalists argue that the ECJ's Cassis de Dijon verdict acted as a catalyst for integration by provoking a pro-market response by the Commission. For Alter and Meunier-Aitsahalia (1994: 552), the Commission interpreted the ruling in its general battle against protectionism, and 'the entrepreneurship of the Commission put the issue on the table and forced a debate'.

Horizontal integration and differentiation

The patterns of horizontal integration in the single market are broadly in line with supranationalist expectations. The growth of the Community to 27 EU member states and the close association of Iceland, Liechtenstein, and Norway through the EEA and Switzerland through the bilateral treaties illustrate the functional dynamics of market integration. All these countries are highly interdependent in economic terms, as there is a high density of transnational exchanges in Europe. The promise of growth has ensured political support in most European countries for the single market. It is primarily for economic reasons that outside states participate in the single market, and this resonates well with the supranationalist focus on economic actors. By including more member states, the EU has made exclusion increasingly costly for trade-dependent non-member states and triggered their demand for closer association with the single market.

In line with supranationalist expectations, Commission President Jacques Delors set the agenda for the EEA in 1989, proposing the establishment of a special regime enabling the extension of the four freedoms to the EFTA states. In the EEA agreement, the EU's supranational institutions supported external integration but, at the same time, they complicated matters for the EEA candidates. In particular, the ECJ clearly objected to attempts to create a joint EEA Court of Justice (cf. Gstöhl 1994: 347). This highlights that the Community institutions strongly watched over maintaining and not diluting the EU institutional framework.

At the same time, supranationalists have greater difficulties in explaining the persistent reluctance of some states *vis-à-vis* the integration project. It is hard to account for the initial reluctance of Denmark or Sweden, or the continuous hesitation of Norway and Switzerland, to becoming full members of the EU solely on the basis of economic figures. All these countries are closely tied to the other European states in economic respects – for instance, the EU is by far the most important trading partner of Norway and Switzerland. Therefore, trade and transnational exchanges alone cannot explain the demand for, or the refusal of, integration.

Constructivism

Constructivist propositions on the single market break with rationalist assumptions and put ideational factors to the fore.

• For constructivists, Europeanist ideas led to the founding of the EEC in the 1950s. Over time, the participating actors became socialized to follow pro-Community norms, facilitating further integration. The reforms of the single market programme can best be explained by an ideational consensus on how successfully to promote growth in the European economies.
• Horizontal integration is also driven by ideas and identities. In particular, 'exclusive national identities' (Hooghe and Marks 2008) can hinder a state to support European integration.

The beginnings of integration: ideas matter

The idea of European unity goes back at least to the nineteenth century. For instance, French author and intellectual Victor Hugo already spoke of the 'États-Unis d'Europe' in 1849. Pan-European ideas blossomed in the inter-war period promoted by enigmatic figures such as the Austrian count Coudenhove-Kalergy. In 1929, French Foreign Minister Aristide Briand promoted the idea of creating a federal association between the states of Europe before the League of Nations. This idea was taken up by the European representatives in the League who mandated Briand to work out his plan in more detail. Under the guidance of Alexis Léger and Briand, a memorandum on the organization of a Federal European Union Regime was elaborated and presented on 1 May 1930. At the time, however, the idea did not achieve lasting success.

In the aftermath of World War II, federalist European ideas were again taken up and even more prominently promoted by the European movement. In May 1948, the Hague Congress under the chairmanship of Winston Churchill united 750 delegates to discuss the future of Europe; amongst them such important figures as Konrad Adenauer, Harold Macmillan, Paul Ramadier, François Mitterrand and Altiero Spinelli (one of the authors of the Ventotene Manifesto of 1941 'Per un'Europa unita et libera'). This development is, to some degree, in line with constructivist expectations that a situation of uncertainty can facilitate persuasion or socialization (cf. Checkel 1999). In such a perspective, the founding of the EEC is primarily an idea-driven response to the decline of Europe after World War II. Note, by the way, that a constructivist reading here overlaps with realist intergovernmentalism, which had also argued that Europe was in search of new solutions after the war, and even Hoffmann (1966: 870) spoke of a 'temporary demise of nationalism'. Both accounts thus agree on the importance of ideas for explaining early European integration.

For constructivists, Robert Schuman and Jean Monnet were primarily driven by pro-European ideas. They wanted to promote European cooperation in strategically important sectors such as coal and steel in order to make another war between France and Germany impossible (cf. also Lindberg 1963: 4). From this perspective, the EEC is not just about economic cooperation, but aims at achieving peace in Europe and, potentially, European political unity. In his account of the Treaties of Rome, Parsons (2003) underlines the important role that pro-European actors played in the process. For instance, Parsons considers the fact that Guy Mollet – and not Pierre Mendès-France – headed the French government as 'Président du Conseil' from February 1956 to May 1957 was a decisive circumstance for a successful conclusion of the ECC negotiations. Mollet, according to Parsons, was driven by a federalist ideology, rather than by geostrategic or economic concerns. He argues that '[r]ather than being lobbied by interest groups, Mollet's team lobbied them' (Parsons 2003: 91). Therefore, for Parsons (2003: 102) 'pro-community leadership' is a key explanation of European integration. It should be noted, however, that while Parsons grants ideas an important role in the integration process, the mechanisms that he puts forward would also fit into a rationalist framework, since he does not argue that the power of the better argument has prevailed, or that persuasion or socialization was taking place. In our view, his historic account basically brings domestic politics back into the equation.

Integrative dynamics: shared understandings of common challenges

The previous paragraphs highlighted that World War II and its devastating effects can be considered a favourable background from which new ideas could emerge on the European scene. In such a reading, uncertainty can bring forward new solutions. The founding of the EEC can thus be considered an ideational response to postwar uncertainties. But how can constructivism explain the dynamics of the single market?

During the early 1980s, European states faced growing uncertainty about the 'right' responses to the economic challenges of the time – the rise of the Asian economies, the perceived decline of the USA, stagflation of their own economies, and the fear of falling behind other parts of the developed world in technological respects (cf. Fligstein and Mara-Drita 1996: 11; Sandholtz and Zyzsman 1989). It is against this background that European leaders turned, one after the other, to neoliberal ideas of economic policy-making. In this logic, politics followed economic thought, since the discipline of public economics had previously and broadly experienced a paradigm shift from Keynesianism towards neoliberalism in the 1970s (cf. Donnelly 2010; McNamara 1999). Market-oriented solutions were dominating the economic discourse of the time, allowing right-wing parties such as the British Conservatives or the German CDU nationally to enact reform agendas and promote more liberal positions on the European level. From a constructivist perspective, the White Paper on the single market strongly resonates with the liberal outlook of the conservative governments, but also with the dominant economic ideas and narratives of the time.

Jabko (1999, 2006) introduces a strategic form of constructivism as a middle-ground between the actor-centred and the ideational approaches. For Jabko, the Commission strategically used the 'market' as a norm to promote European solutions – for instance, in the case of the 1988 Capital Movements Directive. Again, we thus find a package deal emerging between the pro-integration camp, after 1983 prominently represented by the French socialist government, and the pro-liberalization camp, most prominently represented by the UK's government under Margaret Thatcher. In Jabko's (2006: 26) view, political strategy is a causal factor of institutional change, more so than the power of ideas: 'The politics of market ideas, not these ideas themselves, fueled the European Union's quiet revolution.' He continues that the 'key political actors who became the promoters of Europe in the 1980s and 1990s were extremely strange bedfellows. They shared a desire to change the status quo, but for very different reasons' (Jabko 2006: 28).

The Commission's White Paper (COM 85 310) 'Completing the Internal Market' nicely illustrates a strategic use of ideas. At the beginning of this document, the Commission refers to a number of declarations by the European Council relating to the internal market. For instance, it cites the declaration of the Fontainebleau European Council 1984: 'It asks the Council and the Member States to put in hand without delay a study of the measures which could be taken to bring about in the near future ... the abolition of all police and customs formalities for people crossing intra-Community frontiers'. Similarly, the European Council of Dublin 1984 is cited: 'The European Council ... agreed that the Council in its appropriate formations: ... should take steps to complete the Internal Market, including the implementation of European standards.' Also, the Brussels Conclusions of March 1985 are mentioned: 'the European Council laid particular emphasis on the following ... fields of action: a) action to achieve a single large market by 1992 thereby creating a more favourable environment for stimulating enterprise, competition and trade; it called upon the Commission to draw up a detailed programme with a specific timetable before its next meeting'. Since the addressee of the White Paper is the European Council meeting at Milan in June 1985, the Commission underlines with this that the White Paper only executes the European Council's own desires. In the Commission's logic, if the European Council objected to the Commission's proposals, it would only reveal internal inconsistencies. In line with Schimmelfennig's (2003a, b) logic of 'rhetorical action', the Commission thus tried rhetorically to 'entrap' the European Council.

Differentiated integration: constructivism

When surveying the map of Europe over time, we realize that the single market started with six members and at the time of writing covers 30 states (when including the EEA states). There is thus a strong trend towards market integration in Europe. However, the trajectories of different countries vary. How does constructivism explain the choices of the outsiders? We have highlighted the importance of ideas for explaining the vertical integration of the single market. Here, we argue that, in order to develop a political impact, pro-integration ideas need to resonate with the worldviews of those actors whose support is necessary for political integration. In democracies, this is ultimately the public.

For constructivists, the initial reluctance of the UK is easier to explain than its later accession. In terms of identity, Britain as an island country had not considered itself as being part of Europe. To cite Winston Churchill once again: 'If Britain must choose between Europe and the open sea, she must always choose the open sea.' The British outlook in the 1950s was thus rather transatlantic and oriented towards the Commonwealth. Victorious in World War II, it remained a great power. But why then did the UK accede to the EC in 1973? There is, in fact, little evidence for a Europeanization of the British public between the 1950s and the 1970s. Most observers agree that British entry into the EC was far from a love match, and was primarily due to materialistic considerations. Therefore, the explanatory power of constructivism seems limited for the case of the UK.

What about the other outsiders? According to Gstöhl's (2002) analysis of the 'reluctant Europeans', Switzerland or Norway – as small and economically strongly integrated states – would, indeed, have economic incentives to join the EU. However, in her view identity concerns prevent these countries from becoming EU member states. For instance, Gstöhl (2002) identifies three core characteristics of Swiss identity – neutrality, a strong federalism, and direct democracy – which, in her view, can best explain Swiss reluctance towards EU membership. The accession of Switzerland (to the EEA) and Norway (to the EU) were both vetoed in referenda. However, the 'bilaterals' (Switzerland) and the EEA (Norway) were approved by the voters. Economic incentives thus seem to appeal to these publics; however, more far-ranging agreements seem out of reach. Thus, while identity hinders these countries from becoming full EU members, they still have economic incentives for demanding access to the single market. The result of this is external differentiation in the single market.

Conclusion

In this chapter, we analyzed two important historical episodes in the construction of the single market. We highlighted the founding of the common market through the EEC Treaty and the reforms of the single market programme launched in the 1980s. The single market has been at the core of European integration since the 1950s. It can therefore be considered a crucial case for integration theories; an integration theory that proves incapable of explaining integration of the single market would, indeed, seem rather useless. Not surprisingly, the single market has therefore been one of the most important battlefields of integration theories. In this chapter, we surveyed some pronounced debates between the three theoretical accounts. Most differences concern the weighting of different parts of the causal chain that lead to the establishment and the deepening of the single market. In general, the three theories differ in terms of the importance they attribute to the different actors, the types of preferences these actors hold and that drive or restrict integration, and the interactions that take place between these actors.

The most important difference between supranationalism and intergovernmentalism is the importance attributed to the influence of supranational actors and to prior integration. Supranationalism underlines the important role of supra- and transnational actors in the process; intergovernmentalism sees the nation states, represented by the governments, in the driver's seat of integration. Naturally, in the 1950s the influence of supranational actors such as the ECSC's High Authority was very limited. In the 1980s, we find an active Commission presenting an ambitious White Paper: 'Completing the Internal Market'. At the same time, member state governments command market integration and, eventually, sign, ratify, and implement the SEA. We would thus argue that one could possibly take an agnostic position in this debate by acknowledging that both national and supranational actors mattered in the process leading to the SEA, and managed to shape the final negotiation package.

Liberal intergovernmentalism can satisfactorily account for the outcomes of the EEC and the SEA bargaining processes. It also agrees with supranationalism that economic incentives greatly motivated the political decisions. A factor that, however, is mostly neglected by realist and liberal intergovernmentalism is the development of integration over time. To borrow a metaphor from Pierson (1996), liberal intergovernmentalism presents snapshots of integration episodes and refrains from formulating a dynamic theory of regional integration. In contrast, supranationalism takes the endogeneity of preference change into account; previous integration leads to an intensification of transnational exchanges which, in the longer run, entail an adaptation of preference.

Both, supranationalism and intergovernmentalism have difficulties in explaining the reluctance of some European countries regarding the integration project. While the initial reluctance of the UK can still be explained on economic grounds, accounting for the positions of Switzerland and Norway is more difficult. These countries have economic incentives for cooperation in the single market. However, not least for reasons of identity, the voters of these two countries have refused EU membership (see Gstöhl 2002). In order to compensate for resulting losses, they have opted for the EEA and for the conclusion of bilateral treaties. Constructivism can thus help us understand why we find external differentiation in the single market.

This chapter shows that the three theories shed light on different parts of the puzzle and thereby contribute to our understanding of integration of the single market. All three theories managed to take this crucial hurdle; accordingly the good news for this book is that we can continue to scrutinize other policy areas. In the following chapters, the single market – with its mostly uniform application of EU rules – can serve as a baseline against which we can compare integration in economic and monetary issues, defence affairs, and the AFSJ.

Chapter 6

Economic and Monetary Union

The Economic and Monetary Union (EMU) was formally established by the Treaty on European Union, negotiated and signed in Maastricht in 1991. But plans had already been made since the late 1960s. In more abstract terms, EMU concerns the integration of macroeconomic policies. Whereas the market integration presented in Chapter 5 focuses on removing barriers to the free movement of goods, services, capital, and labour across national borders, macroeconomic policy integration refers to monetary and fiscal policies.

Monetary policy consists of all authoritative measures that affect the supply of money in an economy. Normally, monetary policy is a monopoly of the state. The state issues legal tender, controls the amount of money in circulation, and determines or influences the exchange rate of the national currency with other currencies. In most states, monetary policy is delegated to a central bank; in Western countries, central banks generally enjoy political independence from the government. By targeting interest rates, lending and borrowing money to this effect, and revaluing or devaluing the currency, monetary policy affects the entire economy. A policy of cheap money may stimulate growth and employment, whereas the tightening of monetary supply helps prevent the economy from overheating and reduce inflation. Devaluing the currency stimulates exports, but may make imported goods more expensive and deter foreign investment.

Fiscal policy refers to the making of the state budget and its use to influence the economy. It has a revenue side consisting mainly of raising taxes and debt. Expenditures are used to finance state activity and social welfare. Whereas monetary policy is generally delegated to a central bank, fiscal policy is made directly by the government, and controlled and co-decided by the legislature. As with monetary policy, fiscal policy can be used to stimulate the economy – in this case, by reducing taxes or increasing government expenditures. Thus, both monetary and fiscal policies have an effect on growth, inflation, and employment. But they also affect each other. For instance, a restrictive monetary policy makes it more expensive for the government to raise debt (as interest rates will be high). Conversely, highly-indebted countries have an incentive to increase the money supply and allow for high inflation in order to reduce their debt burden.

142

At the beginning of European integration, macroeconomic policy was a monopoly of each member state. Each country had its own currency and central bank, and was sovereign in making and managing its budget. European macroeconomic policy is thus not simply about controlling the supply of money, and budgetary revenues and expenditures, but also about the allocation of monetary and fiscal authority between the national and the European level, and about the coordination of national macroeconomic policies.

This chapter examines integration in both areas of macroeconomic policy. Apart from their obvious political relevance for the EU, European monetary and fiscal policy offer rich and interesting data for the study of differentiated integration. First, monetary policy is one of the most integrated policies of the EU. It has moved, over time, from intergovernmental coordination to supranational centralization. The EMU introduced a supranational currency, the euro, and centralized monetary policy at the EU level. By contrast, fiscal policy has remained at the level of intergovernmental cooperation of member state budgetary policies. Only recently have member states taken the decision to give up more sovereignty in this area. Second, monetary policy is the most horizontally differentiated policy of the EU. Currently, only 17 out of 27 member states participate fully in monetary integration.

In this chapter, we explain the differentiated integration of macroeconomic policies. In the first section, we describe how integration has developed over time. This section also gives an introduction to the institutions and substantive rules of European macroeconomic policy. In the remainder of the chapter, we apply the three integration theories individually.

The Development of Monetary and Fiscal Integration

The Bretton Woods system

At the start of European integration, the Bretton Woods system of global monetary policy was still intact. The Bretton Woods system – named after a town in New Hampshire, USA, where delegates of the Allies met in 1944 to prepare the postwar global economic and financial order – was a system of fixed but adjustable exchange rates centred on the US dollar. The dollar, in turn, was linked to gold at a fixed rate. All member states of the International Monetary Fund (IMF) were required to peg their currency to the dollar, and to maintain the declared parity (within limits of 1 per cent below or above). In cases of disequilibrium, however, the parity could be adjusted after consultation in the IMF. In addition, the Bretton Woods agreements called for the free convertibility of national currencies.

Box 6.1   *Timeline: macroeconomic integration*

1950	European Payment Union	2001	Greece joins
1959	European Monetary	2002	Euro notes and coins
	Agreement	2005	Stability and Growth Pact
1970	Werner Plan		relaxed
1972	Currency Snake	2007	Slovenia, first Eastern
1979	European Monetary		European member state,
	System		joins
1989	Delors Report	2010	Debt crisis, European
1992	Maastricht Treaty (UK		Financial Stability Facility
	opt-out)	2011	Estonia, 17th member
1993	Denmark ratifies Treaty		state of eurozone; decision
	on European Union with		to create European
	opt-out		Stability Mechanism
1997	Stability and Growth Pact	2012	Fiscal Compact signed
1999	Start of European		
	Monetary Union (11		
	member states)		

The Bretton Woods system did not contain any rules directly related to fiscal policy. In the event of balance-of-payment difficulties, however, states could draw on short-term IMF credit facilities so that they would not have to resort to changing the exchange rate, cutting imports, or deflating their economies. The Bretton Woods system thereby sought to avoid the negative impact of balance-of-payment crises on trade and employment that had plagued the world economy before World War II.

In Europe, the European Payments Union (EPU) was established in 1950 in order to facilitate the convertibility of European currencies and intra-European trade. In 1959, the European Monetary Agreement (EMA) succeeded the EPU. Both were established in the framework of the OEEC (since 1961, the Organisation for Economic Cooperation and Development – OECD) rather than the European communities.

In this wider context, monetary policy did not feature in the ECSC in any way, and remained marginal in the EEC. The EEC Treaty called on 'each member state ... to maintain confidence in its currency' (Art. 104). Art. 105 envisaged the intergovernmental coordination of economic policies in general – including collaboration between central banks – as well as the establishment of a consultative Monetary Committee composed of member state and Commission experts. In addition, a Committee of Central Bank Governors was set up in 1964. The member states further committed themselves to the gradual liberalization of cross-border payments and mutual assistance in cases of balance-of-payments crises (to be decided by QMV in the Council). In addition, member states were authorized to take safeguard measures if they were hit by an acute balance-of-payments crisis, or if other member states seriously distorted competition in the Common Market by changing their exchange rates. Finally, even though the EMA remained outside the Treaty framework, the member states of the EEC used it to limit their margins of fluctuation against the US dollar to 0.75 per cent (rather than 1 per cent).

In sum, in the early phase of European integration, fiscal and monetary policy was either national or global, but not 'European'. The core competences remained in the hands of the member states. To the extent that the member states were constrained by international institutions and regulations, this occurred outside the Community under the auspices of the IMF or the OEEC/OECD. Whereas the ECSC did not concern itself with monetary policy, the EEC introduced a few rules and procedures that are best classified as intergovernmental coordination. The EEC rules and procedures applied to the six original member states without exception, but not beyond the EEC.

The Snake and the European Monetary System

Change came with the crisis and eventual breakdown of the Bretton Woods system in the late 1960s. In the course of the 1960s, growing US trade and budget deficits and US inflation had made the dollar–gold peg increasingly untenable. In addition, the convertibility of currencies and the increase in dollar holdings outside the USA led to considerable financial interdependence and speculation, which complicated domestic and international monetary policy. In August 1971, US president Nixon ended the dollar–gold convertibility. The Smithsonian Agreement of the same year, in which ten major economies agreed to widen the fluctuation bands of their currencies to plus or minus 2.25 per cent, was short-lived and collapsed in 1973. As a result, the global monetary system turned into a system of floating exchange rates.

The EC currencies were also affected by imbalances and speculation: in 1969, the French franc was devalued by more than 11 per cent. Such devaluations and revaluations threatened to disrupt the EC market. They created particular problems for the newly established Common Agricultural Policy (CAP) because French farm products suddenly became much cheaper. As a quick fix, the member states introduced a monetary compensation scheme (adding a tax to French agricultural export prices).

At the same time, they entrusted a committee composed of the chairmen of various EEC committees headed by Pierre Werner, the Prime Minister of Luxembourg, to design a plan for EMU. The Werner Report (1970) proposed a three-stage process towards a single currency and a supranational system of central banks (similar to the process and set-up of the Maastricht EMU of the 1990s). In addition, it recommended establishing a Centre of Decision for Economic Policy to coordinate and monitor fiscal policies – including the harmonization of indirect taxes and excise duties, and the adoption of binding guidelines for member-state budgetary revenues and expenditures. The Werner Plan thus envisaged a far-reaching integration of both monetary and fiscal policies. It was, however, first watered down because of conflicting views among the member states, and then abandoned altogether.

In order to reduce the detrimental effects of the looser fluctuation margins of the Smithsonian Agreement, the EEC countries created the Currency Snake regime in 1972 instead. This was seen as necessary because the 4.5 per cent band *vis-à-vis* the dollar could end up in a 9 per cent difference *vis-à-vis* another EEC currency if one EEC currency started appreciating from the bottom and another depreciated from the top margin (Hosli 2005: 20). The Snake therefore limited fluctuation among the EC currencies to plus or minus 2.25 per cent. However, the oil-price shock and the divergent policy reactions of the EC countries – the primacy of price stability in Germany versus fiscal expansion in France and Italy – quickly put enormous pressure on the regime. Denmark, Ireland, Norway, Sweden, and the UK (which had joined the Snake in anticipation of EEC membership) quickly withdrew from the regime. So did France and Italy. Exchange rates had to be adjusted frequently. From the mid-1970s, only Germany, the Benelux countries, and Denmark (which rejoined) remained in the Snake.

Following a joint initiative by France and Germany, 1979 witnessed a new attempt at monetary integration in the EC: the European Monetary System (EMS). Similar to the Snake but without any reference to the dollar, the EMS was based on a grid of bilateral parities between the member state currencies. National central banks were obliged to intervene to support the parity before the exchange rate diverged by 2.25 per cent. This was called the Exchange Rate Mechanism (ERM). Britain did not join the ERM, which forced Ireland to break its peg with the pound sterling, and both Ireland and Italy were allowed a margin of 6 per cent. To facilitate intervention, central banks offered each other short-term credits.

In addition, the member states created the European Currency Unit (ECU), a unit of account whose value was determined by a basket of currencies. It was used for exchanges between central banks and for setting the central rates of the ERM. The Council of Economic and Finance Ministers of the member governments (Ecofin Council) had the authority to change the weights of the national currencies in the ECU, and to adapt the central ERM rates to account for market developments and economic divergence. The EC thus reintroduced a system of fixed but adjustable exchange rates at the regional level several years after the global regime had collapsed.

Initially, adjustments took place fairly often. In the course of the 1980s, however, the EMS became increasingly stable. Moreover, further states joined: Spain in 1989, the UK in 1990, and Portugal in 1992. In addition, the Nordic countries (Finland, Norway, and Sweden) decided to peg their currencies to the ECU in 1990 and 1991. Yet, the EMS again entered a period of monetary turmoil. Speculation against the pound sterling forced the UK to leave the ERM in 1992. So did Finland, Italy, Sweden, and Norway. In 1993, the Irish pound devalued. In the same year, the bandwidth was increased from 2.25 to 15 per cent to ward off speculation against the French franc. Italy and Finland only re-entered the ERM in 1996.

After the failure of the Werner Plan, the introduction of the Snake – and, later, the EMS – constituted only a minor step in monetary integration. The fact that exchange rates were fixed and adjusted in the EC context mainly replaced the previous level of global integration with roughly the same level of regional integration. Yet, the currencies themselves, the defence of the exchange rate, the setting of interest rates, and the fiscal policies that flank monetary policy, remained strictly national competencies. In terms of *vertical integration*, monetary policy remained at the level of intergovernmental coordination and outside the Treaty framework. Exchange rates were set and changed subject to mutual consent in the Council. The governments delegated certain tasks to the central banks – such as the interventions in defence of the exchange rates, or the use of short-term credits. But the central banks also operated on the basis of (transgovernmental) coordination; there was no delegation to any European organization involved. The European Monetary Fund envisaged in the EMS agreement was never established.

Finally, *horizontal integration* was highly differentiated from the start and subject to considerable variation over time. The stable core group comprised only five member states: Germany, the Benelux countries, and Denmark. France, Ireland, and Italy quickly left the Snake but then participated in the EMS. The new member states of the 1980s – Greece, Portugal, and Spain – took several years before they joined the ERM. In a short period between 1990 and 1992 only, the UK and the Nordics participated in the ERM.

Economic and monetary union

In the mid-1980s, European integration gained new momentum. The programme for the completion of the internal market, which resulted in the SEA signed in 1986, also contained a call for closer monetary cooperation. In 1998, the former French and Italian prime ministers

(Balladur and Amato) and German foreign minister (Genscher) launched initiatives in this direction. At the Hannover European Council of the same year, the European heads of state and government commissioned a plan for the establishment of a monetary union. A committee of national central bank presidents and experts headed by Commission President Delors presented this plan (the 'Delors Report') in April 1989. It eventually found its way into the provisions on Economic and Monetary Union (EMU) of the Treaty on European Union signed in Maastricht in 1992. Similar to the Werner Plan of 1970, the Delors Report envisaged a three-stage process towards monetary union. In contrast to the Werner Plan, however, it provided neither for the transfer of fiscal sovereignty to a supranational authority, nor for a sizeable central budget that would have allowed the EU to conduct fiscal policies independently of the member states.

At stage 1, from July 1990, the trans-border movement of capital was fully liberalized. As already agreed in the SEA, all remaining capital controls were abolished. Stage 2, from January 1994, saw the establishment of the European Currency Institute (the precursor institution of the ECB), full independence of all national central banks, and the start of economic policy coordination (monitoring of convergence criteria) between member states. Monetary union (stage 3) started in January 1999 with the irrevocable conversion of the national currencies to the euro. Euro notes and coins replacing national money were issued in 2002.

At the same time, the ECB assumed its work. Formally, the European monetary union is headed by the European System of Central Banks (ESCB), which is composed of the national central banks of the member states and the ECB. It is independent from governments both at the national and the supranational levels (Art. 130 TFEU). The ECB is governed by the six-member Executive Board, composed of experts appointed by the heads of state and government, and the Council, which comprises the Executive Board and the national central bank presidents of the eurozone countries. The day-to-day operation of monetary policy is in the hands of the Executive Board of the ECB. The ECB is obliged to make price stability its main concern (Art. 127 TFEU). It controls the money supply by setting interest rates and by managing the currency reserves of the eurozone. It does not actively manage the external exchange rate of the euro and attends to growth only once price stability is secured.

Before joining the eurozone, EU members need to fulfil the 'convergence criteria' of economic and fiscal performance. They call for convergence of inflation and long-term interest rates towards the rates of the countries with the lowest inflation, medium-term exchange rate stability within the ERM, budget deficits of not more than 3 per cent of GDP, and total government debt not exceeding 60 per cent of GDP.

States outside the eurozone are required to submit a convergence pro-gramme that shows how they will achieve the criteria.

Following an initiative of German Minister of Finance Theo Waigel, the euro countries further agreed on the Stability and Growth Pact (SGP) in 1997, which obliges them to maintain fiscal discipline after adopting the euro. The SGP goes beyond the multilateral surveillance procedure described in Article 121 of the TFEU. According to the mul-tilateral surveillance procedure, the Council (on recommendation by the Commission) decides with QMV on broad, but ultimately non-binding, guidelines for the economic policies of all member states, and makes recommendations in the event that these broad guidelines are not followed. The SGP increases the precision and enforcement of fiscal rules. State budgets are monitored by the EU, and countries with deficits higher than 3 per cent of GDP receive warnings, and eventually face fines decided by the Ecofin Council (Excessive Deficit Procedure). Ultimately, however, monitoring and sanctioning remain political deci-sions made by the member state governments.

In 2005, under pressure of France and Germany, the Council even watered down the SGP rules. Whereas the thresholds (3 per cent for budget deficits and 60 per cent for sovereign debt) were maintained, more exemptions were granted to the member states by taking into account periods of slow growth, contributions to 'international soli-darity' and 'the unification of Europe', and the costs of structural reform (such as pensions reforms). In addition, the deadlines for taking effective action were extended. The comparatively weak centralization and enforcement of fiscal policies goes together with the absence of community liability for member state budgets (Art. 125 TFEU). The ECB is legally prohibited from providing credit facilities to member states or Community institutions, and from buying their debt instru-ments (Art. 123). This is also known as the 'no bailout' clause.

Monetary union started with 11 member states in 1999: the original EC-6, Austria, Finland, Ireland, Portugal, and Spain. Greece joined in 2001, Slovenia in 2007, Malta and Cyprus in 2008, Slovakia in 2009, and Estonia in 2011. Denmark was granted an opt-out after the Maastricht Treaty was rejected in a referendum, but its currency remains pegged to the euro within the ERM margins of 2.25 per cent. Sweden and the UK do not even take part in the ERM. Among the remaining seven new member states, only Latvia and Lithuania have joined the ERM so far.

The establishment of the EMU in 1999 marks a leap forward in the *vertical integration of monetary policy* – and European integration in general. Whereas monetary policy had been a predominantly national competence before, it now became exclusively European. The issue and supply of money, as well as the control of money in circulation, ceased to be a sovereign right and policy. Interest and exchange rates could no longer be set by national central banks (or governments). Moreover, monetary policy is *supranationally centralized* in the EMU. It is fully delegated to the ESCB, with the ECB at its head. Thanks to the independence of the ECB, governments do not have any formal influence on the operation of monetary policy.

By contrast, the *horizontal integration* of monetary policy falls behind other policies of the EU. Only 17 out of 27 member states are part of the eurozone. Some member states do not participate in monetary union on political grounds (Denmark, Sweden, and the UK). Others are on track toward monetary integration but do not yet qualify (Latvia and Lithuania). The remaining new member states are still far away from meeting the convergence criteria, or even hesitant about making the effort to meet them. By contrast, in addition to micro-states such as Andorra, Monaco, San Marino, and the Vatican, two non-member states have adopted the euro without participating in the institutions of monetary integration: Kosovo and Montenegro.

Fiscal policy has remained at a lower level of *vertical integration*. Certainly, multilateral surveillance, the convergence criteria, and the SGP did remove the national budgets from the exclusive purview of the member states. But European competences were limited to setting, monitoring, and enforcing upper limits for budget deficits and, in practice, vertical integration did not go beyond *intergovernmental cooperation*. The decision-making procedures included recommendations by the Commission but no competences for the EP. The EP was merely informed of Council decisions regarding the multilateral surveillance of economic policies and the excessive deficit produce, and consulted on secondary legislation implementing the excessive deficit procedure. The Treaty of Lisbon has not improved the powers of the Parliament in this area. The EU cannot interfere directly with the national budgets of the member states, and its own budget is too limited to create significant macroeconomic effects. Other economic policies focusing on growth and employment operate on the basis of guidelines and recommendations, rather than on binding rules. Regarding *horizontal integration*, the member states are split. Whereas all member states are subject to the multilateral surveillance of economic policies, the excessive deficit procedure only applies to the eurozone plus six further countries. The Czech Republic, Hungary, Sweden, and the UK do not participate.

The debt crisis and the reform of EMU

The combination of supranational monetary integration with intergovernmental fiscal and economic coordination and cooperation is a fundamental characteristic of the EMU. Whereas monetary policy is harmonized for the entire eurozone, fiscal and economic policies (as well as real economic development) continue to vary across the euro countries. The economic crisis of 2008/09 exposed the problems of this asymmetric integration. The introduction of the euro had led to a steep decline in interest rates in the poorer EMU countries, and the ensuing inflow of cheap money had weakened fiscal discipline and facilitated real estate bubbles. When the crash came, the bubbles burst, banks were saved, and budget deficits increased steeply. Interest rates diverged sharply again, reflecting the higher risk accumulating in the Southern eurozone countries and Ireland, but also making it harder for them to refinance their budget deficits. Before monetary integration, they could have taken to looser monetary policy in order to avoid the crunch and stimulate growth. This way out of the crisis was now blocked.

When Greece appeared unable to refinance its debts in early 2010, the EU states decided to disregard the no-bailout clause, rather than risking the bankruptcy of one of its members and the possible break-up of the eurozone. Together with the IMF, they granted Greece a €110 billion loan and created an emergency fund of €750 billion (the European Financial Stability Facility – EFSF) as a guarantee for further countries in difficulty – conditional upon hard austerity measures to re-establish budget stability. Ireland was the first country to use the EFSF from November 2010, followed by Portugal in May 2011 and Spain in June 2012. Later in 2011, the fund was enlarged and allowed to insure credit from other sources.

At the same time, the eurozone countries entered into negotiations on the reform of EMU in order to create higher stability in the longer term. The package includes a permanent, treaty-based European Stability Mechanism (ESM) to replace the emergency fund from 2012 and the reinforcement of the SGP. The so-called 'six pack' of new legislation that entered into force in December 2011 contains stricter criteria of fiscal discipline, as well as earlier and stronger sanctions than the SGP for the '17 + 6' countries that participate in the excessive deficit procedure. In the 'preventive arm' of the revamped SGP, the Commission guides countries in the budget planning process. The 'corrective arm' includes sanctions for countries that do not follow the budgetary recommendations of the Commission and do not take corrective action to reduce their excessive budget deficits. These sanctions can only be reversed by QMV, which is highly unlikely. These provisions thus make sanctions quasi-automatic and close the loopholes of the earlier SGP. The structural difference between monetary and fiscal cooperation is narrowing as fiscal integration is moving from intergovernmental cooperation to the effective pooling of sovereignty.

In addition, the 'Treaty on Stability, Coordination, and Governance in the Economic and Monetary Union' – 'fiscal compact', in short – signed by all member states except the Czech Republic and the UK in March 2012 provides for a ceiling for the annual structural government deficit (0.5 per cent of nominal GDP), and demands that member states introduce a corresponding 'balanced budget rule' and automatic correction mechanisms into their national constitutions, or equivalent laws, within one year after the entry into force of the Treaty (Article 3). Compliance with this demand is subject to monitoring and sanctions by the ECJ (Article 8). All member states additionally agree to report ex ante on their national debt issuance plans to the Council and the Commission (Article 6). Countries that are subject to an excessive deficit procedure under EU law are obliged to put in place a budgetary and economic partnership programme detailing structural reforms to reduce the budget deficit. This programme will be approved and monitored by the Council and the Commission (Article 5). In addition, the fiscal compact takes up provisions from the 'six pack' – such as the qualified majority rule for stopping Commission corrective action – and upgrades them to treaty law. If and when the fiscal compact enters into force in 2013 – only 12 member states need to ratify it – fiscal integration will move from the level of intergovernmental cooperation to the level of *joint decision-making* and, thus, cross the threshold from intergovernmental to supranational policy-making. The role of the EP will remain limited to information and consultation rights, however.

Conclusion

Figures 6.1 and 6.2 summarize the development of macroeconomic integration. Figure 6.1 shows the *vertical differentiation* between the integration of monetary and fiscal policies. Until the Treaty of Maastricht, fiscal policy was not integrated at all. The provisions of the TEU and the SGP moved budgetary policy to the level of intergovernmental cooperation. Starting with the adoption in 2011 of the reversed qualified majority rule in the excessive deficit procedure, budgetary policy is moving towards a supranational policy. Monetary policy was subject to intergovernmental coordination during the first 40 years of European integration. The stages of EMU agreed in the Treaty of Maastricht constituted a qualitative change from the intergovernmental coordination of exchange rates to the complete supranational centralization of monetary policy. In other words, fiscal policy has trailed monetary policy throughout the history of European integration. Whereas monetary policy has reached the highest level of vertical integration, only at the time of writing is fiscal policy moving beyond intergovernmental cooperation.

Figure 6.2 gives an impression of horizontal differentiation in European monetary policy. It shows that the deepening of (vertical) monetary integration has come at the cost of unity and widening. Horizontal integration kept pace with vertical integration until the late

Figure 6.1 *Vertical integration of macroeconomic policies*

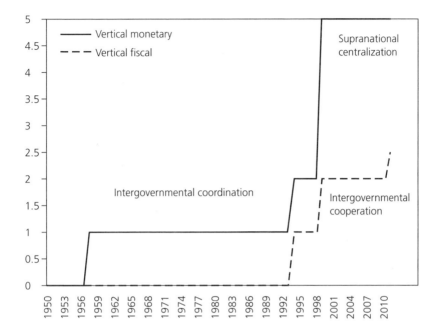

1990s. The two short peaks in horizontal integration indicate the first years of the Snake, and the time after 1990 when the UK and the Nordic countries had briefly aligned themselves with the ERM. With the introduction of the euro, however, vertical integration has leaped far ahead of horizontal integration. Horizontal integration has only increased slowly as new member states have adopted the common currency. Whereas we have observed in Chapter 1 that, on an aggregate level, there is no trade-off in general between deepening and widening, monetary policy clearly deviates from this.

Until the early 1970s, there was no horizontal differentiation across countries in monetary policy because the intergovernmental coordination provisions of the EEC Treaty did not constrain the member states and could not be used by non-member states. By contrast, the introduction of the Snake combined constraints on member states' exchange rate policy with the first enlargement of the EEC and the oil shock. As a result, horizontal differentiation increased both internally and externally until the mid-1980s, before the drop-out of the non-member countries and the introduction of the EMS re-unified the policy. Southern enlargement and the monetary turmoil of the early 1990s temporarily increased horizontal differentiation again. The biggest contribution to horizontal differentiation was the fact that the 12 new

Figure 6.2   *Vertical and horizontal integration in monetary policy*

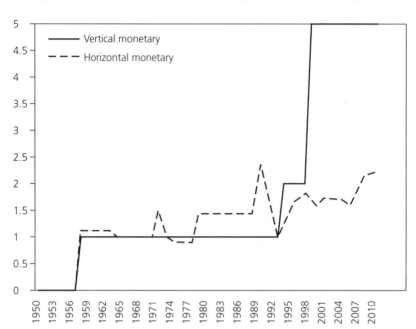

member states joining the EU in 2004 and 2007 did not immediately become part of monetary union.

The development of monetary and fiscal integration thus calls for four major explanations.

- First, why and how did EMU come about? What explains the leap from the intergovernmental coordination of exchange rates to the *supranational centralization of monetary policy and intergovernmental fiscal cooperation*, and why was it decided at the end of the 1980s, having failed 20 years before?
- Second, why do we see such strong *horizontal differentiation* in monetary integration? Why have some countries been part of a rather stable core group from the beginning (Germany and the Benelux countries), whereas others joined this group later (mainly France and the Southern member states) and some (most visibly the UK) have remained aloof? The most interesting cases are those countries that would have been able but were not willing to join EMU: Denmark, Sweden, and the UK.
- Third, how can we explain *vertical differentiation* in macroeconomic policy? Why has fiscal integration followed, but consistently lagged behind, monetary integration?

- Finally, why has *fiscal policy* become *more supranationally integrated* recently?

In the next sections, we will use the three integration theories to shed light on these questions.

Intergovernmentalism

What should we observe if intergovernmentalism were able to explain the integration and differentiation of macroeconomic policy?

- The *leap from intergovernmental coordination to supranational centralization* would need to be explained by a critical increase in international interdependence and convergence of national preferences in the 1980s. We should see the emergence of considerable threats to national autonomy, security, or welfare (which motivated the EC member states to give up their national currencies), and of opportunities to improve member state autonomy and welfare by moving ahead decisively with macroeconomic integration. We should also be able to trace the high level of vertical integration back to massive compliance problems in this area. Moreover, the substantive terms of monetary integration should mirror the preferences of the most powerful state or group of states in European monetary policy.
- Intergovernmentalism attributes *horizontal differentiation* to uneven interdependence and policy preferences, to the high degree of centralization and politicization of monetary policy, and to state size and domestic ratification constraints. Opt-outs from monetary integration would have to be explained by one, or a combination, of these factors.
- From an intergovernmentalist perspective, the *vertical differentiation* of monetary and fiscal policy should reflect higher levels of interdependence, preference homogeneity, compliance problems, and uncertainty together with a lower degree of politicization in monetary policy, as compared with fiscal policy.

The recent steps toward the *supranational centralization of fiscal policy* should, again, result from a critical increase in international interdependence, convergence of national preferences, and compliance problems. The substantive terms of 'fiscal union' should, again, reflect the policy preferences of the most powerful state or group of states.

Realist intergovernmentalism: monetary integration to increase state autonomy?

From the vantage point of realist intergovernmentalism, it is highly unlikely that states give up a core competence of state sovereignty such as monetary policy. Which exceptional circumstances could motivate such a loss of autonomy? There are three candidates for solving the puzzle: external balancing, internal balancing, and hegemonic imposition.

External balancing. First, EMU may be interpreted as a monetary alliance designed to balance the dominance of the US dollar as a global reserve currency and trade currency for important raw materials such as oil. Already in 1971, the Europeans had been told by US Secretary of the Treasury John Connolly that the dollar was 'our currency but your problem'. Whereas the individual European states were not in a position to control the dollar's externalities and create a counter-weight, together they might muster sufficient economic clout. This explanation is underdetermined for timing, however. Why did the member states take the decision to create EMU at the end of the 1980s, rather than during the two previous decades when the dollar was rather more dominant? One possible explanation is Europe's reduced security dependence on the USA at the end of the Cold War, which increased its room for manoeuvre in balancing America. But when the initiative for monetary union was taken in 1988, the Cold War was far from over.

Internal balancing. Second, EMU may not have been directed against external US but against internal German dominance in monetary policy. Indeed, the EMS had developed into a deutschmark zone in practice, whose members followed the Bundesbank's anti-inflationary monetary preferences and its interest-rate policy without being able to influence its decisions. By delegating monetary policy to the symmetrical ESCB, in which each member state formally has equal weight, EMU effectively disempowered the Bundesbank and gave the member states a greater and more balanced say in monetary policy. From this perspective, EMU is a prime example of how supranational integration, even though it involves a loss of formal state autonomy, may result in a net gain of de facto autonomy because formal state autonomy has been hollowed out anyway (Grieco 1996).

In spite of its general plausibility, however, this explanation has a crucial shortcoming: it explains the motivation of all member states but Germany. Why should Germany give up its powerful currency, accept the disempowerment of the Bundesbank, and agree to lose its monetary autonomy? It is often suggested that monetary union was the price Germany had to pay for reunification. Yet, the German foreign minister, Genscher, proposed monetary union in 1988 and the Delors Report on EMU was accepted by the European Council in June 1989 –

i.e. at a time when reunification was nowhere on the political horizon. Reunification could therefore only have been a secondary and additional factor. It has probably speeded up the negotiations on EMU, but certainly did not bring them about.

Hegemonic imposition. Finally, EMU may be viewed as the formalization and stabilization of Germany's hegemonic position in European monetary policy (e.g. Kaelberer 1997). Indeed, EMU mirrored German preferences on monetary policy to a large extent. The ECB is as – if not more – independent from political interference as the Bundesbank and, like the Bundesbank, it is obliged to focus on price stability. Yet, EMU still meant a net loss in autonomy for Germany. German hegemony could have been imposed more effectively in the EMS than through the symmetrical ESCB. Thus, the autonomy-maximizing behaviour assumed by realist intergovernmentalism does not convincingly explain the timing of EMU or Germany's consent.

Liberal intergovernmentalism: interdependence, preference convergence, and credible commitments

According to liberal intergovernmentalism, European states do not care about autonomy and security, as such. They are willing to trade autonomy for wealth and efficiency. From the LI perspective, three conditions needed to come together for a leap in macroeconomic policy integration: critical interdependence, compatible or convergent national preferences, and the need to pool and delegate sovereignty in order to reap the benefits of cooperation (for the following, see Moravcsik 1998: ch. 6).

Monetary policy interdependence in the EU had increased, indeed – or was about to do so – due to the growth of intra-Community trade and the liberalization of capital mobility. The more that the trade interdependence of a national economy increases, the more costly the monetary policy differences, the instability of exchange rates, and the transaction costs of currency exchange become. In addition, the more that cross-border capital mobility is liberalized, the less effective unilateral monetary policy becomes and the more a currency is susceptible to market pressure and speculative attacks. Monetary policy interdependence, however, had been present in the Common Market from its beginnings and had complicated common policies such as the Common Agricultural Policy, but had not led to more than various schemes of monetary policy coordination in the course of integration history. It is also difficult to determine whether interdependence really reached a critical threshold in the late 1980s, which would have necessitated the leap to full supranational integration.

What made the difference from the intergovernmentalist perspective was the fact that the monetary policy preferences of the major member states – France and Germany, in particular – had converged in the years before EMU. Whereas Germany had traditionally been a hard-currency country with a monetary policy committed to price stability and conducted by an independent central bank, France had been a soft-currency country in which the government used devaluations of the national currency and an expansion of monetary supply to improve competitiveness and stimulate the economy. In the course of the 1980s, however, France approximated the German position: it committed itself to the *franc fort* and achieved an inflation rate that was only slightly above that of Germany. In addition, faced with the devaluation of the US dollar, the industries (and the governments) of both countries were interested in a looser monetary policy in order to protect their export interests. Germany's strongly export-oriented industry, in particular, stood to gain from a common currency because it meant that its competitiveness would no longer be undermined by the constant pressure on the deutschmark to appreciate. The economic and policy convergence increased the chances of sustainable monetary integration. By contrast, British inflation rates were much higher than those of Germany and France at the time. Under these circumstances, monetary integration with these two countries was not in the interests of British business or government.

German and French preferences on the process and design of monetary union remained divergent, however. France (together with Belgium, Italy, and – to some extent – Luxemburg) had long championed a 'monetarist' or 'locomotive' strategy. According to this strategy, the establishment of monetary union is, first and foremost, a political decision, to be followed by the macroeconomic policies to make it work and by convergence in the real economy. Moreover, France had consistently favoured a strong role for governments in monetary integration (represented in a *gouvernement économique*), and had tried to limit supranational centralization since the debate on the Werner Plan in the late 1960s and early 1970s. By contrast, Germany (with the support of the Netherlands) defended the 'economist' or 'crowning' theory. From this perspective, economic convergence must come first; monetary union is only possible and sustainable if the member states' economies and economic policies are synchronized. In addition, Germany favoured the delegation of monetary policy to an independent central bank.

The pre-EMU status quo favoured Germany. First, under the EMS regime, France needed to follow the Bundesbank's monetary policy and incurred higher costs on the capital market: the credit standing of French bonds was not as high as that of German bonds. Germany therefore had less interest in changing the status quo than France. Second, Germany already 'benefited disproportionately' from the EMS, which stabilized the deutschmark and 'dampened its appreciation against other participating currencies' (Walsh 2000: 13). Finally, the German government was more constrained domestically. Whereas the export-oriented industries had every reason to welcome monetary union, the Bundesbank stood to become its biggest institutional loser: its representatives were therefore highly sceptical regarding EMU. At the same time, the bank and its policy enjoyed a high reputation in Germany society. The German government could thus not afford to renounce the principles of independent and anti-inflationary monetary policy in a European monetary union. Both its higher satisfaction with the status quo and its domestic constraints accorded the German government strong bargaining power in the negotiations about the conditions and the design of EMU (Wolf and Zangl 1996). EMU without Germany did not make any sense. Therefore, if France wanted supranational monetary integration, it had to accept the German model.

In addition, Germany wanted to make sure that the EMU it preferred would not be undermined and hollowed out once it was in place. As a result, the German government not only insisted on economic convergence as a prerequisite for accession to EMU (the 'convergence criteria'), but also pushed for the SGP in order to constrain member states' fiscal policies subsequently. The no bailout-clause and several other rules were put in place to make sure that the richer and more fiscally disciplined member states would not be obliged to pay for the debts and deficits of the poorer or more profligate ones. Finally, these rules were cast into treaty law together with the principles of price stability and central bank independence, so that it became impossible to change them against the will of any single member state. At the same time, Germany opposed any 'economic government' in the EMU that could have given the ECB political directions and reduced its independence. The ECB and the principles of European monetary policy were thus accorded a legal status that the Bundesbank and German monetary policy had never enjoyed.

The supranational centralization of monetary policy can thus partly be explained by Germany's superior bargaining power. Germany's preferences were closest to the status quo and Germany stood to lose most from EMU in terms of autonomy. The German government could therefore not only successfully impose its monetary policy preferences on the EMU, it could also install institutional safeguards to prevent its preferred monetary policy from being undermined in the future. Realist and liberal intergovernmentalism thus agree on the relevance of German bargaining power for the establishment and design of the currency union. Whereas, however, Germany's policy is difficult to explain on the basis of autonomy-maximizing behaviour, as in realist intergovernmentalism, it appears plausible as a policy that exchanged national autonomy for economic efficiency while imposing German macroeconomic policy preferences on the entire Community, and establishing the strongest possible institutional arrangements to safeguard these preferences in the future.

In addition, the transfer of monetary sovereignty to the EU was also meant to send a signal to the financial market and domestic actors. As long as European monetary policy was limited to intergovernmental coordination, governments could easily be put under pressure to devalue their currency or leave the monetary system, rather than bearing the political or financial costs of mounting a defence of their exchange rate, bringing down wages to restore competitiveness, or implementing budget cuts to restore creditworthiness. Monetary union deprived governments of some instruments and brought about a tremendous increase in the costs of others. They could no longer devalue and, while in practice it was still possible to leave the eurozone, the costs would be enormous. The introduction of the euro and the delegation of monetary policy competences to a supranational agency thus not only bound the member state governments to the rules of EMU, but also demonstrated a strong commitment to domestic interest groups and opposition parties, and to financial market actors. In addition, the sheer size of the new monetary union was thought to deter speculative attacks. As expected by intergovernmentalism, the high degree of vertical monetary integration reflected the severity of enforcement problems in this area.

Finally, the intergovernmentalist explanation is not only in line with the outcome but also with the process of monetary integration. The negotiations mainly took place between 'core executives', i.e. heads of state and government, the relevant ministers, and central bankers. Although business was broadly in favour of EMU, the lobbying of sectoral interests did not play a crucial role. In line with liberal intergovernmentalist expectations, the minor importance of interest groups had to do with the remoteness and uncertain distributional effects of macroeconomic policy (Dyson and Featherstone 1999: 14).

In sum, liberal intergovernmentalism offers a plausible account of the leap from EMS to EMU. Against the background of increasing monetary interdependence in the Common Market, the convergence of macroeconomic preferences, policies, and performance in the 1980s made more monetary integration possible. That it went all the way towards full supranational centralization can be explained by the need for a double credible commitment. First, it was a necessary signal of resolve to the financial market and to domestic politics. Second, it was necessary to dampen the fear and scepticism of the German government and public that EMU would lead to inflation and transfers from rich to poor countries. Because monetary interdependence had already been present when the Werner Plan failed, and Germany had already become the dominant monetary policy actor in the Community during the 1970s, the convergence of macroeconomic policy preferences bears the greatest weight in the liberal intergovernmentalist explanation of EMU. Yet, intergovernmentalism does not tell us what caused this convergence.

Differentiated horizontal integration

In the intergovernmental monetary coordination regimes of the Snake and EMS, entry and exit depended mainly on the individual decisions of the participating governments. Typically, governments decided to leave the Snake or the EMS when market pressures made it too costly to defend the fixed exchange rate. Membership fluctuated strongly and was mainly driven by economic considerations. In general, this issue-specific and intergovernmental dynamic matches well with liberal intergovernmentalist assumptions. There is at least one exception, however. The decision of the Irish government to break the link with the pound sterling and align the Irish pound with the EMS in 1979 was not economically motivated: economic ties between Ireland and the UK were stronger than those with the continent.

Can intergovernmentalism also explain internal horizontal differentiation in EMU? First, the observation that horizontal and vertical integration diverged sharply when the euro was introduced (Figure 6.3) is in line with the general intergovernmentalist conjecture that centralization generates horizontal differentiation. The autonomy loss resulting from centralization politicizes integration, and politicization makes it harder to keep all member states on board. But can intergovernmentalism explain which countries are in and which ones are out?

At first glance, it would seem plausible to assume that *all* member states were subject to monetary interdependence and deutschmark dominance, and that *all* of them participated in the convergence of macroeconomic preferences. For intergovernmentalism to provide an explanation for the variation in participation, we would therefore have to demonstrate that interdependence, autonomy losses, and policy convergence varied among the member states, and that the pattern of variation coincided with the boundaries of the eurozone. Let us look at the new member states and the old member states, in turn.

For the new member states joining in 2004 and 2007, the introduction of the euro was not an automatic by-product of membership. Whereas they were legally obliged to adopt the euro, they also had to fulfil the convergence criteria before being admitted to the eurozone. In the meantime, half of the new member states have introduced the euro. Juliet Johnson (2008) explains the divide between 'pacesetters' and 'laggards' among the new member states with different economic interests having to do with size and interdependence. The smaller and more trade-dependent new member states – the Baltic countries,

Slovakia, and Slovenia – had a strong interest in pegging their currencies to the euro to gain international economic credibility and facilitate trade. By contrast, the larger and less trade-dependent new member states – the Czech Republic, Hungary, and Poland – were more concerned about the potentially growth-inhibiting and inflationary risks of a pegged exchange rate. This explanation is highly compatible with liberal-intergovernmentalist assumptions about the effects of interdependence, and the costs and benefits of integration, on national preferences.

By contrast, intergovernmentalism does not convincingly explain the opt-outs among the old member states, Britain, Denmark, and Sweden. They do not form any clear pattern of preferences and interdependence. Neither do they distinguish themselves from the eurozone members by a common pattern of deviation.

- Going back to the *external balancing* hypothesis, the UK, Denmark, and Sweden abstained from EMU even though they were no less affected by the dollar externalities than the other member states. Whereas the British opt-out could be interpreted as an expression of its special security relationship with the USA, this explanation does not fit the case of Sweden.
- It is also unclear why the countries opting out should have refused to join an anti-hegemonic movement against the deutschmark. Most strikingly, Denmark had long pegged the krone to the mark, and continued to do so with the euro. It should have had the same interest in *internal balancing* as, say, Belgium or the Netherlands. If the euro really was a hegemonic scheme, it is also not clear why large member states such as France and Italy did not resist it more strongly than Denmark or Sweden.
- Members and non-members of the eurozone can be found on both sides of the *large/small country divide*.
- Denmark and Sweden are small and highly *trade-dependent economies*, just as the 'pacemakers' in the new member states. They conduct roughly 70–75 per cent of their foreign trade with the rest of the EU and should therefore have had a similar interest in adopting the euro.
- The *macroeconomic policy preferences* of the opt-out countries did not deviate from the German model. Indeed, their preferences were more in line with Germany's, and had been so for longer, than those of many of the (Southern) euro countries.
- Whereas British opposition against EMU can be partly attributed to a lack of *economic convergence* with the rest of the EU, neither Denmark nor Sweden would have had major difficulties in meeting the convergence criteria.

If we take the conflicting preferences on monetary union as given, can intergovernmentalism explain why horizontal differentiation was possible? To answer these questions, we need to take into account externalities and bargaining power. In general, the negative externalities of horizontal differentiation are weak in the case of the EMU. The fact that some countries keep their national currencies does not undermine the eurozone; neither does the existence of the euro undermine the welfare of the non-members. In other words, whereas horizontal differentiation potentially reduces the benefits of a larger unified currency area, it does not harm either the euro countries or the outsiders relative to the status quo of national currencies. First, whereas the weight and functioning of the eurozone would probably benefit if it could count the economically and fiscally strong countries of Denmark and Sweden as well as the large market of the UK with its powerful financial services among its members, it is sufficiently large without the opt-out countries and is not undermined in its functioning by the survival of the pound sterling or the Danish or Swedish krone. Second, whereas the non-euro countries forego the efficiency gains of a common currency, they still benefit from lower exchange rate risks and transaction costs, as well as increased economic stability in their trade with the euro countries. In the absence of important negative externalities, horizontal differentiation is easy to establish and maintain.

The countries that are most likely to suffer from horizontal differentiation are those that would like to join but are excluded until such time as they meet the convergence criteria. This was true initially for Greece and for the new member states after 2004. These countries stood to gain significantly in attractiveness and credibility as an economic and financial partner by introducing the euro. Potentially, the financially and economically weaker member states could have vetoed EMU unless they were given immediate access. But given German bargaining power, it was more beneficial for them to agree to the convergence criteria set by Germany and its allies (as long as such criteria seemed achievable), rather than having no EMU at all. The candidate countries seeking EU accession did not have the bargaining power to demand immediate accession to the euro area either. In order to gain membership, they accepted several discriminatory provisions, such as temporal constraints to the free movement of labour and the phasing-in of agricultural subsidies. Delayed and conditional accession to the eurozone was one of them.

In sum, whereas intergovernmentalism does not account for the preferences of the (old) EU member states that chose to opt out from the euro, it explains why horizontal differentiation was possible, and why Greece and the new member states could be excluded initially.

Differentiated vertical integration

Why, finally, is fiscal policy less vertically integrated than monetary policy? According to intergovernmentalism, the difference would have to be explained by lower autonomy costs and politicization of monetary integration, or lower interdependence, preference homogeneity, and compliance problems of fiscal policy.

Intergovernmentalism offers a plausible account based mainly on considerations of autonomy and interdependence. The de facto loss of monetary autonomy has been more pronounced than that of fiscal autonomy. National currencies have long been integrated into international regimes and transnational markets that exposed them to foreign exchange trade and speculation. By contrast, the member states' fiscal sovereignty has remained much more intact. Fiscal policies were not subject to international regimes, and could be managed by adjusting state-controlled resources (taxation) and expenses. The supranational centralization of fiscal policy would thus have involved a major loss of not only formal, but also material autonomy.

Moreover, the policy convergence that is generally seen as the crucial enabling factor for monetary integration appears to be absent in fiscal policy. The differences in government debt across Europe widened in Western Europe between the 1970s and the 1980s, and only narrowed during the 1990s. In addition, a recent paper finds little evidence for convergence among EU member states regarding tax burden or structure between the 1960s and the 1990s (Delgado and Presno 2010).

By contrast, there is no clear evidence of differences in politicization. According to the received wisdom, fiscal policy should indeed be more politicized than monetary policy. Taxation and redistribution are core state activities and the main line of political conflict in the modern welfare state. The provision of social security to the population, and of fiscal benefits to political supporters, is the main source of legitimacy for the EU's member states and its governments. Comparative studies show, however, that the alleged partisan difference regarding fiscal policies diminished considerably between the 1960s and the 1990s (Cusack 2001), and even disappeared in the 1980s for the EU member state governments (Clark *et al.* 2002).

Finally, the vertical differentiation between fiscal and monetary integration cannot in any way be explained by diverse enforcement requirements. Governments are often under strong domestic pressures regarding tax and social policies. The domestic political incentives to deviate from international fiscal policy rules are thus considerable. In addition, governments in a currency union are tempted to free-ride on the fiscal discipline of others. Finally, as the history of EMU has shown, the deficit rules of the SGP have been extremely difficult to enforce. If there were sufficient interdependence and preference convergence, there would thus be a strong incentive to move toward supranational centralization in fiscal policy, too.

Centralization of fiscal policy in the debt crisis: intergovernmental bargaining

From an intergovernmentalist perspective, the preferences, negotiations, and decisions on fiscal supranationalization in the context of the European sovereign debt crisis bear a strong resemblance to the constellations and processes at the origin of EMU. First, we see a dramatic increase in interdependence among the euro countries as a result of an exogenous shock originating from the banking crisis in the USA, which spilled over to European banks and compelled European states to undertake the systemic rescue of relevant banks to prevent a meltdown of the financial system. These rescue operations, in turn, sent public debt skyrocketing and destroyed the markets' confidence in the ability of many European countries to service those debts. The potential default or exit of one rather small country, Greece, threatened to trigger a chain reaction in the markets, lead to the default of larger countries such as Italy or Spain, put pressure on further countries such as France, spur recession in the eurozone, and even cause the breakdown of monetary union. There is broad agreement among the euro countries that such a course of events would come at a prohibitive cost, and that more integration is needed in order to stop it now and prevent it for the future. The call for more integration results not only from increased interdependence, but also from the revealed enforcement problems in the eurozone's fiscal policy: the intergovernmental SGP has obviously proven incapable of imposing sufficient fiscal discipline on the member states to guarantee the stability of the eurozone in times of financial crisis.

Second, however, member state preferences on the design of supranational fiscal policy diverged sharply. Germany and other fiscally conservative Northern euro countries with sustainable debt levels – such as the Netherlands and Finland – have propagated fiscal discipline, budget austerity, and stricter European surveillance of national budgets as the lessons to be drawn from the debt crisis. By contrast, France and the Southern euro countries have favoured budget expansion and transfers at the European level as the way out of the crisis: e.g. in the form of eurobonds or unlimited purchases of debt by the ECB. Whereas the Northern countries are disinclined to pay for the debt of the poorer and more profligate Southern members, the Southern members seek to avoid painful austerity measures and to elicit transfers from the wealthier euro countries.

Third, this conflict has been resolved in a process of hard inter-governmental bargaining, in which the most powerful country prevailed. As in the EMU negotiations of the late 1980s and early 1990s, this country was Germany. Clearly, the stability of the eurozone in the financial crisis depended crucially on the soundness of Germany's public finances and its willingness to provide the largest share of money to feed the eurozone's rescue funds. In return, Germany was able largely to determine the conditions and instruments of the rescue, and the institutional reforms of the eurozone, according to its preferences. Germany ruled out any formal 'communitarization' of public debt and successfully rejected the introduction of eurobonds, or a change in the mandate of the ECB. In contrast, it imposed austerity policies on the over-indebted countries, as well as the strengthening of the excessive deficit procedure and a German-style balanced budget rule on the entire eurozone. Whereas Germany had a strong economic interest in preserving and stabilizing the eurozone for fear of the disruptive consequences a breakdown would have on its banks and export-oriented industries, it had weathered the financial crisis comparatively well, continued to pay low interest on its bonds, and was under much less pressure to act – let alone make concessions – than the more vulnerable Southern euro countries, Ireland, or France.

Supranationalism

In general, supranationalism attributes the leap to EMU to spillover and institutionalization processes. For the specific mix of integration and differentiation in macroeconomic policy, we can translate the supranationalist assumptions and hypotheses about transnational exchange, and the preferences and capacities of supranational actors into the following expectations:

- From the supranationalist perspective, the decision at the end of the 1980s to move from intergovernmental to *supranational centralization* in monetary policy may be explained as the functional spillover of integration in a related policy area, possibly transmitted through the activities of transnational actors. Alternatively, it may have resulted from institutional spillover of earlier integration steps in monetary policy driven by the interests and capacities of supranational actors. We should observe an influential role of transnational interest groups and networks, as well as effective policy entrepreneurship of supranational actors. In addition, the substantive terms of monetary integration should mirror the interests and capacities of transnational groups and supranational actors.

- Supranationalism attributes *horizontal differentiation* to the unequal distribution of transnational exchange, or to the uneven preferences or capacities of supranational actors to integrate states. States remaining outside the eurozone should thus be less involved in transnational exchange and policy networks than those inside.

- The *vertical differentiation* of monetary and fiscal policy would have to be explained by a lower level of transnational exchanges and supranational actor capacity in the area of fiscal policy. For any given level of integration, both horizontal and vertical differentiation will decrease over time. In other words, membership in EMU, as well as the vertical integration of fiscal policy, should increase as a result of functional and institutional spillover processes.

- Finally, supranationalists would explain the recent decisions to *centralize fiscal policy* as the result of functional spillover from monetary integration or as the result of institutional spillover from the supranational institutions and rules in the area of monetary integration. The centralization of fiscal policy should have been driven by transnational societal and supranational actors, and reflected their preferences.

EMU: spillover and transnational networks

Two kinds of spillover may have produced the leap from intergovernmental coordination to supranational centralization in monetary integration: functional spillover from other policies and institutional spillover from previous integration steps in monetary policy.

Pressures for monetary integration may have resulted from previous market and policy integration in other areas. It is certainly true that the coexistence of different currencies in a Common Market creates risks and transaction costs that reduce the efficiency of the market. In addition, changes in exchange rates have complicated the working of the CAP from its beginnings, and have required the introduction of compensation schemes. Monetary integration had therefore been on the agenda of the Community for a long time. For the same reason, however, functional spillovers from other policies cannot explain the timing of EMU. If functional pressures had existed for some time, why was the decision to establish EMU only taken at the end of the 1980s – in particular, as the EMS had achieved unprecedented monetary stability?

If we want to explain EMU as a result of spillover, we need to turn to anticipated and cultivated spillover. The internal market programme agreed in the SEA (1986) promised to boost market transactions and transnational exchanges in Europe, thereby increasing the relevance of transaction costs of currency exchange for firms. In addition, the removal of barriers to the free movement of capital envisaged in the

SEA threatened to increase the risk of currency speculation and undermine the stability achieved in the EMS (Dyson and Featherstone 1999: 3). EMU can thus be seen as a precautionary policy to counter these anticipated costs and risks. Cultivated spillover can be found in the German foreign minister's 1988 initiative for monetary union, as well as in the Commission's report 'One Market, One Money', published in October 1990. In this report, a group of economists working for, or advising, the Commission argued that a single currency would add microeconomic efficiency and macroeconomic stability to the internal market, and showed that industrialists shared this perception. In their view, 'complete capital liberalization requires virtually a unified monetary policy if exchange rates are to be stable'. In sum, 'one market needs one money' (Commission of the European Communities 1990).

Turning to institutional spillover, the Werner Plan of 1970 provided an institutional template that the plan for EMU followed in many ways. In particular, the single currency, the institution of a European system of central banks, and the three-stage process strongly resembled the predecessor project. This can be regarded as an instance of institutional spillover or path dependency. However, the fiscal union also proposed in the Werner Plan did not make it into EMU. And the mere existence of the template, again, does not explain why it was taken up in the late 1980s, rather than sooner or later. The timing of EMU may, however, be explained by the existence and success of the EMS. The increasing stability of the EMS in the 1980s strengthened the member states' confidence that EMU could work; the ERM and ECU laid important institutional groundwork for the first stages of EMU; and the management of EMS provided ample experience that could be used for the design of EMU.

To sum up, whereas the Common Market and common distributive policies exercised general functional pressure, and the Werner Plan provided a general institutional template for a supranational monetary policy, it was the anticipated (or cultivated) effects of the Internal Market and the institutional experience of the EMS that triggered the specific EMU project in a supranationalist perspective. Note that both triggers are endogenous: they result from previous decisions and policies in European integration.

There is, furthermore, rich evidence that transnational and supranational actors were active and influential in the run-up to EMU (Cameron 1995). For example, the Association for the Monetary Union of Europe, founded in 1987 by large European multinational companies, lobbied for monetary integration. In the area of macroeconomic policy-making, the most relevant transnational actors are, however, not private firms but transnational networks of public officials and academic experts: mainly central bank officials and economists. To the extent that central banks are independent agencies, central bank officials can also be categorized as (public) non-governmental actors. These groups had established institutionalized links long ago: the Monetary Committee (in which the national finance ministries are represented, too) and the Committee of Governors of the Central Banks had been meeting since the early days of the EEC. The Werner Committee and the Delors Committee were likewise composed of independent experts and public officials, most of them taken from the ranks of the regular Committees. In the Delors Committee, 12 out 17 members were central bank governors; the others were experts and members of the Commission. They proposed the main parameters of what was later endorsed by the European Council and written into the Treaty of Maastricht. The rules of the SGP were prepared by the Monetary Committee, too. Finally, the Commission was not only represented in the Monetary Committee and the Delors Committee, but also produced its own expertise – such as the 'One Market, One Money' study.

Both supranationalist conditions for progress in vertical integration were thus present. First, regular committee meetings of a transnational network of experts produced frequent transnational exchanges. The coordinative management of the EMS had further increased the relevance and intensity of these exchanges. Second, this transnational network had high capacity – the power of expertise. Whereas the formal powers of transnational or supranational actors were weak in the run-up to EMU, the expert committees possessed the knowledge and knowledge-based authority that governments were lacking. Whereas supranational actors were arguably less influential than this transnational network, the Commission participated in the committee work and helped in its coordination, channelled its expertise into the political arena, and provided expertise of its own.

Horizontal differentiation

If anticipated functional spillovers, institutional templates, and transnational networks explain the leap from intergovernmental cooperation to supranational centralization, how could horizontal differentiation have occurred? After all, every member state participated in the Internal Market programme and had been part of the committee-based expert network. Yet, there is both functional and institutional variation among the member states that could provide the basis for differentiation. First, member states are differentially involved in transnational exchange. Some are more trade-dependent than others. Second, member states have been differentially involved in institutionalization. Some had not been members when the Werner Plan was made, and some had not participated in the EMS. The question is whether the differential involvement in transnational exchanges and institutionalization match the pattern of membership and non-membership in the eurozone.

For the new member states, the distinction between early joiners and laggards based on size and trade-dependence (Johnson 2008), which we described in the section on intergovernmentalism (pp. 161–2), fits the supranationalist framework as well: participation in the eurozone varies with the density of transnational exchange. By the same token, supranationalism does not explain the opt-outs of Britain, Denmark, and Sweden more convincingly than intergovernmentalism, because they cannot be attributed to weak transnational interactions with the eurozone (see the section on intergovernmentalism).

Differential institutionalization does not account for horizontal differentiation, either. All opt-out countries had been represented in the specialized committees of the EU on the same footing as the eurozone countries. The British central bank governor Leigh-Pemberton, who participated in the Delors Committee, is even on the record for having supported both a single currency and an independent ECB. Whereas the UK had not participated in the EMS, Denmark had. Spain, Portugal, and Greece, which joined the ERM late, nevertheless strove to become members of the eurozone. The new member states have, in general, been subject to the same institutional effects (duration of membership, participation in EU institutions, and so on): there is no variation in institutional exposure that could explain why some new member states strived to adopt the euro quickly while others have dragged their feet. In sum, supranationalism cannot explain horizontal differentiation in monetary policy.

Vertical differentiation

From a supranationalist perspective, the vertical differentiation between monetary and fiscal policy should, again, reflect different levels of transnational exchange and institutionalization. It is, however, difficult to measure – let alone compare – levels of transnational exchange for monetary and fiscal policy. We therefore need to pass judgement on this aspect of the supranationalist explanation of vertical differentiation. Suffice it to say that both foreign exchange and foreign debt have long been high and increasing in the EU. EU member states are among the most externally indebted countries of the world, both in terms of per capita external debt and in relation to GDP.

There is a clear qualitative difference with regard to institutionalization, however. Whereas specialized expert and governmental committees have existed in monetary policy since the 1950s, this has not been the case in fiscal policy. It is also noteworthy that the monetary policy committees and experts that advocated the currency union in the second half of the 1980s did not speak out in favour of fiscal union (see e.g. the Commission's 'One Market, One Money' report, cited above). Vertical differentiated integration could thus be partly attributed to the lack of supranational and transnational institutional support.

From differentiation to uniformity?

Supranationalism assumes that differentiation will become more difficult and less likely as institutionalization increases. There is, indeed, partial evidence for such institutionalization effects in macroeconomic policy integration.

First, the Snake and the EMS were only weakly institutionalized. From the supranationalist perspective, these monetary regimes did not create costly institutional hurdles that would prevent countries from leaving or prevent the regimes from collapsing altogether. This changed with the supranational centralization characteristic of EMU. When the decision in favour of currency union was taken, the costs and risks seemed to be small in light of the economic and policy convergence of the member states and the recent history of exchange rate stability. Had the heads of government been aware of the problems of EMU that were to follow, they might have reconsidered the issue. When the investments in EMU were made, however, the political and economic costs of retreat became prohibitively high. In 1992 and 1993, currency speculation and financial market turmoil had brought the ERM to the verge of collapse; it could only be saved by giving up the narrow bands of fluctuation. Having just signed the Treaty of Maastricht and made the commitment to establish a currency union, the member states nevertheless decided to move to Stage II of EMU. This stands in marked contrast to the early 1970s, when the Werner Plan faltered quickly. More importantly, when the debt crisis hit in 2010 and the survival of the eurozone seemed threatened, the member states went out of their way to save the currency union with guarantee funds worth hundreds of billions of euros and with severe austerity measures in the highly-indebted countries. The alternative of leaving or dissolving the currency union was deemed even more costly.

Second, there has been progress in fiscal integration, which – in the absence of relevant institutionalization – can be explained as a result of functional spillover. Indeed, intergovernmental cooperation in fiscal policy is inextricably linked to the prior decision to create a currency union and to transfer national monetary policy competences to the ECB. In this view, fiscal cooperation is a functional necessity of monetary integration: monetary union without fiscal union is likely to fail. Fiscal policy divergence can lead to a situation in which member states with a loose budgetary policy free-ride on the fiscal discipline of the others. Profligate members stimulate their economies at an interest rate that is subsidized by the creditworthiness of the disciplined members who, in turn, have to pay higher interest rates than they would outside monetary union. Conversely, countries in an economic and fiscal crisis cannot devalue the currency unilaterally in order to ease their fiscal burden through inflation or to boost their exports. In both cases, monetary union would come under severe strain. In anticipation of such a situation, the eurozone countries agreed on the SGP in 1997 – in particular, because it became clear at this time that some of the economically and financially weaker Southern member states would adopt the euro from the start (Heipertz and Verdun 2010: 83). Whereas supranationalism explains that and why fiscal integration follows monetary integration, it is, however, indeterminate regarding the precise level of fiscal integration. If there is a functional link between monetary and fiscal integration, why have the member states not agreed on full fiscal union or supranational budgetary policy enforcement in order to match the currency union and supranational monetary policy?

Finally, the fact that initial horizontal differentiation has been narrowing in macroeconomic policy integration supports supranational expectations. In 2011, the eurozone grew from an initial 11 member countries to 17. At the same time, however, it appears as unlikely as ever that the opt-out countries among the old member states – Britain, Denmark, and Sweden – will adopt the euro in the foreseeable future.

Functional spillover and supranational autonomy in the debt crisis

From a supranationalist perspective, the debt crisis has displayed several core mechanisms stipulated by historical institutionalism: institutional autonomy, unanticipated effects, and endogenous preference formation.

First, in response to the crisis, the ECB has clearly demonstrated institutional autonomy and deviated from its original mandate. Intergovernmentalists are right to point out that the ECB has been designed according to German preferences for an independent bank committed to price stability before anything else, and prohibited from bailing out indebted countries. Even so, the ECB first bought bonds worth more than 200 billion euros from the highly-indebted countries to reduce interest rates, and then flooded the money market with extremely cheap liquidity in late 2011 and early 2012 in order to stabilize the banking system, and to enable and encourage the banks to buy bonds from indebted countries, too. Although the ECB was careful to justify these measures as being in line with its mandate to maintain and stabilize monetary relations in the eurozone, it seems clear that they were intended to support the indebted countries and carried significant inflationary risks. Because the ECB decides with majority, the defenders of the orthodoxy could be outvoted: it is telling that two prominent representatives of Germany in the ECB resigned in the process.

Second, the debt crisis resulted in the dramatic exposure of the problems of partial macroeconomic integration. It proved that the parallelism of supranational monetary integration and intergovernmental fiscal cooperation was destabilizing. It is not clear that this development was entirely *unanticipated*: a chorus of expert warnings that partial macroeconomic integration was unsustainable had accompanied the establishment of EMU in the 1990s. At any rate, tight fiscal integration was not *desired* by the member states at the outset, and the weak enforcement rules of the SGP had been further weakened in 2005. From 2010, however, the euro countries generally agreed that more fiscal integration was essential. This is a typical case of functional spillover. Politically desired partial integration creates negative externalities, and because dismantling the more integrated policy (monetary policy, in this case) would be prohibitively costly, states are compelled to move ahead with the supranational integration of the less integrated adjacent policy (fiscal policy, in this case).

Finally, supranationalists would argue that the intergovernmentalist account of how national budgetary policy was integrated supranationally is short-sighted. While it rightly points to the exogeneity of the financial crisis shock, and the causal relevance of German preferences and bargaining power, it tends to overlook the endogeneity of the policy response. Whereas the shock was exogenous, it was partial macroeconomic integration that turned it into a crisis of the eurozone. In addition, the existence of EMU and the prohibitive costs of reintroducing national currencies reduced the set of feasible reactions to the crisis. In this situation, all eurozone governments agreed that more fiscal integration was needed – a preference change that would not have occurred in the absence of monetary union. In the end, German preferences and bargaining power were only decisive for deciding on a specific type of fiscal integration from a variety of options on the table; and Germany had to retreat several times from its anti-bailout preferences during the crisis.

Constructivism

From the constructivist perspective, integration and differentiation in macroeconomic policy is explained by ideational factors. A constructivist approach to European integration generates the following specific propositions on EMU:

- The decision at the end of the 1980s to move from intergovernmental to supranational centralization in monetary policy reflects either the strengthening of European identities, or the convergence of monetary policy ideas among the member states. The pro-integration consensus may have been promoted further by the institutionalization of the relevant policy ideas at the European level. The substantive terms of monetary integration fit with these policy ideas.

- Horizontal differentiation results from variation in European identity among the member states, or from the contestation of policy ideas. The opt-out countries have a lower level of European identity, or do not share the policy ideas underlying supranational monetary integration. Opt-outs are further facilitated by high domestic ratification constraints.
- Vertical differentiation results from a lower level of (institutionalized) ideational consensus, or a higher degree of ideational contestation and relevance, in fiscal policy.
- Constructivist integration theory would explain the recent supranational centralization of fiscal policy by the strengthening of European identity as a result of the common experience of using the euro, trans-European solidarity triggered by the financial crisis and the danger to the euro, or the convergence of fiscal policy ideas.

EMU: macroeconomic policy consensus

Constructivism explains the establishment, the timing, and the design of EMU by ideational consensus. This consensus may have been built on a general European identity favouring supranational integration, or on a policy-specific paradigm supporting EMU. Whereas, however, there is no evidence that a surge in European identity occurred ahead of EMU, macroeconomic and, more specifically, monetary policy ideas did converge.

Kathleen McNamara (1999) claims that the previously dominant Keynesian policy paradigm was replaced by a neoliberal or monetarist consensus in the course of the 1980s. In the 1960s and 1970s, most European governments followed Keynesian macroeconomic policy beliefs. In times of economic downturn, they tried to stimulate the economy through loose monetary policy and increased government spending – even if that meant higher inflation. In the 1970s, however, Keynesian polices had created 'stagflation' in many European countries, i.e. high inflation but no growth. As a consequence, the neoliberal paradigm gained ground. It demanded tight monetary policy and budget discipline. More specifically, the member states emulated the German model of macroeconomic policy, which had proven highly successful in combating inflation and thus acquired high legitimacy throughout Europe.

There are limits, however, as to what the neoliberal paradigm, the policy consensus on 'sound money and public finances' (Dyson and Featherstone 1999: 3), or the legitimacy of the German model can explain (Sandholtz 1993: 11). Monetarist economic theory generally prefers a system of flexible exchange rates to a system of fixed exchange rates, let alone an international currency. In line with this belief, the vanguard countries of monetarism, the USA and the UK, have been highly sceptical of EMU. In other words, whereas the neoliberal paradigm may have generated the ideational convergence that made more monetary integration possible, it does not explain supranational centralization.

A full ideational account of *supranational* monetary integration therefore needs to combine macroeconomic policy consensus with shared pro-integration attitudes. Constructivist explanations highlighting the emergence of an 'epistemic community' provide such a combination. An 'epistemic community' is a network of experts with common principled and causal beliefs about an issue, together with a common policy project based on these beliefs (Haas 1992). These characteristics fit the network of monetary experts who designed the basic principles and rules of EMU in the Delors Committee, which were later adopted without major modifications by the heads of state and government (Verdun 1999; see also Dyson and Featherstone 1999: 27). At the level of principled ideas, they were in favour of economic and monetary integration. Amy Verdun further detects several common causal beliefs: 'inflation was detrimental to growth'; an independent central bank was necessary to achieve low inflation; 'stable exchange rates were necessary to ensure the proper operation of the internal market'; the 'dominance of the Deutschmark' was 'politically unsatisfactory'; and national governments should remain fully responsible for other national macroeconomic and fiscal policies – albeit with 'binding rules ... to contain budget deficits'. Finally, the common policy project of this epistemic community was an EMU with an independent European central bank and the primary objective of price stability (Verdun 1999: 320).

Constructivism thus offers an explanation both for the timing and the substance of the preference convergence that made EMU possible at the end of the 1980s. In contrast to intergovernmentalism, it does not simply take preference convergence as exogenously given but explains it as the result of an ideational shift in the dominant macroeconomic policy paradigms. Moreover, it attributes the fact that EMU followed German preferences, not to German bargaining power but to the legitimacy of the German model. Constructivism also attributes the initiative of the German government in favour of EMU to its traditional pro-integration ('federalist') attitude, rather than to calculations of economic benefit (Dyson and Featherstone 1999: 771). Moreover, Germany did not need to coerce the other member states into accommodating its preferences for EMU because they had been persuaded of the superior performance of the German model during the 1980s.

With regard to supranationalism, the constructivist explanation is more complementary than competing. However, it relies on learning and persuasion, rather than institutional spillover and capacity. From the constructivist perspective, transgovernmental exchange and cooperation in the EC committees and the EMS may have facilitated the formation of a network, and having an expert committee isolated from domestic politics and government interference certainly helped the elaboration of a blueprint for EMU (Dyson and Featherstone 1999: 755–6). But the intensity of exchange and the institutional context did not cause the learning process and the emergence of a policy consensus.

Differentiated integration

Neither intergovernmentalism nor supranationalism provides convincing explanations for the opt-outs of the old member states: Britain, Denmark, and – *de facto* – Sweden. Can constructivism fill the gap? The major constructivist explanation for EMU, i.e. the emergence of a neoliberal macroeconomic policy consensus on sound money and public finances backed by an epistemic community of monetary experts, does not. After all, the governments and national experts of the opt-out countries shared the neoliberal policy consensus. Yet, the three states did not subscribe to the programme of *supranational* monetary integration advanced by the 'federalist' proponents of EMU and the monetary epistemic community meeting in the Delors Committee. Furthermore, the rejection of supranational monetary integration did not follow a policy-specific rationale but, rather, reflected deeply-rooted scepticism against wide-ranging transfers of national sovereignty to the European level. Whereas identity does not account for the leap to supranational monetary integration, it is the best explanation for the opt-outs.

As shown in the series of *Eurobarometer* surveys, Britain has a consistent and long-standing record of being the country with the strongest exclusive national identity and the lowest support for (supranational) European unification. According to a poll in 1992 (*Eurobarometer* 38), UK, Danish, and Irish citizens most strongly expressed fear of the loss of national identity in European integration. Denmark and the UK were the only two countries in which both the Treaty of Maastricht and the single currency were opposed by majorities. Sweden joined in 1995, following a close accession referendum. From the outset, Swedish Euroscepticism has been similar to that of the British and the Danes. In 1995 (*Eurobarometer* 43), support for European unification was lowest in the UK, Sweden, and Denmark; and the share of respondents with exclusive national identities was even higher in Sweden than in the UK. Weak support for further European integration, a comparatively negative image of the EU, and extremely low support for the euro have remained consistent features of the public opinion in these three countries.

These data show that the opt-outs from supranational monetary integration are not only firmly anchored in mass-level public opinion, but also strongly correlated with weak pro-European identities and attitudes. In contrast to the inconclusive intergovernmentalist and supranationalist explanations, which failed to identify a commonality of the three countries that could account for their opt-outs, constructivism can make a plausible argument based on mass identities. The data support the constructivist claim that 'the Euro is about identity politics and political visions of European order' (Risse *et al.* 1999: 175). The picture for the new member states is less clear-cut, but public opinion in favour of the euro is (on average) lower in the laggards than in the countries that joined early. Popular support in the two most important laggard countries, Poland and the Czech Republic, is similarly as weak in the UK, Denmark and Sweden (see *Eurobarometer*s 72 (2009) and 73 (2010)). Both countries also have a history of highly Eurosceptic governments. On the other hand, Latvia combines low popular support with membership in the ERM and efforts to introduce the euro, whereas Hungary has been reluctant to prepare for eurozone membership in spite of medium levels of general support for the EU among the population.

The existence of high domestic ratification constraints has clearly boosted the political relevance of mass-level identities. In Denmark and Sweden, it took popular referendums for the mass-level identity-based opposition to the euro to assert itself against euro-friendly elites. Even though the British government has rejected supranational monetary integration from the very start, it also constrained its room for manoeuvre with the promise to hold a referendum should it want to introduce the euro. By contrast, the German constitution does not provide for treaty ratification by popular referendum. As a result, popular majorities against the euro have never been able to assert themselves against the pro-euro mainstream parties.

Monetary integration thus clearly supports the constructivist explanation of identity-driven horizontal differentiation. On the other hand, however, the consistency and persistence of this identity-based opposition does not lend any support to the constructivist expectation of socialization effects strengthening European identity and thereby working to overcome differentiated integration. The growth of the eurozone has mainly been an effect of countries with a clear support for the euro meeting the convergence criteria, rather than evidence for a change of identity or ideas. Under the condition of strong domestic ratification constraints, any socialization effect of EU-level institutions that is by definition limited to the elites will fail to become politically consequential.

Can constructivism also explain the vertical differentiation between supranational monetary integration and intergovernmental fiscal policy coordination? An identity-based explanation is certainly less useful than in the case of horizontal differentiation. It is hard to argue that fiscal policy is more identity-relevant than monetary policy. In addition, the national currency is a stronger symbol of national identity than the national budget. To account for the gap in vertical integration, the epistemic community approach is more useful again. As shown above, the beliefs of the monetary expert community differed for monetary and fiscal integration. Whereas the central bankers and other like-minded experts believed in an independent European central bank and binding European rules to constrain national budget deficits, they did not support transferring other macroeconomic policies or fiscal sovereignty to the European level. This comes out of the Delors Report and also the Commission's 'One Market, One Money' study. According to constructivism, the difference in vertical integration is reflective of a difference in policy paradigms and expert beliefs.

The centralization of fiscal policy: socialization and solidarity?

Constructivist integration theory gives us little analytical leverage to explain the recent supranational centralization of budgetary policy in the EU. First, it cannot be explained as the result of increased diffuse support of the EU, or the euro, or by the strengthening of European identity, or transnational solidarity. In contrast, support for the euro and trust in the EU has markedly diminished during the financial crisis; the image of the EU has worsened significantly (*Standard Eurobarometer* 75 and 76 (2011)). Rather than fostering transnational solidarity, the crisis appears to have re-emphasized national stereotypes and cleavages. Second, whereas the euro crisis has generated a shared understanding that intergovernmental fiscal cooperation was insufficient to stabilize the eurozone, this shared understanding was a reaction to the crisis rather than the result of an institutional socialization process. Moreover, it goes together with divergent views on how to reform the system. Ultimately, it seems more plausible to explain the provisions of the fiscal compact by German bargaining power, rather than by the convergence of policy ideas.

Finally, the explanatory power of politicization and Euro-scepticism appears limited, too. The euro crisis and the measures taken to combat it have politicized European integration in an unprecedented way. They have triggered violent protests in Greece and changes in government in the most affected countries. And yet at the time of writing, these developments have not caused stagnation or additional differentiation in the EU. To the contrary, the fiscal compact – which constrains national fiscal autonomy considerably – was signed by all euro countries and all but two non-euro countries. Only the Czech

Republic and the UK rejected the treaty for reasons having to do with Euro-scepticism. By contrast, Denmark and Sweden decided to support the treaty in spite of their opposition to the euro. It seems that under the impact of the grave financial, economic, and – ultimately – political threat of the euro crisis, high politicization, ideational contestation, and increasing Euro-scepticism have not prevented the member states from reaching agreement on further vertical integration in an area with significant relevance for national identity and sovereignty. Ultimately, however, voters and parties in Greece and elsewhere will decide on whether transnational and supranational pressures will carry the day.

Conclusion

Macroeconomic policy integration is a highly relevant area for understanding the driving forces and obstacles of integration and differentiation in the EU, and for testing theories of European integration. Monetary policy is not only one of the most vertically integrated policies of the EU, but also shows the most pronounced horizontal differentiation. In addition, macroeconomic policy integration has been characterized by a marked gap between the supranational centralization of monetary policy and intergovernmental cooperation in fiscal policy. In this chapter, we therefore applied supranationalism, intergovernmentalism, and constructivism to explain not only monetary policy integration, but also the horizontal and vertical differentiation in macroeconomic policy.

Intergovernmentalism explains the leap from intergovernmental coordination to supranational centralization as the result of intergovernmental bargaining. It was made possible by the convergence of national monetary preferences and policies in the 1980s, and its design and substance reflected both superior German bargaining power and the severe enforcement problems of monetary policy. The latter two factors also explain the supranational integration of budgetary policy in the euro crisis. According to supranationalism, the driving force behind supranational monetary integration was a transnational network of monetary experts and central bankers, which had been formed and become influential in the institutional (committee-based) system of the European Community. They elaborated the blueprint for EMU against the background of anticipated functional spillover from the Internal Market, the institutional template of the Werner Plan, and the experience of EMS. The recent steps toward supranational fiscal integration resulted partly from autonomous actions of the ECB and partly from the attempts of the member states to come to terms with the negative functional spillover of partial macroeconomic integration. Finally, constructivism offers an explanation based on policy beliefs and identities. Whereas the leaps to supranational monetary integration cannot be attributed to a leap in pro-integration European identity, it reflects the shift in macroeconomic paradigms from Keynesianism to neoliberalism or monetarism, and the adoption of the German model of monetary policy during the 1980s. It was reinforced and converted into a blueprint for EMU by an epistemic community of monetary experts organized in EU-level committees.

All three theories offer plausible partial accounts of supranational monetary integration. But these accounts are not fully competitive or controversial. To some extent, the accounts complement each other. Then again, they interpret the same factors in different ways. Core elements in each account are interdependence, preference convergence, and the power of Germany.

Interdependence

There seems to be broad agreement that interdependence is an important driving force of monetary integration. Both intergovernmentalism and supranationalism emphasize this factor and, although constructivism does not theorize this condition explicitly, heightened and critical monetary interdependence is the background condition to which the epistemic community reacts with its belief-based policy proposals. The question that divides the theories, however, is the nature of interdependence. Whereas intergovernmentalism emphasizes exogenous and 'real' material interdependence, supranationalism focuses on endogenous interdependence generated by prior steps of integration and – at least in part – cultivated by supranational actors. In our view, the evidence speaks strongly in favour of the supranationalist interpretation. The timing of EMU is best explained by the Single Market programme agreed on before, the abolishment of capital controls that were part of this programme, and the expectation that intensified market integration would require or benefit from monetary integration. This line of argument was used by all proponents of monetary integration, whether supranational or governmental actors, and it was used before the Single Market was completed and the freedom of capital movement was established. Moreover, the recent steps toward fiscal policy integration have clearly been motivated by additional interdependence and negative externalities resulting from prior monetary policy integration. It is safe to say that the financial crisis would not have produced the supranational integration of national budgetary policies in the absence of existing monetary integration.

Convergence of policy preferences

The convergence of macroeconomic policy preferences is another factor that all three theories agree on. If heightened interdependence generated demand for monetary integration, the convergence of monetary policy preferences made it possible to realize the EMU project. The theories differ, however, on the causes of convergence. Again, one issue is exogeneity or endogeneity. Intergovernmentalism regards convergence as exogenous and does not offer a theory-based explanation for the shift in preferences; but in line with intergovernmentalist assumptions about the material nature of preferences, convergence can be attributed to the failure of Keynesian macroeconomic steering, which motivated governments to change their policies in order to increase their welfare benefits.

By contrast, supranationalism and constructivism offer a highly complementary endogenous explanation. In part, the convergence of policy preferences is part of a global paradigm shift from Keynesianism to neoliberalism, but this shift alone does not explain the choice of supranational monetary integration. More specifically, preference convergence has been the effect of monetary cooperation within the EMS and the formation of a transgovernmental monetary epistemic community organized in EC committees. Whereas constructivism emphasizes the ideational basis of preference convergence and the existence of an epistemic community, supranationalism points to the effects of institutionalization in the EMS and the EC committees. Even though the shift towards neoliberalism may well have been a rational response to the economic failure of Keynesianism, the fact that it ended up in a blueprint for EMU (rather than national solutions) can hardly be explained without reference to existing European level institutions: the EMS experience and the integration-friendly monetary expert community. Finally, the convergence of preferences for a more centralized fiscal policy was, again, endogenous: it resulted from the revealed failure of intergovernmental cooperation in this field. In this case, however, institutional constraints – as expected by supranationalism – clearly offer a more plausible explanation than socialization processes – as theorized by constructivism.

German power

Again, all theoretical explanations agree on the relevance of the German model of monetary policy for European monetary integration. But they debate why the design of EMU follows German preferences. Intergovernmentalism tells a story of German bargaining power resulting from satisfaction with the status quo and domestic constraints, whereas constructivism emphasizes the legitimacy of the

Germany model resulting from a long record of superior performance. Constructivism sees emulation where intergovernmentalism sees coercion. Correspondingly, the Bundesbank appears as a domestic veto-player in the intergovernmentalist account, as the anchor of a transgovernmental network according to supranationalism, and as a legitimate policy authority from the constructivist perspective. The evidence seems to suggest that the competing perspectives apply to different actors and issues. It appears as though the German model was largely uncontested in the monetary epistemic community, which was not the case in the intergovernmental arena. Whereas macroeconomic policy preferences had converged, indeed, the institutional preferences of the major camps, the 'economists' represented by Germany and the 'monetarists' represented by France, remained similarly opposed as in the 1970s on the process and design of monetary union (Walsh 2000: 15–17). Expert deliberations alone did not settle these issues. They were ultimately resolved in intergovernmental negotiations, in which the German bargaining position prevailed on most issues thanks to its superior bargaining power. As the history of EMU and the recent debt crisis show, monetary integration has remained a conflictive process with divergent interests and positions among the eurozone countries – and a process, in which Germany's bargaining power is of crucial importance for the outcomes.

In sum, then, the story of EMU is difficult to tell without German bargaining power, but it played a role in a context of largely endogenous interdependence and preferences.

The clearest results for theory competition can be found for horizontal differentiation. Neither supranationalism nor intergovernmentalism offers a full and systematic explanation of horizontal differentiation in monetary integration. Whereas the difference between countries that joined early and laggards among the new member states can be attributed to differences in economic interdependence, the opt-outs among the old member states do not distinguish themselves consistently from the eurozone countries with regard to interdependence, size, policy preferences, or institutional density or capacity. Constructivism solves the puzzle of horizontal differentiation. The comparatively high level of exclusive national identities and opposition to supranational integration, in combination with strong domestic ratification constraints, is a common feature of the three opt-out countries and sets them apart from the other member states.

Turning, finally, to vertical differentiation, we find again that all theories provide plausible explanations as to why fiscal policy has remained less integrated than monetary policy. Intergovernmentalism attributed the difference to higher national autonomy, lower interdependence, and more pronounced preference divergence in fiscal policy;

supranationalism can point to the lower international institutionalization of fiscal policy; and constructivism can argue that vertical differentiation mirrors the macroeconomic policy beliefs of the epistemic community. These explanations have different causal depth, however. Whereas intergovernmentalism focuses on fundamental structural factors, institutionalization and policy paradigms appear secondary: the weaker institutionalization of fiscal policy and the shared belief that fiscal policy should remain a (constrained and regulated) intergovernmental competence may itself be a consequence of the low levels of international interdependence and autonomy loss. When the financial crisis exposed how interdependent the eurozone countries had become in fiscal policy, and how limited the autonomy of the highly-indebted countries had become *de facto*, supranational fiscal integration became possible.

Chapter 7

Security and Defence

The areas of security and defence are commonly referred to as an issue of 'high politics' and, as such, they are characteristic of policies that are deemed vital in determining the autonomy, integrity – and hence the survival – of nation-states (Hoffmann 1966). The development of defence capabilities and the capacity of rulers to deploy armies is a significant milestone in the history of modern statehood. War, in Charles Tilly's words, made states and states, in turn, have waged wars to secure their position in the incipient system of national states, thereby to secure and protect their nascent and often fragile sovereignty. While war and the process of state-building are inextricably linked, international cooperation, or even integration in matters of security and defence policy, mark particularly intriguing puzzles for every student of International Relations, more generally, and European integration in particular. According to realists, the anarchical and uncertain nature of international politics offers no protection to the security and integrity of states and therefore, governments have to invest in capabilities and forge alliances to defend themselves against potential competitors. This view of international politics is, however, increasingly challenged. Security threats are said not to rest on asymmetric distributions of material capabilities but, rather, reflect deep-rooted 'strategic cultures' (Meyer 2005), leading to different threat perceptions. Still, security and defence policy integration can be considered a 'hard' case: capabilities and security threats differ, as do states' strategic cultures, which are often deeply rooted in foreign and security policy traditions reaching far back in history. Why, then, would states decide to give up sovereignty in an area that lies at the heart of its coercive power and is constitutive of its sovereignty? Why would states engage in establishing multi-national military forces and military decision-making structures? The ensuing sections draw on our set of hypotheses from European integration theory to shed light on these questions.

The Development of Security and Defence Policy in the EU

Even though defence policy is still among the least integrated policy areas in the EU, the origins of European integration are intimately

linked to security concerns among the founding member state governments. The history of European integration cannot be written without
appreciating that postwar Germany was perceived to pose an ongoing
security threat to large sections of the political elites and publics among
the former wartime enemies. The plan to create the ECSC – and
thereby pool German and French coal and steel resources, and submit
investment, production, and supply-related decisions in these sectors to
a supranational High Authority – can be rightfully considered a 'break
with the past' (Duchêne 1994: 205). Not only did the institutional
structure of the ECSC possess supranational quality – a novelty in the
orbit of inter-state cooperation – the ECSC also marks a decisive break
with the past by proposing a solution to the eminent economic and
security concerns that France entertained *vis-à-vis* Germany. (See Box
7.1 for further details.)

The ultimate objective of the Schuman Plan, culminating in the
adoption of the ECSC treaty in 1951, was to alleviate French concerns
that postwar Germany would employ its regained industrial strength as
a threat to French autonomy and security. These concerns arose, in
particular, against the backdrop of imminent German economic
recovery and the prospect that Germany would be 'freed' from Allied
oversight. Yet, the initial route taken to 'bind' Germany firmly to the
West was an economic one, which – according the hopes of many

Box 7.1 *Timeline: security and defence integration*

1950	Pleven Plan	1998	Franco-British St
1952–54	European Defence		Malo Declaration
	Community	1999	Cologne and
1961–62	Fouchet Plans		Helsinki European
1970	Davignon Report		Councils (Headline
	and European		goals; establishment
	Political		of European
	Cooperation		Security and
1986	Single European Act		Defence Policy)
	(EPC in treaties)	2001	Treaty of Nice
1992	Treaty on European		(treaty base for
	Union: Common		European Security
	Foreign and		and Defence Policy)
	Security Policy as	2003	First European
	second pillar		Security and
1992	Danish opt-out from		Defence Policy
	defence		operations
1997	Amsterdam Treaty	2009	Treaty of Lisbon
	(i.e. High		(Common Security
	Representative)		and Defence Policy)

French politicians at the time – would generate not merely economic benefits underpinning France's economic modernization plan, but also security externalities by ensuring that former wartime industries were put under the control of an independent High Authority. Security concerns also dominated plans to progress with European integration even before the ECSC treaty was finalized. This time, the governments addressed security concerns head on by proposing the creation of a European army in the context of a European Defence Community (EDC).

A bold move: the Pleven Plan and the EDC

The outbreak of the Korean War in 1950 infused the Cold War with new heat, and triggered activities to adjust security strategies and policies among the former wartime allies. The governments of the USA and Great Britain brought up the prospect of rearming West Germany under a framework of equal partners. At the same time, the ongoing security concerns France harboured *vis-à-vis* Germany would have to be alleviated by launching 'a broader Schuman Plan' (Pastor-Castro 2006: 389), which included an explicit military component. The resulting Pleven Plan, named after the French Prime Minister René Pleven, was presented on 24 October 1950. In the case of German rearmament, the plan envisaged a joint supranational framework preventing unilateral military action by denying West Germany prospects for an independent army or general staff. On 15 February 1951, France, West Germany, Italy, Belgium, and Luxembourg entered into negotiations on what was to become the ill-fated Treaty establishing the EDC. On 27 May 1952, the six founding members of the ECSC signed the Treaty establishing a European Defence Community.

The EDC treaty stipulated that the participating states ought to delegate control over their armed forces to the European level (Ruane 2000: 15). However, the prospective member states were permitted to run and command nationally organized military forces for deployment in non-European areas, and to live up to international commitments. Moreover, the EDC member states also committed to the drawing up of a common armament programme. The EDC treaty thus envisaged a relatively strong set of competencies in the area of defence with national governments merely exercising residual competencies for procurement of armaments, and the organization and command of their own armed forces. Institutionally, the ECSC largely served as blueprint for the institutional structure of the EDC. The EDC was to comprise a Court, a parliamentary assembly, a supranational Commissariat and a Council, representing the governments of the member states. Akin to the High Authority of the ECSC, the Commissariat was to become the centrepiece of the new organization, initiating and carrying out a broad set of policies ranging from procurement to deploying military resources and troops. Decisions were to be taken mainly by (qualified) majority in the Council, with the assembly playing a particularly important role in controlling the Commissariat and in co-deciding on the EDC's budget. The prominent part accorded to supranational organizations in making, monitoring, and adjudicating decisions, as well as the introduction of 'pooled' decision-making rules, amounts to a level of *vertical* integration reflecting 'joint decision-making II'.

Turning to *horizontal* integration, the provisions of the EDC treaty left no room for external or internal differentiation, but envisaged a uniform application of the treaty rules. At first sight, it is hardly surprising that only a small number of European states decided to sign the EDC treaty: Even prior to the formation of the Warsaw Pact in 1955, the world witnessed the formation of an 'Eastern Bloc'. This bloc was characterized by politico-military dominance of the Soviet Union over most central and eastern European states, and by the installation of autocratic or totalitarian 'satellite' regimes and command economies in these states. During the decades of the Cold War, the 'Eastern Bloc' remained outside the group of European states for which European integration was a political option. Both, the creation of the ECSC and EDC have to be seen in context of heightened confrontation between 'East' and 'West'. Binding Germany into a system of European cooperation and integration promised to alleviate French security concerns; subsequent US administrations considered binding West Germany to the 'Western' bloc as highly instrumental, from a political, military and economic perspective. Still with a view to horizontal integration, subsequent decisions of the British government to stay outside the EDC (a decision that had its precursor in the case of ECSC membership and was replicated in the case of the EEC) are of interest, as they foreshadow the often difficult relationship between Britain and the EU – an issue to which we will return in the second part of this chapter.

The highly ambitious EDC treaty was successfully ratified in all but one member state: France; Italy was waiting for the French parliamentary vote before the Italians cast theirs. The French National Assembly rejected the treaty on a procedural motion on 30 August 1954, 364 votes to 219. Even though the EDC treaty was abandoned as result, this did not mean that security and defence cooperation was dropped from the agenda. Instead of integrating the former wartime enemies Germany and Italy into the EDC framework, both countries became members of the Western European Union in 1954, which emerged from the military assistance treaties of Dunkirk und Brussels signed in 1947 and 1948, respectively – both of which were initially elaborated against fears of German aggression. As an organization with a mission to provide military assistance to its members, the Western European Union (WEU) recognized its subordinate status *vis-à-vis* NATO, since the WEU member states passed the responsibility for planning and carrying out military tasks on to NATO 'with West Germany thus being militarily integrated into NATO through a back door opened by WEU', thereby stripping the Europeans of 'the opportunity to use their own military capabilities to pursue their own foreign policy choices' (Keukeleire and MacNaughtan 2008). As a consequence, NATO became the focal point for cooperation in security and defence matters for a long time to come. Instead of adopting a supranational European framework, NATO provided for an intergovernmental decision-making structure and mutual military assistance through nationally contained armies.

De Gaulle's 'certaine idée' and the Fouchet Plans

De Gaulle's rise to power in France in 1958 had a lasting impact; not only on French domestic politics – effectively putting an end to the crisis-ridden Fourth Republic by installing a semi-presidential system with the Fifth Republic – it also had important repercussions for the future course of European integration. Not only was the newly-founded EEC considered to be instrumental to the achievement of key French economic objectives – most notably, the subsidization of agricultural production and industrial modernization, de Gaulle also saw the chance to promote European political union by challenging the role of the transatlantic alliance and, hence, NATO. De Gaulle's aim was to deepen foreign policy cooperation among the member states of the newly-founded EEC on the basis of an intergovernmental framework that was to be independent of NATO and the USA (Dinan 2004: 83, 99). Following-up on an initiative by de Gaulle, a committee headed by French Ambassador Christian Fouchet worked on a proposal for closer cooperation among the EEC member states in areas ranging from foreign and defence policy to cultural policy, human rights, and democracy. The Fouchet Plan, issued in 1961, called for a new international organization structured on strictly intergovernmental lines and so included proposals for an institutional set-up that was to differ fundamentally from the institutions and decision-making procedures of the EEC (not to mention the even more supranationally designed ECSC and EDC).

Commentators argue that the Fouchet Plan was a reflection of de Gaulle's '*certaine idée*' of France in the world, which rested on the primacy of the nation state (as the only legitimate actor in world politics), French independence and '*grandeur*', as well as military power to promote French power status in world politics (Moravcsik 2000). As a corollary of this 'certain idea', de Gaulle was said to consider an independent European foreign and defence policy not only to control Germany, but also to establish Europe as a 'third force' in international politics – and thus as a counterweight to the two existing superpowers (Hill and Smith 2000: 47). Moreover, de Gaulle envisaged that France would play the dominant role within a European political union, given the French president's ambition to establish France as the most potent military power in Europe. A Council composed of the heads of state or government would dominate the organization the Fouchet Plan wanted to establish. The plan did not accord any role to institutions such as the supranational Commission or the Court; a European Parliament would be permitted to table questions and make recommendations to the Council, which would decide by unanimous vote (Reynolds 2010: 121–2). The Fouchet Plan thus represents the very counter-image of the EDC. The intergovernmental nature of its decision-making structure is reflected in the absence of both pooling or delegation of decision-making authority. The level of *vertical* integration thus meets what we have labelled 'intergovernmental coordination'. Following the criticisms of the other Community member states, a second Fouchet Plan was issued in January 1962, which did not reflect concessions demanded by the other parties, but 'hardened up the commitment to intergovernmentalism and to French leadership' (Hill and Smith 2000: 47).

The failure of the Fouchet Plan(s) can, among other factors, be traced back to the issue of *horizontal* integration; more specifically, the question of British membership. The Dutch and Belgian governments insisted on the participation of Britain in the political union envisaged by the Fouchet Plan (as well as in the Common Market of the EEC), partially to counter the possibility of Franco-German dominance within the union (Reynolds 2010: 123). Given the attachment of the British government to sustaining and fostering its transatlantic ties and cooperation in security and defence matters, de Gaulle dropped the Fouchet Plan in April 1962 (Dinan 2004: 99–100).

One decade after the entry into force of the ECSC, integration in the area of defence had thus experienced a double failure. While the Pleven Plan failed in its attempt to establish supranational integration of security and defence policy, the Fouchet Plan did not succeed in imposing an intergovernmental structure on the existing Community institutions. Moreover, these two episodes foreshadow two cleavages that came to dominate debates on security and defence cooperation until the time of writing. Should cooperation follow a more intergovernmental or more supranational institutional set-up? Should the cooperative arrangement be more 'Atlanticist' or more 'European' in outlook (see Reynolds 2010: 124–5)?

Informal intergovernmental coordination: the EPC

Following de Gaulle's departure from the political scene in 1969, the ensuing years saw the first successful attempts of the six founding members to coordinate their foreign policies. Following the experiences with the EDC and the Fouchet Plans, the heads of government decided at the summit meeting at The Hague in 1969 to return to foreign policy coordination, putting a committee headed by Etienne Davignon, political director in the Ministry of Foreign Affairs of Belgium, in charge with the elaboration of proposals for the member states to progress towards foreign policy cooperation. To avoid 'doctrinal debates' on the methods and 'finality' of the European integration project, the report tabled by Davignon in 1970 (also referred to as the Luxembourg Report) 'provided for light, non-binding consultations rather than a treaty ... The institutional architecture was also expressly kept separate to that of the Community, apparently for fear of supra-national contamination' (Reynolds 2010: 127). To avoid the latent conflict between 'Europeanists' and 'Atlanticists' over the role of NATO, foreign policy cooperation excluded issues with security and defence implications.

According to the Davignon Report, the aim of European Political Cooperation (EPC) was to coordinate – and, eventually, to 'harmonize' – views on matters of common concern, yet the formal competencies to conduct foreign policy were to remain firmly located at the national level. In the years to come, EPC did undergo a transformation, by allowing foreign policy coordination to encroach upon issues with security implications. This is reflected in a series of official Community documents, such as the London Report of 1981 or the Solemn Declaration of Stuttgart of 1983, which made explicit that many foreign policy issues inevitably touch upon security matters and, hence, cannot be excluded from discussion of common foreign policy objectives (Hill and Smith 2000: 114, 125). In the face of political events and crises in the 1970s and early 1980s, ranging from the Arab-Israeli War in 1973, the Soviet invasion of Afghanistan, the coup in Poland or the revolution in Iran, disputes among European states and between European states and the USA arose over coordinated foreign policy responses. Yet, these crises encouraged the member states to renew efforts promoting cooperation and broadening the political agenda of EPC to include foreign policy questions with security implications (Giegerich and Wallace 2010: 433–4; Keukeleire and MacNaughtan 2008: 47).

Initially, EPC did not contain any provisions for an institutional structure or resources, such as a secretariat, permanent staff, or a budget. In M.E. Smith's words, EPC 'was little more than an exclusive "gentlemen's club", run by diplomats for diplomats, subject to the goodwill of its members and closed to outside scrutiny' (Smith 1998: 307–8). Member state governments were to be assisted by high-level diplomats forming the 'Political Committee' to prepare the ministerial meetings and coordinate policy positions. The intergovernmental format implied that any form of pooling or delegation – i.e. supranational actor involvement – was anathema, or reduced to a minimum. Should the competencies of the Commission be touched upon, the Commission would be 'invited to make known its views' (Part II, section V, Davignon Report). Even though the provisions of EPC were not formally linked to the Community and hence did not have a treaty base, EPC represents the earliest form of (informal) intergovernmental foreign policy coordination.

European cooperation in the area of foreign policy was accorded treaty status for the first time with the entry into force of the SEA in 1987. Akin to the rules and practices developed in the context of EPC since the 1970s, the SEA formalized EPC practices ('intergovernmental coordination'): Title III, Article 30, paragraph 6, of the SEA stipulates that member states should be 'ready to coordinate their positions more closely on the political and economic aspects of security'. Moreover, it was reaffirmed in the SEA that the cooperation within the framework of the Community was not to 'impede closer cooperation in the field of security between certain High Contracting Parties within the Western European Union or Atlantic Alliance'. These two statements already point towards the trajectory future cooperation in the area of foreign (and security) policy was about to take. Even before the Cold War came to a sudden end in 1989, Community member states were outspoken in their ambitions in the medium to long run: European integration remained incomplete unless closer cooperation in the areas of security and defence were to be taken (Reynolds 2010: 134). When the Iron Curtain finally fell and German unification was imminent, 'questions about the delicate balance between France and Germany and about American security leadership through NATO' (Giegerich and Wallace (2010: 434) were reopened.

Picking up speed: Maastricht, Amsterdam, and the CFSP

The end of the Cold War and German unification acted as a catalyst in bringing about the Maastricht Treaty. In 1990, the French and German governments, under the respective leadership of President Mitterrand and Chancellor Kohl, proposed to convene an intergovernmental conference (IGC) on political union (alongside the IGC on economic and monetary union), with the objective of establishing and advancing the EU's common foreign and security policy. The Maastricht Treaty, which was signed in 1992 and entered into force in 1993, replaced EPC with the Common Foreign and Security Policy (CFSP), constituting the 'second pillar' of the new three-pillar structure, which – from then onwards – would be officially labelled 'EU'. The provisions for CFSP were laid down in Title V, Article J of the Maastricht Treaty. The relevant treaty provisions state explicitly that questions related to the security of the EU also include defence-related issues, which 'might in time lead to a common defence' (Article J.4) For the time being, the elaboration and implementation of defence-related policies and actions was restricted to the WEU, which was considered the appropriate forum and the respective 'defence arm' (Reynolds 2010: 138) of the EU. The WEU was, at the same time, considered the 'bridge' between CFSP and NATO (Hill and Smith 2000: 152). In contrast to the EPC, the main provision of which was a forum for consultation and coordination of different foreign policy positions, the CFSP provided concrete tools for action by introducing the instrument of 'Joint Action' (Article J.3), which had to be adopted unanimously by the member state governments acting through the Council and based on the guidelines adopted by the European Council. In cases where a Joint Action constitutes an implementing measure of a Joint Strategy adopted by the Council, member states could choose to move to qualified majority voting (QMV) instead of unanimity (the same applies for procedural issues). With a view to decision-making procedures, the Maastricht treaty thus contains some cautious steps towards 'intergovernmental cooperation' with limited pooling (vertical integration). Even though falling short of joint decision-making, the Commission and the European Parliament (EP) are more closely associated with CFSP than EPC. Article J.8 states that the Commission may submit proposals to the Council, thereby exercising a right of (joint) initiative (Hill and Smith: 152). Moreover, the EP shall be consulted 'on the main aspects and basic choices' (Article J.7) of CFSP. The decision to fund CFSP from the EU's common budget gave the Commission and Parliament a potential lever with which to exercise influence on CFSP measures. It is also noteworthy that the member state governments decided to exclude the CFSP from the jurisdiction of the ECJ.

The Maastricht Treaty also marks a break with the past with regard to *horizontal* integration. At the 1992 European Council meeting in Edinburgh, Denmark was granted an opt-out from all common foreign policy initiatives that carry defence implications. This first step away from the uniform application of the *acquis* in the area of CFSP towards 'internal differentiation' set the scene for more comprehensive, albeit treaty-based forms of internal differentiation in ensuing treaty reforms. The Maastricht Treaty contained an in-built review mechanism, which stipulated that the member states should revisit the Treaty at a subsequent IGCs, starting in 1996. Against the widely-perceived failure of the EU to find a joint and adequate response to the wars and atrocities in the Balkans, and with a clear definition of defence-related tasks for which the member states would deploy troops under shared WEU and EU responsibility still pending, a revision of CFSP provisions appeared to be overdue only shortly after the Maastricht Treaty had entered into force. The Amsterdam Treaty, which was signed in 1997 and entered into force in 1999, modestly extended the space for QMV. Yet, 'pooling' remained restricted to matters of implementation, where joint strategies, joint actions, or common standpoints had already been agreed upon (by unanimity). The Treaty also provided for the post of a High Representative for CFSP, a function to be exercised by the Secretary General of the Council. The post was established not to provide CFSP with a 'supranational' impetus, but to instil a certain degree of continuity into the EU's foreign policy operations against accusations that the rotating Council Presidency generated too much confusion and inconsistency (Reynolds 2010: 146). The fact that the High Representative was firmly rooted in the Council Secretariat reflects the intergovernmental quality of the position. The High Representative was to be assisted by a new institutional infrastructure, the Policy Planning and Early Warning Unit. The Policy Unit, as it is most often called, had its staff drawn from EU institutions (mainly from the Council Secretariat and the Commission), the member states, and the WEU (Hill and Smith 2000: 169), and was to provide the CFSP with a 'forward-planning capability' (Reynolds 2010: 147). Moreover, the Amsterdam Treaty further specifies the link between the EU and WEU by incorporating the so-called 'Petersberg tasks' into the Treaty (Hill and Smith 2000: 169). Defined in 1992 at a WEU summit meeting at Petersberg, near Bonn, they comprise mainly peacekeeping, humanitarian, and rescue tasks. In terms of vertical integration, the Amsterdam Treaty thus continues the trend towards establishing a system of 'intergovernmental cooperation' with modest levels of supranational delegation and pooling.

In the light of the enlargement round in 1995, whereby formerly neutral or 'non-aligned' states (Austria, Finland, and Sweden) acceded to the EU, a mechanism was introduced in the Treaty to prevent the potential for paralysis by enabling selective opt-outs for states unwilling to adopt a particular joint foreign policy initiative: 'Constructive abstention' created the opportunity for recalcitrant states to opt out from a common position without preventing the other governments from moving ahead. In the light of our conceptualization of *horizontal integration*, constructive abstention is a major innovation in the area of foreign, security, and defence policy as it explicitly allows for internal differentiation. The Treaties of Amsterdam and Nice, as well as the Lisbon Treaty, formally enshrined and extended the possibility for internal differentiation in matters of security and defence policy. While the Amsterdam Treaty made the start with 'constructive abstention', 'enhanced cooperation', which was also introduced at Amsterdam but only extended to CFSP at Nice, makes it easier for subgroups of EU member states to march ahead in security- (but not defence!) related policy issues. The Lisbon Treaty continues to highlight the formal possibility of forming subgroups of the 'willing'.

Change of tide: St Malo, ESDP, and CSDP

With the Treaty of Amsterdam barely ratified, the Kosovo War, which erupted in March 1998, prompted the EU member states to re-define the EU's role in the Balkans. The German government, headed by a coalition of the Social Democrats and Greens, decided – following a fervid domestic political debate – that it would not stand aside in case of a military operation. The new British Prime Minister, Tony Blair, declared that the EU needed to enhance its military capabilities, thus displaying a more pro-European attitude than any previous British government, while the French government under President Chirac demonstrated a more conciliatory and cooperative stance towards NATO (Keukeleire and MacNaughtan 2008: 56). This 'rapprochement' of national positions resulted in the famous Franco-British St Malo Declaration of December 1998. This declaration calls for the EU to 'make its voice heard in world affairs' and, as a result, it 'must have the capacity for autonomous action, backed up by credible military forces, the means to decide to use them and a readiness to do so, in order to respond to international crises'. At the same time, the declaration also makes clear that enhancing the EU's defence capabilities does not imply a challenge to NATO. On the one hand, it pledges 'conformity with our respective obligations' and points out that NATO continues to be the focal point for the collective defence of its members; on the other hand, it calls for the creation and deployment of institutional and military infrastructures upon which EU actions can rely in those cases where NATO, as a whole, is not engaged.

The major tenets of the bilateral St Malo Declaration were echoed and rendered more specific in the Presidency Conclusions of the Cologne European Council summit of June 1999, as well as that of the ensuing Helsinki European Council of December 1999. The member states pledged to create the appropriate institutional and military infrastructure for the European Security and Defence Policy (EDSP). The ESDP was to be realized and assisted by a range of new institutions and decision-making forums. A permanent body in Brussels, the Political and Security Committee (PSC), consisting of national representatives of ambassadorial rank, was to become the linchpin of the new institutional structure of the EDSP. Its task lies in monitoring the international situation, and in contributing to the definition of foreign and security policies and the monitoring of the implementation of the Council's decisions. The PSC also plays an important role in defining the strategic direction of crisis management operations and may, in this context, be authorized by the Council to take decisions on the management of a crisis. The PSC is assisted by a European Union Military Committee (EUMC), composed of Chiefs of Defence or their military representatives, and provides the PSC with advice on all military matters. Moreover, an EU Military Staff (EUMS) is installed in the Council Secretariat – consisting of seconded officials from member states, the Council Secretariat, or the Commission – to assist and work under the direction of EUMC (Reynolds 2010: 164–8). With a view to enhancing the EU's military capabilities, the member state governments decided on the so-called Helsinki Headline Goals (HHG), which set specific force targets to ensure the viability of EU-led operations. The Presidency Conclusions to the summit underline that the member states 'must be able, by 2003, to deploy within 60 days and sustain for at least 1 year military forces of up to 50,000-60,000 persons capable of the full range of Petersberg tasks'. Amidst problems in realizing these objectives and demand for addressing a broader range of defence challenges – ranging from 'war on terrorism' to campaigns involving ground troops on a larger scale – the HHG were revised in 2004 and the new Headline Goal 2010 (HG 2010) was adopted. The HG 2010 focused on 'small, rapidly deployable units capable of high intensity warfare', thereby shifting the objective from 'quantity to quality' (Howorth 2005: 192). The Nice Treaty incorporated and formalized the existence of the new institutional structure developed in between the Amsterdam and Nice Treaties. But even before the eventual ratification of the Nice Treaty, the ESDP institutions were all up and running. Moreover, in 2003, the EU launched its first military operation, a peacekeeping operation in the Former Yugoslav Republic of Macedonia, which it took over from NATO (Operation Concordia). By early 2012, no fewer than 24 civilian missions and military operations were either ongoing or completed in the ESDP context.

The Treaty of Lisbon, which entered into force in 2009, took onboard most of the changes proposed in the ill-fated Constitutional Treaty. While the 'pillar' structure introduced by the Maastricht Treaty was formally abolished, the differences in the decision-making methods were maintained, with the 'intergovernmental method' still dominating decision-making in the area now re-labelled 'Common Security and Defence Policy' (CSDP) (Title V, chapter 2, section 2 of the Consolidated Version of the TEU). Under the new treaty, the High Representative wears a 'double hat' as Vice-President of the Commission and as High Representative of the Union for Foreign and Security Policy presiding over the Foreign Affairs Council. Moreover, the High Representative will be assisted by a European External Action Service (EEAS), which is composed of seconded diplomats from the member states, Commission, and Council officials. The EEAS was inaugurated in December 2010. The EU's first High Representative, following the entry into force of the Lisbon Treaty, is Catherine Ashton.

The trajectory of the EU's security and defence policy since St Malo shows some clear trends with regard to *vertical* and *horizontal integration*. With a view to vertical integration, there is still a strong tendency to resist the centralization of decision-making competences. Yet, the fact that some of the institutional innovations, such as the PSC and the EEAS, are composed of officials from national governments and supranational actors (the Commission), suggests that decision-making may depart from its purely intergovernmental premises and display tensions between more 'intergovernmentally' and 'supranationally' oriented actors and their views – a conflict that can already be witnessed in the battles between Council, Commission, and EP over the organization of the EEAS. Nevertheless, observers are still mostly cautious in their assessments about changes in vertical integration: The institutional set-up of CSDP 'shows a growing trend towards more coordination at the EU level ... and thus represents a marginal shift from the original wholly intergovernmental model of EPC towards closer association with the established Brussels institutions' (Giegerich and Wallace 2010: 444). Turning to horizontal integration, Article 42 (6) of the Consolidated Version of the TEU introduces the instrument of 'permanent structured cooperation', which envisages that member states 'whose military capabilities fulfil higher criteria and which have made more binding commitments to one another in this area with a view to the most demanding missions shall establish permanent structured cooperation within the Union framework'. Permanent structured cooperation thus allows a core group of states meeting certain criteria – specified in Declaration No. 10 annexed to the Lisbon Treaty (e.g. budgetary commitments to military investments; deployability targets, coordinating defence means and logistics) – to enter into closer cooperation to enhance European defence capabilities. To launch this form of differentiated horizontal integration, the Council can adopt (by qualified majority) a decision establishing permanent structured cooperation and determine the list of participating member states.

Conclusion

Figure 7.1 summarizes the development of security and defence integration in its vertical and horizontal dimensions. Since the mid to late 1980s, foreign policy cooperation took place outside the formal treaty structures and expressly excluded security and defence related issues. This is also reflected in the predominance of NATO in providing for Western Europe's collective security and defence. Despite its informal quality, we classified the level of integration as 'intergovernmental coordination'. Since the 1990s we can witness some cautious moves towards more 'intergovernmental cooperation', albeit with very limited pooling. Hence, we chose an intermediate category – between intergovernmental coordination and cooperation – to refer to the changes in the Maastricht Treaty. Following the Treaty of Nice and subsequent plans to develop EU-wide defence capabilities, vertical integration

Figure 7.1   *Vertical and horizontal integration of defence policy*

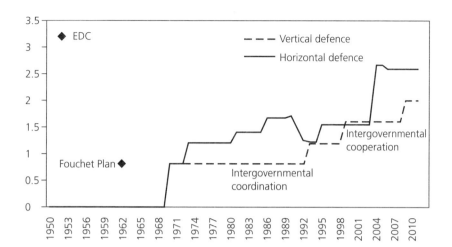

moves towards 'intergovernmental cooperation'. As a result of the latest treaty reform, security and defence policy are now firmly enshrined in CSDP. Moreover, we can witness a mounting tension between the hitherto intergovernmental decision-making structures and attempts to empower actors, such as the High Representative and the staff in the EEAS and the other permanent organizations, who may hold a more 'supranational' outlook.

With regard to horizontal integration, we witness very little internal differentiation. The only EU member state to have demanded and been granted an opt-out in the area of security and defence was Denmark in 1992. The opt-out implies that Denmark does not participate in the EU's foreign and security policy when the relevant activities carry defence implications. It also implies that Denmark does not participate in the newly-created European Defence Agency. At the same time, the introduction of opportunities for the member states to engage in 'enhanced cooperation' – and, since the Lisbon Treaty, 'permanent structured cooperation' – demonstrates that member states actively encourage moves towards promoting internal differentiation that have, yet, to be used.

The above-sketched development of security and defence integration calls for the following explanations:

- First, why and how did integration in this policy area come about? What explains the initial failure to integrate security and defence policies in Western Europe (most notably the EDC)? Compared with other policy areas, why did it take the EU member states a relatively long time to achieve fairly modest levels of vertical integra-tion in security and defence policy cooperation in the ensuing decades? Despite the ongoing dominance of the 'intergovernmental method', how can we explain the more recent shifts towards further cooperation in defence matters?

• Second, with regard to horizontal integration, it is worthwhile exploring why we observe so little internal differentiation. Why has Denmark, alone, opted out from foreign policy initiatives carrying defence implications?

How do the integration theories introduced in the first part of this book help us to better comprehend the pattern of integration in the area of defence policy? In this section, we will focus on two important episodes in the construction of a common security and defence policy. First, we explore, theoretically, the initial success that led to the signing of the EDC treaty in 1952, followed by the Treaty's prominent ratifica-tion failure in 1954. Second, we will scrutinize the answers integration theories have on offer to address the puzzle as to why, once the EDC was declared dead, it took four decades for defence to be placed on the agenda of EU policy-makers in the 1990s, and why, since 1998, there has been quite remarkable progress in institutionalizing defence coop-eration in the EU.

Explaining the European Defence Community and its Failure

In this section, we will shed light on the initial success and subse-quent ratification failure of the EDC against the backdrop of our three integration theories. We begin with intergovernmentalism, before turning to supranationalist and constructivist hypotheses. The ensuing sections are structured as follows. First, we define the observ-able implications of each theory, which means that we derive expec-tations from the theory for our empirical cases at hand. Second, we confront these theoretically derived expectations with the empirical record offered by the literature and assess the plausibility of the dif-ferent integration theories.

Intergovernmentalism

In the case of the EDC, what should we observe if intergovernmen-talism offered a convincing explanation for integration (and its failure), as well as differentiation?

- The decision of the founding members of the ECSC to press for a common European army would need to be accounted for by a critical increase in interdependence among the 'Six' and the convergence of their welfare- or security-related preferences in the early 1950s. Supranational centralization and the concomitant waiving of unilateral defence policy options should be considered by governments if they expect that defence cooperation will be highly beneficial to them, and if individual member states were to have unilateral incentives to fail to comply with the rules laid down in the treaty.
- An intergovernmentalist explanation for the rejection of the EDC Treaty by the French National Assembly in August 1954 would be based on the following considerations: changes in the geopolitical or economic environment that would have adverse effects on the expected gains of integration and reduce the positive economic or security externalities, thereby rendering the creation of a European military force less beneficial.
- Intergovernmentalists would also argue that the reluctance of the British government to join the EDC is due to an insufficient level of international interdependence. Britain's size as an economically and militarily potent European country would lead intergovernmentalists to expect that the autonomy and sovereignty costs incurred from integration in the security and defence field would prove prohibitively high and, hence, work against renouncing unilateral military and defence options.

Realist intergovernmentalism. As we have argued in the case of monetary policy, realist intergovernmentalists consider it highly unlikely that states give up sovereignty in an area that symbolizes 'high politics' like no other: the ability of a state to defend itself against outside threats. In the ensuing section, we discuss the realist intergovernmentalist argument that the initial 'success' of the EDC can be accounted for by *internal* as well as *external balancing*.

According to realist intergovernmentalism, the success (and failure) of the EDC can be explained by balance of power politics, which encompass both external and internal balancing. Turning to *external balancing* first, Western Europe faced an 'overwhelming competitor' (Rosato 2011: 105) in terms of the global distribution of military power and resources – the Soviet Union. Only when Western European states stood together, would they have the capacity to establish an effective balancing coalition *vis-à-vis* the Soviet Union (Rosato 2011: 105). With mounting fears that a Soviet attack were to leave Western Europe more or less defenceless, the US government shifted its policy from focusing on promoting economic recovery in Western Europe to planning European (including German) rearmament. The Prague coup in 1948, the Berlin blockade in 1948–49, the successful test of a Soviet nuclear bomb in 1949, and – ultimately – the outbreak of the Korean War in 1950, prompted the US government to put the issue of German rearmament on top of the security policy agenda. The external threat emanating from the Soviet Union and its high military capabilities thus fuelled attempts to balance externally – which implied, among other things, that West Germany had to be a part of the balancing coalition.

These dynamics, and the US government's decision to move forward with German rearmament in particular, triggered moves towards *internal balancing*, primarily to address French security concerns. Establishing a favourable balance of power – not only *vis-à-vis* the Soviet Union (external balancing), but also with a view to West Germany (internal balancing) – was a core objective of French postwar foreign policy (Rosato 2011: 124). Historians have underlined that the prospect of German rearmament 'gripped the Quai d'Orsay' (Hitchcock 1997: 610). Once the US government shifted its attention to German rearmament, the French government's objective, to maximize France's autonomy by keeping Germany's economic and political development under allied control, was no longer a viable option. The Pleven Plan was introduced against the background of a rapidly shifting geopolitical context, and the acknowledgement that Germany would ultimately regain its sovereignty and military forces. The slogan 'EDC or Wehrmacht!' espoused the notion that France could only meet its security needs *vis-à-vis* Germany by creating a European army under the command of a supranational defence authority, which would allow for a joint control of German military forces (Hitchcock 1998). To reduce the perceived uncertainty that emanated from the prospect of a rearmed Germany, the French government pressed for co-binding ECSC-like institutions and, hence, for far-reaching levels of *vertical* integration: the creation of a multinational army under European command, which – at the same time – offered sufficient controls to delimit independent military action on behalf of Germany.

The internal balancing argument also offers a plausible explanation for the decision by the German government to sign up to the EDC. For the German government under Chancellor Konrad Adenauer, the most important foreign policy objective was to achieve political equality by a revision, and eventual termination, of the Occupation Statute to end allied control over Germany's internal and external policy-making (Rosato 2011: 123). The ECSC treaty negotiations, which were up and running by the time the Pleven Plan was tabled, marked a crucial step towards this objective. Germany was accepted as equal partner in the concert of European states, which jointly agreed to delimit their sovereignty in all matters relating to coal and steel. Even though it may appear counterintuitive, the prospect of relinquishing sovereignty in the area of coal and steel and, subsequently, in the military field, was the precondition to obtain sovereignty in matters of external – foreign and security – policy matters. The partial delegation of sovereignty along-side other states' commitment to do likewise constituted a promising avenue for Germany to gain self-government over its external affairs. For France, given the external Soviet threat und uncertainty about the US commitment to defend Western Europe in case of a Soviet attack, surrendering military independence seemed to lower the security threat emanating from Germany. For Germany, there was no military independence to surrender, but – ultimately – an army and autonomy over its external policy to gain (Hitchcock 1998: 168).

Turning to horizontal integration, why did the UK not join the EDC? For the British government, the realization of the EDC did not imply a challenge to its security, rather the contrary. Britain, as well as the US government, came to endorse the EDC as 'a method of safely arming the Federal Republic' and 'also [as] a vitally necessary means of cementing the Bonn Republic's full political and military alignment with the West' (Ruane 2000: 10). Against this background, the EDC was not perceived as a competitor or threat to the transatlantic alliance (NATO), of which all EDC signatories – with the exception of Germany – were members. According to the EDC Treaty, the deployment of troops under the banner of the EDC had to take place in accordance with NATO strategy and under the responsibility of the Supreme Allied Commander in Europe (SACEUR). While it is often argued that the British government's suspicion regarding any cooperative arrangement carrying 'federalist' or 'supranational' features was an anathema, the government's calculus when evaluating the proposals for joining the ECSC and EDC was strongly affected by security considerations. Throughout 1951–52, the British Foreign Office argued that, for 'strategic' reasons, both economic- and security-related, joining EDC was out of question. The Schuman and Pleven Plans were seen as means to strengthen the continent's economy and provide for its defence, both of which were in the economic and security interest of Britain. Rosato argues that the British government 'took comfort in the knowledge that in the event of a Soviet attack the United States would return in force and rescue them at acceptable cost' (Rosato 2011: 155). Even though this did not mean that the UK was invulnerable, the British government considered itself to be more secure than France and Germany (Rosato 2011: 155). Moreover, a common European defence scheme of which Britain was not a member was seen to generate no negative externalities. The Labour government under Clement Attlee, and later the Conservative government under Sir Winston Churchill, endorsed the non-membership policy (Ruane 2000: 27–8). Yet, the EDC signatories and the British government agreed that Britain should be closely associated with the EDC. An 'association-not-membership' formula was developed and foresaw joint security guarantees by NATO and EDC as implying that 'an attack on one grouping would be considered an attack on the other. This would mean that ... German aggression against France could not be dismissed as an intra-EDC issue from which Britain and the United States ... could remain aloof' (Ruane 2000, 31). The British government thus agreed to the signing of an Anglo-EDC treaty, which envisaged the provision of automatic military assistance. 'Anything more', Foreign Secretary Anthony Eden warned, 'risked *de facto* membership of a federal Europe' (Ruane 2000, 34). This episode supports our intergovernmentalist conjecture for *horizontal* integration: Britain neither opted for membership in the EDC, nor openly opposed the EDC since no sizable negative externalities were expected to incur once the EDC was in place.

Finally, we have to answer the following question: Why was the EDC not ratified by the French National Assembly? Following realist intergovernmentalist reasoning and its corollary, balance of power politics, we argue that the French government preferred military integration (and hence the EDC) over the creation of an independent West German military force (Rosato 2011: 138). Yet, reservations about the EDC Treaty had been voiced in French political quarters even before the ink was dry. From an internal balancing perspective, the EDC could not provide a guarantee to French policy-makers that Germany would not defect from the agreement. If it did, it would have gained a military that could pose an immediate security threat to France (Rosato 2011: 138–40). From a balancing perspective, then, the most favourable alternative to the EDC for France 'was to secure a strong American presence on the continent and rearm Germany within the Atlantic alliance system' (Rosato 2011, 145), implying that both Britain and the USA carried the potential to counter-balance Germany effectively. Moreover, the NATO option implied that France would not have to surrender its sovereignty in military matters. Hitchcock argues that, during the course of only two years, a majority of French legislators and policy-makers came to the assessment that the EDC gave away too much of France's sovereignty in security and defence affairs (Hitchcock 1998: 5). The French government under Prime Minister Pierre Mendès France thus decided to change track. It sacrificed the EDC by submitting it to a vote it knew would fail, and then presented a solution to the 'German question' bringing Germany into NATO while maintaining restrictions and German military capacity and general staff through the extension of the Brussels Treaty Organisation, which subsequently became the WEU. At the same time, this arrangement freed France from the constraints on its military sovereignty that the implementation of EDC would have entailed (Hitchcock 1998: 170; Rosato 2011: 146–7).

Why did the French government alter its assessment of the costs and benefits of supranational integration? Hitchcock emphasizes the importance of geopolitical events in the period between 1952 and 1954. The death of Stalin in 1953 led to hopes about an improvement of East–West relations and 'slowed progress on the EDC' (Hitchcock 1998: 182). Another geopolitical development that stalled the EDC and occupied French domestic politics for most of the latter half of 1953 was the rapidly deteriorating military situation of French troops in Indochina, which also led to fears that a new *Dien Bien Phu*, which became emblematic for the French military disaster in Vietnam, could arise in Europe, leaving France defenceless (Hitchcock 1998: 191). As a result, the belief that the EDC was the only viable alternative against a resurging German *Wehrmacht* lost appeal and momentum. Prime Minister Mendès France, supported by the British government under Winston Churchill, developed an alternative to the EDC that involved integrating Germany into NATO via the WEU – the fate for the EDC was finally sealed (see Rosato 2011: 142–51).

Liberal intergovernmentalism. According to liberal intergovernmentalism, governments opt for policy coordination when economic interdependence reaches critical levels such that, for example, internationally competitive producer groups push governments to liberalize trade. Following this line of argumentation, domestic interest groups representing the armament industry would push for defence integration if this furthered their economic interest. The empirical record suggests that armament producers played a negligible role, favouring German rearmament and Franco-German cooperation over a supranational defence community, since French industry would lack competitiveness in a supranational arrangement, including a common procurement policy (Rosato 2011: 164–5). This suggests, furthermore, that, in the phase prior to the signing of the EDC Treaty, governments were pressing for defence integration while domestic interest groups were hesitant, which does not permit concluding that they were driving the process of integration. If we extend the interest group argument to a broader domestic politics argument, including key actors in the politico-administrative realm to explain government preferences for security and defence integration, liberal intergovernmentalists would argue that top-level military staff and executive actors in the defence ministries should react to heightened levels of security interdependence in the light of an overwhelming external or internal security threat by supporting EDC. However, it is argued that top-level French military staff did not endorse the supranational EDC solution (Milner 1997).

Turning to ratification failure, the lack of support from the French military is also considered crucial to explain this outcome. Helen Milner argues that ratification depends on the 'presence or absence of endorsement from important domestic actors' (Milner 1997: 200) such as well-organized interest groups. In the case of the EDC, domestic actors failed to endorse the Treaty; the French military in particular was ferociously in opposition to the EDC Treaty. This lack of endorsement is considered to be the result of successive French govern-ments' lack of willingness to make side payments to these actors in an attempt to win the military over to supporting the EDC. Furthermore, mounting divisions inside the French government in the period pre-ceding Premier Mendès France's lacklustre attempt to ratify the EDC treaty constituted a growing obstacle for successful ratification. In the period 1953–54, the centre of gravity of the governing coalitions shifted to the right, thereby undermining the parliamentary majority in the National Assembly in support of ratification (see Milner 1997: 197–200). In sum, neither domestic interest groups nor critical levels of security interdependence were decisive in explaining the French govern-ment's push towards EDC. When it comes to explaining why the Treaty failed to be ratified in France, Milner cites, inter alia, the lack of interest group support and the importance of coalitional shifts, which made the ratification outcome less likely. These arguments offer support for a liberal intergovernmentalist interpretation of ratification failure.

Supranationalism

Supranationalists argue that the main factors driving European integra-tion are the scope and intensity of transnational exchanges, as well as the preferences and capacity of supranational actors to advance an integrationist agenda in a given policy area.

- Supranationalists expect that the push for security and defence inte-gration originates from transnationally operating defence industry actors who see benefits in the creation of a common market for armaments production by exploiting economies of scale and enhancing their profitability.
- Furthermore, the logic of functional spillover leads supranational-ists to expect that there will be a demand for further integration if the gains resulting from integration in a particular policy sector remain sub-optimal, unless adjacent policy sectors will also be inte-grated. This logic implies that integration of the coal and steel sectors, which had been launched only a few months prior to the presentation of the Pleven Plan, should have had a formative impact (spillover) on the debate to integrate national defence policies and forces.
- Moreover, supranationalists expect that the pro-integration prefer-ences, decision-making capacity, and the discretion of supranational actors promote security and defence cooperation.

The empirical record suggests that none of these factors has been deci-sive in explaining the success and failure of the EDC. First, in the decades following World War II, market liberalization in the area of defence was an anathema, since defence firms were state-owned and, hence, dependent on their governments to build up and support national armaments programmes. Lacking opportunities for, and incentives to engage in transnational exchange, the defence industry did not press domestic or supranational policy-makers to promote European-wide market-making measures (institutional spillover). As we will show, this situation began to change once the Cold War came to an end (Fligstein 2008; Mörth and Britz 2004). Second, the logic of functional spillover is not instructive in accounting for the rapid move from integration in the coal and steel sectors to a common defence policy and army. It is not clear, theoretically, why and how the benefits from integrating national coal and steel markets would remain suboptimal unless the member state governments of the prospective ECSC created a common multinational military force. Empirically, we have illustrated above that the French government was pressing for the EDC once German rearmament became imminent following the outbreak of the Korean War in June 1950. The French government was at pains to define an initiative that would be in sync with its security concerns. The parallel discussions on the ECSC did not affect the initial decision to launch the Pleven Plan. Third, given that the ECSC organs had not even been decided upon when the Pleven Plan was issued (let alone operational), supranational actors, such as the High Authority and Common Assembly, could not take any initiative to press for further integration in new policy sectors.

Constructivism

In contrast to intergovernmentalism and supranationalism, constructivism stresses the primacy of ideational structures over material (economic and geopolitical) structures and emphasizes that social action follows a 'logic of appropriateness', rather than a 'logic of consequences'. From a constructivist perspective, we argue that several factors influence differentiation in European integration. The extent of consensus over the course of integration is the central factor and depends not only on sector-specific ideational consensus, contestation, and relevance, but also on domestic ratification constraints. In addition, it has been demonstrated in Chapter 4 that argumentation and socialization effects matter when it comes to account for explaining negotiation outcomes and institutionalization. What do constructivists expect with regard to the success and failure of the EDC?

- If constructivism possesses explanatory leverage, the initial success of EDC should be rooted in a strong ideational consensus among the member states' governments negotiating the EDC Treaty. This consensus is based on the notion that a European approach – the creation of a multinational military force – is the most appropriate way to organize and implement defence policy combined with a highly centralized system of decision-making whereby authority is vested in a supranational Commissariat and a European Defence Minister.

- Conversely, constructivists attribute the failure to ratify the EDC in France to a faltering domestic consensus and, hence, mounting domestic contestation over the appropriateness of a European solution in defence matters. In this context, constructivists also argue that policy-makers critical of a supranational military should have been successful in framing the EDC as an 'identity issue' that appealed to fundamental domestic (instead of European) community values and norms, and in construing the autonomy of the French army as symbol of national independence.

- The incompatibility between domestic and community norms, as well as the portrayal of the EDC as a domestic identity issue, should have also played a role in accounting for the British government's reluctance to subscribe to the supranational defence arrangement in the first place.

Whereas realist intergovernmentalists see the initial move towards EDC as a response of policy-makers to shifts in the geopolitical environment and heightened levels of security interdependence, constructivists conceptualize elite agreement on the EDC as the expression of an ideational consensus among key policy-makers. Even though a 'community environment' with supranational decision-making structures was absent prior to the setting up of the ECSC, it has been argued in the literature that informal transnational policy networks have played an important role in promoting an ideational consensus on the quality and substantive form of European integration. Research by Wolfram Kaiser and collaborators posits that the most relevant actors in postwar European integration were the leaders of political parties in Europe, who operated transnationally and shared the same ideological affiliation: 'Only they could use the various channels to translate transnationally deliberated and negotiated ideas and policies into national governmental policy-making and European-level decision-making' (Kaiser 2007: 8–9). More specifically, he argues that Christian democratic parties assumed a 'hegemonic' position in shaping the European integration agenda, and in forming a consensus on the nature and form of European integration in the postwar era (Kaiser 2007). In the early 1950s, Christian democrats were the dominant political party in the ECSC founding states – with the exception of France, where the electoral support of the *Mouvement Républicain Populaire* (MRP) was in steady decline. Congruent with our construc-

tivist expectations, Kaiser argues that the glue for transnational cooperation between Christian democrats was a shared 'ideological predis-
position' (Kaiser 2001) that helped spur supranational integration in
Europe. Postwar Christian democrats throughout Western Europe
shared a set of principled ideas and norms that sided well with the
notion delegating sovereignty to the European level. Christian democrats subscribe to the idea of subsidiarity, which is a hallmark of
Catholic social doctrine, they accept the 'quasi-supranational'
authority of the Church exercised by the Pope, and they engage in a
discourse linking the exigencies of integration with the experiences of
the early-medieval organization of secular authority in the Frankish
Empire. This set of ideas and ideological predispositions facilitated a
convergence of preferences in favour of supranational integration. Via
the informal Christian democratic transnational party network, which
regularly assembled top-level politicians in the co-called 'Geneva
Circle', the Christian democratic political leadership – dominated by
Konrad Adenauer, Robert Schuman, and Alcide De Gasperi – was in a
position not only to debate and define common objectives, but also
effectively to set the policy agenda on matters of European integration
(Kaiser 2007; Kaiser and Leucht 2008: 39–42).

Congruent with these claims, Craig Parsons (2002; 2003) argues
that ideational factors possess more explanatory leverage to explain the
EDC than 'materialist' accounts, which accord primacy to geopolitical
(or economic) structures. While Kaiser stresses the emerging consensus
among Christian democratic political leaders, facilitated by a deliberative forum such as the 'Geneva Circle', Parsons explores the nature of
contestation of the 'Community' idea in French domestic politics. He
argues that there was all but a domestic consensus on how France's
security concerns should be best addressed, let alone interpreted.
Sharing the constructivist premise that 'actors interpret their interests
through ideas that can vary independently from their objective positions' (Parsons 2002: 50), he probes the causal effect of ideas on policy
preferences by focusing on instances where ideas cut across different
groups of actors who faced similar material ('objective') conditions:
'Take two French diplomats, with similar social backgrounds and
party sympathies, in the same office of the foreign ministry in 1950.
One insists on French interests in a new 'supranational' Franco-
German federation; the other sees French interests in policies based on
an informal partnership with Britain. These similarly placed individuals face *all* the same objective pressures but seem to interpret them
differently' (Parsons 2002: 51, emphasis in the original). Parsons
demonstrates that different sets of ideas about European institution
building – traditionalist, confederal, and community notions of cooperation – were all viable in the domestic political debate in France
(Parsons 2002: 57–8; see also Ruane 2000: 19). He goes on to argue

that geopolitical (and hence intergovernmentalist) explanations of the EDC put too much emphasis on the effect of exogenous events (such as the war in Korea and the concomitant prospect of German rearmament) in explaining the French move towards EDC. Forming a supranational military force was by no means the 'natural' response to this challenge: 'All else equal, the French were selecting between outcomes as divergent as a European Army and simple German entry into NATO' (Parsons 2002: 63).

It follows from this discussion that there was no domestic consensus in France in favour of the 'community' solution by opting for a supranational EDC. What is more, the domestic debate over the EDC in France demonstrated vividly that defence policy was clearly an identity issue arousing hefty and passionate debates in the political and public arenas. Pro-European and anti-European camps formed and confronted each other. While the former pleaded for the formation of a European state to overcome national idiosyncrasies and lay the foundation for a European identity, the latter continued to see the nation-state as focal point for identity constructions and the sole legitimate carrier of national sovereignty (see Parsons 2003: 82–3). These findings also corroborate the constructivist expectation that policies construed as identity issues mobilize domestic opposition to European integration. Maurice Faure, a pro-EDC politician illustrates this point vividly: '[W]ith the EDC we were stirring up sacred things: the flag, the blood' (cited in Parsons 2003: 82). The final vote in the National Assembly, which brought the EDC to its fall, was even characterized to have taken place 'in a near-hysterical atmosphere' (Parsons 2003: 80).

How do constructivists approach the question of *horizontal* integration, i.e. British reluctance to sign up to the EDC? The situation in the UK was characterized by the existence of a strong domestic consensus, which was sceptical of supranational or even 'federalist' experiments (mirroring the British domestic debate on the ECSC) and which touched upon key tenets of what policy-makers came to construe as British political identity. The federal conception of European cooperation and integration, the fusing of domestic sovereignty, the autonomous decision-making capacity of supranational organs – all of these notions were an anathema to the vast majority of British policy-makers and public opinion alike. As Anthony Eden (Foreign Secretary under Prime Minister Winston Churchill) was reported to have said, even though Britain supported the continental states in their efforts to bring the EDC to life, joining the EDC was 'something we know, in our bones, we cannot do' (cited in Ruane 2000: 22). The principled objection against supranational integration is often cited as a sufficient cause for the government to reject EDC membership (Ruane 2000: 22). Other factors, as we have seen in the previous section, are more in line with intergovernmentalist expectations, as they link the government's security interests with 'Britain's position as a world power with extensive overseas commitments to uphold, an important relationship with the Commonwealth to maintain and a central position in the Sterling Area to protect' (Ruane 2000: 22). Hence, constructivism and intergovernmentalism both offer plausible conjectures about Britain's reluctance to join the EDC: a strong and principled ideational consensus among domestic elites and the public alike against subscribing to a federal Europe, buttressed by geostrategic (and economic) factors that stood against joining the supranational project. A close association in security and defence matters with the prospective EDC signatories, which eventually resulted in Britain joining the WEU, enabled the British government to maintain its sovereignty for both principled and instrumental rationales.

Explaining St Malo: The Return of Defence Policy

In this section, we employ our different theoretical perspectives to account for a fundamental shift in the integration project towards closer cooperation and integration in the defence sector. Since the failure of the EDC, defence cooperation in the EU context was a non-issue until the 1990s. While NATO had occupied the defence plane since the EDC-project was buried, the EU had made cautious moves towards foreign policy coordination and cooperation, which had only be formalized with the entry into force of the SEA. The end of the Cold War and the wars in the Balkans were catalysts for the establishment of the CFSP in Maastricht. At that point, defence cooperation and collective crisis management were still considered NATO's *domaine reservé*. Yet, this notion was gradually fading. The Franco-British St Malo summit declaration of 1998 is often considered a breakthrough in this regard, since it reversed the hitherto very cautious approach of the EU towards defence policy by calling for the establishment of military capabilities for autonomous action. How can we explain this shift, which is reflected in cautious moves towards enhanced (*vertical*) integration? Turning to *horizontal* integration, the move towards closer defence cooperation has thus far produced one case of an EU member state deciding to opt out: Denmark does not partake financially or operationally in any EU-sponsored actions and missions that carry defence implications. What leverage do our integration theories possess to account for cases of opt-outs in general, and the Danish opt-out in particular?

Intergovernmentalism

What expectations can we derive from intergovernmentalism to account for the St Malo initiative and the subsequent advances in defence integration?

- According to intergovernmentalism, the French and British governments expected positive economic or security externalities to accrue from extending integration to the defence field. More concretely, intergovernmentalists expect governments to alter their stance towards defence cooperation as a result of external events or geopolitical shifts that threaten to undermine domestic security or autonomy.
- How would intergovernmentalists go about explaining the governments' choices to delimit integration in the defence field by keeping decision-making intergovernmental, instead of delegating or pooling authority? The preferred level of pooling and delegation depends on the value governments place on the issues and substantive outcomes in question, and on their uncertainty about the future behaviour of other governments. The more a government benefits from a centralizing decision-making authority in the area of security and defence, and the higher the risk of non-compliance by other governments, the higher is its readiness to cede competences to the EU to prevent potential losers from revising the policy.
- With regard to *horizontal* integration, intergovernmentalists argue that opt-outs or arrangements for 'enhanced cooperation' can be accounted for by the variation in state preferences, i.e. differentiation is deemed beneficial, since it allows states to opt for a level of integration that corresponds to their level of interdependence and their preferences. Moreover, differentiation is easier to come by if it produces no, or very few, negative externalities for the actors concerned.

Realist intergovernmentalism. Barry Posen (2006) and Seth Jones (2007) address these questions from the perspective of realist intergovernmentalism. Both argue that the EU's choice to enhance integration in the area of defence is a response to the demise of 'bipolarity' after the end of the Cold War and the emergence of a 'unipolar' system dominated by the USA. Even though Europe's power position improved following the political transformations in the Soviet Union and its former satellite states, the power position of the USA improved even more: 'Europe is collectively much stronger relative to Russia now than it was; it is weaker relative to the United States than it was' (Posen 2006: 153). Changes in relative power positions generate uncertainty among the weaker states on how the stronger states will deploy (or not deploy) their superior capabilities. This does not necessarily imply that the greatest power will pose a direct military threat to the weaker states: it may simply mean that the weaker states are increasingly uncertain about the intentions and plans of the stronger states as the latter's options increase with superior power capabilities. Posen (2006) and Jones (2007) claim that the status of the USA as leading world power makes it 'an unreliable partner' for European states and their ambitions in the field of security and defence. This is not because Europeans fear that the US government garners malign intentions towards them. Rather, European states are motivated to improve their military capabilities in ways that make them less security dependent on the USA to meet their imminent security threats, i.e. political instabilities in its immediate neighbourhood, such as the recurrent crises in the Balkans or the prospect for crises in North Africa (Jones 2007: 182, 197).

The response realist intergovernmentalists thus expect from European states is one of 'soft' or 'weak' *external balancing* against the stronger state, the USA, by building up capabilities and by forming a balancing alliance (Posen 2006: 184; Jones 2007: 198–200). To overcome security dependence on the USA, 'unilateralism' – i.e. relying on, or building up, national military forces – is not seen as an option, as this would perpetuate the security dependence on the United States of the major European powers. The same holds for exclusive reliance on NATO. And, indeed, with the USA shifting its focus on other regions in the world, such as Asia and the Middle East, and given its increasing reluctance to deploy troops to 'small-scale problems in Europe' (Jones 2007: 198), continued reliance on the USA through NATO was a worrisome prospect in the eyes of European governments. In fact, NATO operations in Bosnia and Kosovo have highlighted a rift in security interests between the USA and European powers. While the former did not consider the Balkans to be of strategic importance, which was reflected in US unwillingness to commit ground troops, European states were ill-equipped in military terms and politically not in a position to go it alone. This left a third, *European*, option to lessen security dependence on the United States. Realist intergovernmentalists see the St Malo initiative in this light since the Franco-British St Malo summit meeting 'jumpstarted the construction of European Union military forces that could act independently of NATO and the United States' (Jones 2007: 200). The result has been the gradual build-up of 'low-end' military capacity to respond to the threats faced by European states: humanitarian disasters and conflicts in Europe's immediate vicinity. To meet these strategic and operational challenges, European states decided to create a rapid reaction force and rapidly deployable battle groups, together with a political-military structure to decide on, implement, and command peace-keeping and humanitarian operations headed by the EU.

Liberal intergovernmentalism. To account for advances in integration, liberal intergovernmentalism points at the importance of heightened levels of interdependence, levels of preference homogeneity among member state governments, and demand of domestic interest groups. We have already highlighted that the preferences between EU member states and the USA on what kind of military operations were in their respective 'strategic interest' diverged strongly throughout the 1990s. The experience of the wars in the Balkans created a situation in which the EU member states realized that they could no longer 'free ride' on the USA deploying its troops to address and meet the security objectives of EU member states. Lacking superior bargaining power, the EU member states saw themselves compelled to opt for closer defence cooperation, which also implied an investment in defence capabilities. Contrary to the realist intergovernmentalist argument, European security dependence on the USA did not trigger an external balancing strategy, since the USA neither constituted a security threat nor was a competitor to the EU. Instead, the negative security externalities emanating from European security dependence on the USA forced member states to opt for a European response, which can be interpreted as a form of internal differentiation within NATO (not directed against the USA and NATO) in order to realize European security objectives. The US government accepted the move towards ESDP because it created no negative security externalities on its part. From the liberal intergovernmentalist perspective, the move towards ESDP can thus be accounted for by an increase in preference heterogeneity between the USA and EU member states, and the concomitant attempt by EU member states to redress a situation whereby 'free riding' on the USA was no longer possible (Weiss 2011).

What is the liberal intergovernmentalist answer to the question as to why the EU governments opted for limited pooling and delegation in the area of security and defence? According to liberal intergovernmentalism, the level of pooling and delegation depends on the value governments place on the issues and substantive outcomes in question, and on their uncertainty about the future behaviour of other governments. The more a government benefits from a cooperative agreement, and the higher the risks of non-compliance by other governments, the higher is its readiness to cede competences to the EU to prevent potential losers from revising the policy. While uncertainty about the US government's commitment to helping Europeans solve their security and defence problems triggered the move towards deepening security and defence cooperation in the EU, we still need to account for EU member states' preferences about the desired level of vertical integration. Moritz Weiss (2011) argues that EU governments were less concerned with the potential for opportunism or non-compliance of their European partners than with assessments of the governance costs associated with establishing and running new institutions, and deploying EU-specific military assets. France, for instance, 'was faced with a low level of opportunistic risks' emanating from either Germany or the UK (Weiss 2011: 160). The French government was fairly certain about the level of commitment displayed by Germany and Britain to engage in the development of joint military capabilities. This low risk of opportunism also implied that France did not wish to bind Germany and the UK more strongly in institutional terms, thereby relinquishing unilateral control of security and defence policy-related decisions. However, when the ESDP was actually established in the period between 1998–99, the French government harboured some concerns 'about potential exploitation by Germany and sudden abandonment by a Britain that would in the end side with the Americans rather than Europe' (Weiss 2011: 166). This prompted the French government to demand more binding commitments and agreements with its partners. Short of delegating new competences to EU institutions, the French government preferred to retain its veto option and, hence, keep the institutional decision-making structure of ESDP largely intergovernmental. Yet, in order to improve the flow of information and improve the capacities for policy coordination, some limited reinforcement of the institutions was considered beneficial (see Weiss 2011: 166–7), which helps to explain the moderate shift in vertical integration.

What impact did domestic interest groups have on the timing and content of the St Malo initiative, and the move towards ESDP? The literature seems rather straightforward since 'there is no evidence that domestic-level groups have ever mobilized for or against the development of ESDP' (Reynolds 2010: 65; see also Mérand 2006). Yet, as we will demonstrate when discussing the explanatory potential of supranationalism, it is not inconceivable that the development of competitive defence firms could play an important role in affecting the course of defence integration in the EU in the long-term future.

What is the liberal intergovernmentalist explanation for the Danish opt-out? In the absence of externalities from differentiation, we expect differentiation to be easy to negotiate. This appears to be the case with Denmark. Even though Denmark and other EU member states hold different preferences with regard to the conduct of their defence policies, the action of neither actor has negative effects on the other. Moreover, even if Danish opt-out would be conceived of as free riding, generating negative externalities for the EU states providing the collective good 'security', institutional factors can affect the bargaining power of the 'free rider' making differentiation easier to negotiate: For example, high ratification constraints, such as the credible threat of holding (and losing) a referendum may compel the other EU member states to consent to differentiation, rather than jeopardize defence integration altogether. The Danish opt-out, which it obtained following a failed referendum campaign, can be accounted for in these terms.

Supranationalism

Supranationalists attribute importance to transnational and supranational actors in advancing integration. What expectations for the breakthrough to the ESDP can we derive from supranationalist integration theory?

- Given the limited decision-making capacity and discretion of the Commission, the European Parliament, and the Court in the area of security and defence, we expect the impact of supranational actors on advancing integration and exploiting spillover potentials to be very modest.
- Integration can also be spurred if transnationally operating defence firms have an interest in expanding the reach of supranational rules. Transnational actors, such as business corporations in the defence industry sector, tend to push for further integration if they expect to benefit from the creation of common European forces and an EU-level policy for military procurement.

Does supranationalism fare better at explaining the establishment of a European defence policy at the turn of the century than the failed move towards building a multi-national European army in the 1950s? It is suggested in the literature that some of the factors crucial for European integration to unfold its transformative impact, while absent in the 1950s, are present fifty years later. For example, supranational actors, such as the European Commission, have begun to press more strongly for integration in the field of security and defence policy. Hanna Ojanen (2006) argues that even the moderate inclusion of supranational actors in the EU's security and defence policy, as well as the potential for complex issue-linkages, begets the potential for spillover and, thus, further integration. The Commission has been actively exploiting its competences 'in the slice of defence that is linked to the common market, trade, procurement and co-operation within the armaments industry' (Ojanen 2006: 65). On the civilian side of conflict prevention, crisis management, and peace-building, the Commission assumes an increasingly important role. On the basis of the so-called 'rapid-reaction mechanism', based on a Council regulation, the EU finances civilian tasks to avoid crises in Latin America, Africa, and Asia. The Commission is responsible for the implementation, coordination, and evaluation of this mechanism. Given the recent creation of the European External Action Service, the Commission is likely to become 'a major partner in ... conflict management and prevention, were it to assume a strong position in the development of the EU diplomatic service' (Ojanen 2006: 65).

Moreover, supranationalists expect that the Commission will push for extending the rules of the Common Market to the area of defence – which is shielded from international competition, given distinct national security concerns and agendas. The Commission is expected to adopt 'a more proactive role in promoting defence industrial cooperation in Europe, opening the market and increasing competition' (Ojanen 2006: 65) According to Ulrika Mörth (2003), the creation of a common market for armaments was precisely what the Commission had planned and pushed for since the mid-1990s. Politically and discursively, the Commission attempted to impose a 'market frame' onto defence policy to exercise influence in an area that has 'traditionally been framed as a ... security issue' (Mörth 2003: 84). Akin to the Commission's role in promoting the SEA, the objective pursued by the Commission in the area of armaments is to establish a common set of rules and standards within the defence industrial sector, and to establish a more coordinated European industry policy in this area. From the purview of supranationalism, it could be argued that the creation of the European Defence Agency (EDA) in 2004 is, at least, a partial response to meeting this challenge. One of the EDA's key tasks is to promote European defence-relevant research and technology, which involves coordinating national efforts in research and technological development, as well as promoting the restructuring of the European defence industry to match the political demand for coordinated military action with the supply in forms of high-quality, interoperable defence material.

It has to be noted, however, that closer cooperation and integration in the area of military procurement has to be seen as a response to the rising demand for multinational and multi-functional military forces, which has been triggered by governmental and not by supranational actors: 'The political process toward a European armaments policy has ... been dependent on the general CSFP process and the political break-through that came with the Amsterdam Treaty' (Mörth 2003: 56). Yet, as we have seen, the Commission depicted cooperation in the defence industry as a necessity, given the concomitant demand for interoperability and standardization to act effectively in a military context. Moreover, fifty years after the failure of the EDC, the renewed emphasis on common defence capabilities has been received very favourably by the defence industry, which has supported the creation of the EDA, and is a strong supporter of ESDP and a staunch ally of the Commission in its intent to promote multinational projects for military procurement – such as the transport aircraft A400M, or the Galileo positioning system (the European response to the US-developed GPS) (see Mérand 2008: 142–3, 146; see also Fligstein 2008).

Constructivism

The expectations that can be derived from constructivism to account for the St Malo initiative and ESDP can be summarized as follows:

- Advances in defence integration result from the emergence of an ideational consensus among the member states governments pressing most vehemently for enhanced defence cooperation in the EU, i.e. France and the UK. The emerging ideational consensus is, *inter alia*, the result of socialization among the actors involved most closely and frequently in EU foreign and security policy cooperation.
- Successful integration in the defence sector contributes to the further institutionalization of shared ideas on the desirability and institutional design of a common European defence policy. This, in turn, increases commonality and compatibility of these ideas among the relevant actors in the defence policy area. This process re-enforces the integration process and may beget further integration.
- Opt-outs from individual countries in defence cooperation reflect the strength of these countries' (exclusive) national identity, a lack of commonality and compatibility of domestic with European policy ideas, the (domestic) construction of defence policy as an identity issue, as well as domestic ratification constraints, such as referenda. Similarly, constructivists see the establishment of the opportunity for enhanced cooperation – and, hence, the potential for enhancing EU-wide differentiation – as a consequence of an increase in the variation of the strength of national identities, commonly held values, norms, and policy ideas, as well as the construction and perception of defence as an identity issue.

What does constructivism contribute to explaining ESDP? Is the progress of integration driven by an ideational consensus, based on an EU-wide 'strategic culture' (Meyer 2005)? Meyer argues that EU member states are characterized by different 'strategic cultures', which implies that their 'national security and defence policies rest on deep-seated norms, beliefs and ideas about the appropriate use of force' (Meyer 2005: 523). Recently, scholars have come to ask whether, and under what conditions, differences in national strategic cultures persist, or converge, towards a *European* strategic culture (Meyer 2005), or the formation of a European 'defence field' (Mérand 2006, 2008) replacing or complementing different national defence fields. According to Meyer (2005: 529–31), differences in national strategic cultures are rooted in differences about objectives for and instruments of the use of force, as well as differences in modes of cooperation (e.g. based on neutrality, cooperation with preferred partners, or on multilateral treaties/international rules). Similarly, Mérand posits that European defence policy represents a 'conflict of visions' and 'state traditions' among the member states that hold different ideas about the objectives to be pursued through

ESDP: 'For the French, ESDP must lead to European *defence*; for the Germans, it serves to further European *integration*; for the British, it must remain a *policy*' (Mérand 2008: 141; emphasis in the original).

Given these differences in domestically-held ideas and visions, how can the move towards ESDP be explained? Since the norms and values that underwrite national security cultures tend to be relatively stable by definition, how likely is their convergence? And, once we observe convergence, what are the mechanisms underpinning this process of convergence? Various authors mention that the density of interactions among domestic defence officials and diplomats, which span decades of cooperation in European foreign policy and defence cooperation in NATO, has been conducive to socialization effects (Howorth 2001, 2004; Meyer 2005; Mérand 2008). For instance, Meyer underlines that there is a 'growing acceptance for the EU as a framework for defence cooperation at the level of high officials' and emphasizes 'the power of such committees to exert conformity pressures on newcomers to support the overall thrust of ESDP' (Meyer 2005: 536.) Mérand and Howorth echo this point. They argue that a small group of defence officials from the different EU member states formed an 'epistemic community', sharing a common set of objectives and views about European defence, i.e. on the type and nature of security challenges, and the role of the state in matching these challenges (see Mérand 2008: 143–4). For these security and defence policy 'professionals', defence policy was not an issue that aroused national identity issues, rendering prospects for further integration unlikely. The notion of 'epistemic community' can also shed light on *vertical* integration and, hence, the question why ESDP chose a particular institutional design that strongly resembled the decision-making structure of NATO, given the pro-NATO bias of defence ministries due to 'history and socialization' (Reynolds 2010: 200). According to Reynolds, the partial copying of NATO structures and rules reflected deeply institutionalized norms and identities shared among defence officials: 'In a densely institutionalised policy space, and with defence ministry officials involved in the ESDP having also a substantial and long-standing degree of relations with NATO ... it is therefore unsurprising that NATO should be the model of choice' (Reynolds 2010: 182–3).

The common professional outlook of security and defence officials, based on common practices and beliefs, also aligned well with broader socio-political developments that came to construe defence as an area of 'low politics'. Many countries have abandoned the era of conscription and declared the era of territorial defence as terminated (see Ojanen 2006, 63). Studies in public opinion have also underwritten the claim that defence has come to be less perceived as a key part of national identity, but is compatible with a European vocation (Schön 2008). On top of the closely-knit web of 'Europeanized' defence officials, EU member state governments have also begun to adapt their defence policies to the exigencies of ESDP as a consequence of socialization. EU member states that tradition- ally considered themselves as champions of the 'civilian power' char- acter of the EU – such as Germany, Austria, or Sweden – came to subscribe to a new guiding principle, which entailed that the EU should consider the use of military force as a legitimate option to address security challenges and develop autonomous military capabil- ities for this purpose: 'Sweden, for instance, has used the new institu- tions to re-shape the country's strategic doctrine by exporting its strong preferences for a multi-lateral rule-based order to the EU level and importing notions of using military force for humanitarian pur- poses as well as watering down its neutrality attachment within a new European defence policy framework' (Meyer 2005: 539).

Finally, we turn to the question about the Danish opt-out from the defence arm of foreign and security policy cooperation. The popular rejection of the Maastricht Treaty by Danish voters in 1992 led the government to opt out from several areas of the integration process, including monetary and security policy, which they have upheld since then. According to constructivism, the opt-out reflects a strong popular resentment towards EU integration in general and a European superstate in particular (Olsen 2007). Moreover, the domestic discourse on European security and defence cooperation was not compatible with the domestically held (majority) view that the integration project is, first and foremost, an economic enterprise. From this perspective, it can be argued that the opt-out is the conse- quence of a lack of compatibility of domestic notions with European policy ideas, the (domestic) construction of defence policy as a non- economic issue, as well as the staging of a referendum, during the course of which identity issues were activated by Eurosceptic con- stituents.

Conclusion

This chapter has offered a detailed overview of the differentiated character of European integration in the area of security and defence policy. We then explored the explanatory leverage of different inte- gration theories and hypotheses to explain the two most important episodes and attempts to form a European defence policy: the EDC, which eventually failed, and the St Malo initiative leading to the for- mation of the ESDP, which has led, over the course of less than a decade, to the establishment of common military capabilities, as well as to a decision-making structure with a civilian and a military component. Moreover, these structures have been used heavily since their creation, most visibly in the launching and implementation of EU-led civilian and military operations.

Our theoretical analysis has shown that intergovernmentalism, in the form of its realist variant and its emphasis on autonomy concerns and 'exogenous shocks', offers a good assessment for the timing of change. The move towards a common army in the 1950s followed the prospect of German rearmament in the wake of the Korean War (internal balancing), and the realization that the Soviet Union was an overwhelming power that necessitated an external balancing strategy. The end of the Cold War also prompted changes in the way EU governments assessed security threats. This led to the creation of a common foreign and defence policy and, following the US government's shift of attention (away from Europe), left EU states to ponder the development of EU defence capabilities to reduce dependency on the USA and NATO. Yet, intergovernmentalism has a problem in explaining the timing of the St Malo initiative. EU member state governments realized in the mid-1990s that they could no longer rely on US commitment, which effectively enabled the EU partially to free ride on the USA deploying troops in the EU's 'backyard'. This is where the constructivist emphasis on socialization processes offers explanatory leverage. While intergovernmentalists focus on the material sources of national preferences, constructivists emphasize their ideational foundations. Constructivists have shown that, in the two episodes under scrutiny, cross-national differences in 'strategic culture' rendered cooperation and further integration difficult – or, as in the case of the EDC, even unlikely. However, constructivists have alluded to processes of learning and socialization through which domestic security and defence officials increasingly came to see the EU as the 'natural solution to their concerns' (Mérand 2008: 5). Moreover, constructivists have shown that institutional choices, as in the case of the ESDP, are not necessarily the product of strategic interaction but, rather, a reflection of what politico-administrative actors, diplomats, and military officials perceived to be the most appropriate or legitimate institutional solution.

Intergovernmentalists and constructivists have also alluded to the factors that help us to explain why certain member states choose to opt out (Denmark on defence related matters), or why potential members refrain from joining a cooperative arrangement (the UK in the case of the EDC). By contrast, supranationalists focus on the preferences and capacities of supranational actors to explain integration. While supranationalist actors that could have fuelled change were literally absent during the time the Pleven Plan was launched, we have shown that the Commission, in particular, has strived to depoliticize security and defence questions by linking them to 'low politics', i.e. market integration. Moreover, the Commission continues to point at the links between the civilian dimensions of humanitarian crises – in which the Commission entertains considerable competences – and the military dimensions, where it has only few.

Chapter 8

The Area of Freedom, Security and Justice

The Area of Freedom, Security and Justice (AFSJ) – formerly called Justice and Home Affairs – has become one of the most dynamic fields of European integration in recent years. Hardly on the official agenda before the 1990s, it has since then experienced a rapid integration in vertical and horizontal terms. Given the 'late-comer' status of this policy area, followed by some dazzling dynamics, and an extraordinary amount of vertical and horizontal differentiation, this policy area poses some intriguing and challenging questions for integration theories. In this chapter, we will first outline the development over time of the AFSJ. Given the complexity and diversity of this policy area, we will then concentrate our theoretical analysis on a selection of issues and events relating to the AFSJ. A particular focus of this chapter will be on the Schengen border regime. For the purposes of this book, 'Schengen' is of major interest, since it can be considered a paradigmatic example of external and internal differentiation. Non-EU member states participate in it, while some EU member states have preferred not to join. The UK and Ireland have opted out of Schengen, Cyprus has not yet implemented it, and Bulgaria and Romania still have to fulfill the necessary criteria for joining the Schengen group. At the same time, the non-EU members, Iceland, Norway, Switzerland, and Liechtenstein (in late 2011) have signed and implemented the Schengen agreement. In addition, Monaco, San Marino, and Vatican City are *de facto* participants of the Schengen area.

The Development of the Area of Freedom, Security and Justice

According to the Treaty on the Functioning of the European Union, the AFSJ encompasses policies on border checks, asylum and immigration, judicial cooperation in civil matters, judicial cooperation in criminal matters, and police cooperation. For traditional political theory, such matters constitute core components of state sovereignty. Providing internal and external security is considered a state's *raison d'être* at least since the time of Thomas Hobbes. For Max Weber, states are

221

characterized by the monopoly of the legitimate use of violence within their territory. But with the abolishment of border controls, territorial delimitations have become less visible between the members of the Schengen group. And while the EU does not contest the role of national police services, there has undoubtedly been a trend towards closer cooperation in internal security matters. By creating the so-called 'third pillar' of Justice and Home Affairs, the Treaty of Maastricht marked an important turning point in the history of this policy area. Before Maastricht, the policies falling under this heading were only loosely coordinated between the member states and were not formally included in the Treaty framework. Since Maastricht, the policies of AFSJ as it stands at the time of writing have been consistently more deeply integrated. In our short historical overview, we will first review the early beginnings of cooperation in matters relating to justice and home affairs. Then, in greater detail, we will trace the trajectories of vertical and horizontal integration of this policy area from the 1980s onwards.

Early intergovernmental beginnings

By 1971, an intergovernmental 'Co-operation Group to Combat Drug Abuse and Illicit Drug Trafficking' had already been established at the initiative of French President Georges Pompidou. At its beginning, the so-called 'Pompidou Group' united experts from the six EC member states and the UK. Later, it was extended to include more countries and was incorporated into the institutional framework of the Council of Europe in 1980 (note that, because the Council of Europe is a different organization than the EU, the Pompidou group, which, at the time of writing, comprises 35 member states, is not part of the AFSJ). In 1976, the so-called Trevi group was set up by the Interior Ministers of the EC member states as a network of senior police and security officials from the member states for coordinating the fight against terrorism. Similar informal groups – such as, for example, the Customs Mutual Assistance Group or the Judicial Cooperation Group – were later founded, and paved the way for closer cooperation between national experts.

A significant step towards the establishment of the AFSJ was the signing of an agreement on the gradual abolition of checks at their common borders by the representatives of the three Benelux countries, France, and Germany in the small town of Schengen in 1985. The European Commission had for some time promoted the establishment of a European passport union but had faced sturdy opposition, especially from the UK and Denmark. Because agreement on an EC-based border system seemed impossible to French President François Mitterrand and German Chancellor Helmut Kohl, they decided bilaterally to facilitate border proceedings between France and Germany in the Saarbrücken Agreement of July 1984. In response to this agreement, the three Benelux countries, which had already removed checks at their common borders in the 1960s, addressed a memorandum to France and Germany demanding the establishment of a common travel area without internal borders. This was to become the Schengen Agreement (see Gehring 1998). As an international legal agreement, 'Schengen' at its inception did not fall under the EC's competence. In fact, it explicitly sidelined the EC framework.

The implementation of the Schengen Agreement proved more complex than initially anticipated by the signatories, and the Convention on the implementation of the Schengen Agreement was only signed in 1990, entering into force in 1995. In the Schengen Convention, the signatory states had decided to abolish the border controls between the members of the Schengen Area, to establish common rules on visas and police cooperation, and to set up the Schengen Information System. In 1997, Austria, Italy, Portugal, and Spain joined the pioneers, to be followed by Greece in 2000 and the members of the Nordic Passport Union (Denmark, Finland, Sweden, Iceland, and Norway) in 2001. In 2007, all accession states from the first round of Eastern enlargement (with the exception of Cyprus) joined the Schengen Area. Switzerland became a member in 2008, Liechtenstein in 2011. While Bulgaria and Romania want to join 'Schengen', the UK and Ireland prefer to remain outsiders.

Since the Schengen regime only united a subset of EC member states at the outset, it is often considered a prominent experiment of internal differentiation. In this case, internal differentiation was reduced over time, and the regime even attracted states from beyond the EC. In addition, the Schengen *acquis* was finally incorporated into the EU framework through a protocol annexed to the Amsterdam Treaty. The legal basis for integrating Schengen was established through Art. 2.15 of this Treaty, creating a title on 'visas, asylum, immigration and other policies related to free movement of persons'. In terms of the organizational structure, after the Treaty of Amsterdam the Council Secretariat replaced the Schengen Agreement's Executive Committee. The Treaty of Amsterdam granted an opt-out to the UK and Ireland. At the same time, however, the treaty allowed these countries to opt in in the future, i.e. to take part in some or all of the arrangements of the Schengen *acquis* after unanimous agreement in the Council by the Schengen member states.

Closely linked to Schengen, the Dublin Convention on asylum, was signed in 1990 and entered into force in 1997. Dublin represents a decisive breakthrough towards the establishment of a common asylum policy. By determining which member state is responsible for processing an asylum claim, the Dublin system is designed as a mechanism to prevent asylum seekers from applying for asylum in various states – so-called 'asylum shopping'. The original Dublin Convention was replaced by the amended Dublin Regulation in 2003 that continues to apply at the time of writing.

Integration of justice and home affairs into the EU: Maastricht and beyond

The 'third pillar' of the Treaty of Maastricht established the official foundations for justice and home affairs. Initially, justice and home affairs were designed as a purely intergovernmental policy area. However, by including a so-called *rendez-vous* provision in the Maastricht Treaty, the heads of state and government at that time ensured that the institutional framework was to be revisited at the next IGC. In addition, *passerelle* clauses allowed the Council unanimously to shift areas of common interest from the third pillar (Title VI TEU) to the 'supranational' first pillar (Title IV EC Treaty). This paved the way for future vertical integration. And, indeed, the provision was used during the Amsterdam IGC when migration, asylum, rights of third country nationals, external border controls, and judicial civil cooperation were transferred to the first pillar. At the same time, police and judicial cooperation in criminal matters were retained in the third pillar. As already highlighted, in the Treaty of Amsterdam the Schengen Convention and *acquis* were incorporated into the Treaty through a protocol. Further steps towards the creation of the Area of Freedom, Security and Justice were taken at a special meeting held by the European Council in Tampere in October 1999. In its conclusions to this summit, the Finnish Council presidency identified as the main goals for the development of the AFSJ: the creation of a common EU asylum and migration policy, a genuine European area of justice, and a union-wide fight against crime. The Treaty of Nice further extended the use of the codecision procedure in judicial cooperation in civil matters (with the exception of family law) and in issues relating to asylum and in establishing standards for temporary protection of refugees.

In addition, terrorism has become a more pertinent issue for EU cooperation, following the terrorist attacks of New York, Madrid, and London. In 2002 the Council of the EU passed a framework decision on combating terrorism (cf. Kostakopoulou 2006: 245–6). In 2005, in the German town Prüm, seven member states decided to enhance cross-border police cooperation in order to combat terrorism, cross-border crime, and illegal immigration. The Prüm Convention was modelled on the Schengen experience and constitutes an intergovernmental agreement outside the EU's jurisdiction. Its supporters hoped that the matters falling under the Convention would be incorporated into the

Box 8.1   *Timeline: integration in the AFSJ*

1972	Pompidou Group	1999b	Tampere European
1976	Trevi Group		Council ('ten
1985	Schengen Agreement		mile stones' towards
1990	Schengen		the Area of Freedom,
	Implementation		Security and Justice)
	Convention	2002	Framework Decision
1990	Dublin Convention on		on Combating
	Asylum		Terrorism
1993	Treaty on European	2003	Treaty of Nice
	Union: third pillar –	2004	Hague Programme
	Justice and Home	2005	Treaty of Prüm
	Affairs	2009a	Treaty of Lisbon
1999a	Treaty of Amsterdam	2009b	Stockholm Programme

EU's institutional framework in the future. The first parts of the Prüm Convention – e.g. information exchange on DNA profiles, fingerprints, and vehicle number-plates – became part of the legislative framework of the European Union in 2007 (see Box 8.1 for the integration of matters in the AFSJ).

The European Council's multi-annual Hague Programme (2004) and Stockholm Programme (2009) formulate more concrete goals concerning fundamental rights and citizenship, the fight against terrorism, migration management, (internal and external) borders, asylum policy, data protection, the combat against organized crime, and a European area of justice (cf. Buono 2009). With its focus on cross-border problems, the Hague Programme also upgraded the status of Europol – at that time, still an international organization. First referred to in the Maastricht Treaty and implemented by the Europol Convention of 1995, Europol is the European law enforcement agency based in The Hague, Netherlands. Its role is to support the member states in preventing and combating serious international crimes and terrorism. The 170 initiatives of the Stockholm Programme aimed at an 'open and secure Europe serving and protecting the citizen' were endorsed by European leaders in December 2009. With the Lisbon Treaty entering into force, the AFSJ has become Title V of the Treaty on the Functioning of the European Union. Lisbon has further extended the usage of the co-decision procedure and QMV in this area under the ordinary legislative procedure. It also incorporated the Charter of Fundamental Rights into the EU's legal framework.

How can the trajectory of the AFSJ be translated into the terms of our vertical integration scale? When combining the different policies contained in the AFSJ, we can say that there was no EU-level policy coordination before the 1970s. Purely intergovernmental groups, such as the Trevi group, indicate a development towards intergovernmental coordination, but without establishing an explicit link to the EC framework. Government representatives coordinated their activities, albeit only loosely. The Treaty of Maastricht established the third pillar, which has transformed justice and home affairs into a matter of intergovernmental cooperation. The Treaty of Amsterdam transferred a range of policies from the third to the first pillar, and thus we witness a noticeable shift towards joint decision-making. After the Treaty of Amsterdam, the Commission, together with a specified number of member states, was given the right to propose new pieces of legislation; also, the ECJ began to exercise its jurisdiction in this area. Finally, the Lisbon Treaty abolished the intergovernmental third pillar altogether, and the community method has broadly become the rule. The European Parliament is a key player in the ordinary legislative procedure, and most matters relating to the AFSJ are decided by QMV in the Council. Even in selected issues of judicial cooperation in criminal matters and police cooperation, the ordinary legislative procedure has been used following the Lisbon Treaty.

The AFSJ is one of the most productive fields of EU policy-making. Besides the member states and the EU organs, a multitude of 'semi-autonomous' agencies and bodies are active in this area (cf. Lavenex 2010). A prominent example of such an agency is the Warsaw-based European border security agency Frontex. Frontex provides expertise, equipment, and even manpower, for operational cooperation at the EU's external borders. Because of its focus on protecting the EU's borders – partly at the expense of the human rights of refugees – Frontex was previously often criticized by human rights activist groups. In fact, the tension between the guaranteeing of civil liberties and protecting of security of the EU's citizens makes the AFSJ one of the most divisive areas of EU policy-making (see also Lavenex 2010).

Horizontal integration

The AFSJ also raises some interesting questions from the perspective of (differentiated) horizontal integration. The Schengen Agreement and the Prüm Convention introduced closer cooperation among a subset of member states. Both of these agreements started outside the framework provided by EU institutions, but were fully (Schengen) or partly (Prüm) incorporated into the *acquis* at a later point. In addition, in the third pillar, a 'rolling ratification' mechanism was introduced that allowed conventions that were adopted by at least half of the participating member states to enter into force in those member states (Art. 34.2(d) TEU). This is a fine example of a (temporal) horizontal differentiation. A more pick-and-choose or *à la carte* integration is illustrated by the combinations of the opt-ins and opt-outs of Ireland, the UK, and Denmark (cf. Peers 2007: 55–64). After the Maastricht Treaty was rejected by referendum in Denmark in 1992, this country was subsequently granted a number of opt-outs. Globally, Denmark negotiated an opt-out from supranational decision-making in the third pillar. In addition, the newly-designed EU citizenship was not to be applied to Danish citizens. A 'national compromise' adopted by seven of the eight parties in the Danish parliament, the *Folketing*, stipulates: 'Denmark cannot agree to transfer sovereignty in the area of justice and policy affairs, but can take part in the intergovernmental cooperation which has existed to-date. This means that Denmark cannot agree to parts of the third pillar being transferred to the area of supranational cooperation in the first pillar.' In the Treaty of Amsterdam, Denmark obtained opt-outs for first pillar provisions through protocols attached to the Treaty. However, it participates in the free movement area and may adopt relevant European provisions as international law (in order to avoid the direct effect of EU law and being submitted to the European Court of Justice's rulings). It thus only participates in EU judicial cooperation in intergovernmental terms.

While the non-EU member states Iceland, Norway, and Switzerland are part of the Schengen area, the UK and Ireland do not participate in the common border policy. We thus have a case of internal combined with external differentiation. In practice, differentiated horizontal integration in the case of Schengen is even more complicated, since the UK and Ireland in the Treaty of Amsterdam obtained the opportunity for opt-ins in asylum, immigration, and judicial cooperation in civil matters. Opt-in protocols are case-by-case exemptions and they allow member states to select from the 'menu of new EU proposals' (Adler-Nissen 2009: 66). This puts countries such as Ireland and the UK in a very favourable position, since they can decide on a case-by-case basis whether a particular policy suits their domestic interests. The UK has opted into most civil law measures, all asylum affairs, and most issues concerning illegal migration, but has barely adopted protective measures concerning legal migration, visas, and border controls (Adler-Nissen 2009: 69). In the Schengen Agreement, they chose to opt-in with regard to the Schengen Information System II, a database containing detailed information related to visa questions. Denmark has a 'bizarre position' in the context of the Schengen Agreement (Adler-Nissen 2009: 75). While it signed the Schengen Agreement in 1996, it negotiated an opt-out from 'supranationality' in the Treaty of Amsterdam. Article 5 of the protocol on the position of Denmark attached to the Treaty of Amsterdam provides Denmark with a choice to implement new Schengen proposals or initiatives in its national law. Opt-outs also exist concerning the ECJ's role in the European law enforcement agency Europol. A protocol to the Europol Convention gives member states wide discretion to opt out of the ECJ's preliminary rulings for the interpretation of this Convention.

Conclusion

Figure 8.1 shows the pattern of vertical and horizontal integration in the area of 'criminal and domestic security'. The solid line plots horizontal integration as the percentage of all European states participating in this policy area, normalized to range from 0 to 5. The dashed line illustrates the progress in terms of vertical integration reached with the Treaties of Maastricht, Amsterdam, Nice, and Lisbon. Figure 8.1 underlines the dynamic development of the AFSJ since the 1990s from a non-integrated to a strongly integrated policy area. It also suggests that vertical and horizontal integration have evolved largely in parallel. However, the figure conceals the considerable differentiation in this area.

In the ensuing section, we attempt to explain the empirical patterns that have emerged in this sector and that raise so many compelling questions for integration theory. Why are justice and home affairs 'latecomers' of integration? Why has this policy area lagged behind other policy areas – e.g. the Common Market, transport, or competition? Why did vertical integration unfold in such a dynamic way in the AFSJ once the first steps had been taken? Why are some AFSJ policies more vertically integrated than others? How can we explain the fact

Figure 8.1   *Vertical and horizontal integration in the AFSJ*

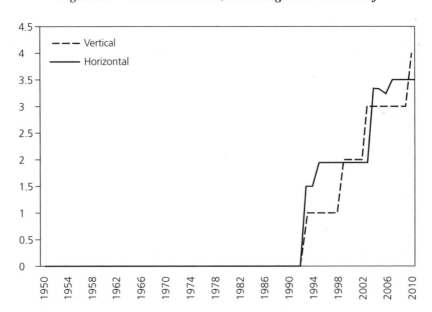

that states were willing to give up sovereignty in this important and politically sensitive area? Why are some states – e.g. the UK, Ireland, and Denmark – more reluctant to integrate than others? And why do some non-EU member states participate only in parts of the AFSJ? We will now turn to intergovernmentalism, supranationalism, and constructivism to shed light on these questions.

Intergovernmentalism

How does intergovernmentalism explain integration and differentiation in the AFSJ? We will first formulate a set of expectations derived from intergovernmentalism, and will then submit these claims to an empirical evaluation. What should we observe if intergovernmentalism were able to explain integration and differentiation in the AFSJ?

- Given that issues of internal security are a core attribute of statehood, intergovernmentalism would expect a general reluctance towards integration in this area. If at all, integration should be driven by strong interdependence, conducting to a convergence of national preferences. Common threats to national autonomy, security, or welfare could thus motivate state actors to agree to work together more closely. From an intergovernmentalist perspective, a shifting of competences to the European level would be a means of assuring the enforcement of such sensitive policies, but governments should still seek to remain in control of these policies and limit delegation to supranational organizations. In substantive terms, the outcomes of the AFSJ should mirror the preferences of the most powerful state or groups of states.
- For intergovernmentalism, state preferences and bargaining power determine the horizontal patterns of integration. Differing preferences can either be attributed to varying structural incentives – uneven interdependence is a key explanatory variable – or to different domestic conditions. For instance, high ratification hurdles can constrain the participation of states in the AFSJ.
- According to an intergovernmentalist perspective, vertical differentiation of different policies falling under the umbrella of the AFSJ can be attributed to varying levels of interdependence, preference homogeneity, compliance problems, uncertainty and domestic support.

Formation and development of the AFSJ: sovereignty, interdependence, member state preferences, and bargaining

Given that justice and home affairs can be classified as 'high politics', realist intergovernmentalists should rather be sceptic about the integration of this policy area. Until the 1990s, their scepticism seems well-founded. We hardly find any cooperation in this field or, if so, only under intergovernmental auspices. The first tentative steps towards cooperation were taken by administrative actors from national interior ministries during the 1970s and 1980s. Realizing that transnational criminals undermined the states' capacity to provide internal security to its citizens, these actors agreed to accept more coordination for the sake of securing the fulfilment of the states' obligations *vis-à-vis* their citizens. Explaining the development of justice and home affairs until the Maastricht Treaty therefore seems like a walk in the park from a realist intergovernmentalist perspective. And even the institutionalization of the third pillar at Maastricht is in line with intergovernmentalist logic, given that the third pillar was intergovernmental in nature and supranational agents were kept out of the game. By contrast, the subsequent 'communitarization' of the AFSJ at Amsterdam is hard to explain for realist intergovernmentalism. Why would autonomy-maximizing member states be willing to give up sovereignty in core areas of statehood by granting more rights to the Commission, the ECJ, and other member states?

Liberal intergovernmentalism is better suited for this task. First, liberal intergovernmentalism explains the relative insignificance of societal actors by the nature of the issue area. According to Moravcsik (1993: 483), the AFSJ falls into the category of non-economic, political, and institutional policies. For such policies, Moravcik (1993: 495) finds that '[e]xcept where implications are calculable, governments and parliamentary elites enjoy relatively broad autonomy to pursue symbolic goals or side payments'. Since gains and losses per capita are difficult to calculate in the AFSJ, the interests of social groups are limited; therefore, politicians and the administration possess a high level of discretion. This argument conforms to the impact the Interior ministries had in the process.

Second, liberal intergovernmentalism explains the increase in vertical integration by increased interdependence (cf. Moravcsik 1998: 452). The fall of the Iron Curtain led to a substantive inflow of immigrants and asylum seekers. With the prospect of Eastern enlargement – declared to be one of the main driving forces behind the Treaty of Amsterdam – the salience of such issues was likely to rise. By further communitarizing justice and home affairs (JHA), the commitments could more easily be enforced. In addition, a more institutionalized cooperation could reduce uncertainty and transaction costs (cf. Keohane 1984).

Differentiated horizontal integration

Heterogeneity of state preferences and bargaining power are core factors in explaining differentiated horizontal integration from an intergovernmentalist perspective. According to liberal intergovernmentalism, national preferences are determined by interdependence, domestic interest groups, and institutions. How does this relate to the patterns of internal and external differentiation that we find in the Schengen regime? In fact, the liberal intergovernmentalist and the supranationalist explanations of horizontal differentiation overlap to some degree: the unwillingness of Greece, Ireland, and the UK to align themselves with their EC partners can be attributed to their isolated geographic position, which limits interdependence. In addition, Denmark initially declined Schengen membership in order to keep up its ties with an alternative (Nordic) grouping. Given the unanimity requirement of treaty changes, the drivers had no other option of reaching their goal than by forming a regime outside the EC legal framework (remember that, at that time, enhanced cooperation did not formally exist). The step was further facilitated by the fact that differentiation did not impose extra costs or negative externalities on the Schengen countries: they did not need the non-members to realize the free-travel zone; neither could the non-members free ride on Schengen.

Over time, more and more countries joined the Schengen area and, in the mid-1990s, the ratio of drivers versus brakemen had changed in favour of the drivers. When Sweden and Finland became EU members, and Norway and Iceland were invited to become members of the Schengen area, the obstacle of the Nordic Passport Union was removed. Denmark, however, maintained its 'bizarre position' in the Schengen cooperation scheme. While it signed the Schengen Agreement in 1996, in the Treaty of Amsterdam it negotiated an opt-out from 'supranationality'. Article 5 of the protocol on the position of Denmark attached to the Treaty of Amsterdam provides it with a choice of implementing in its national law new proposals or initiatives building upon the Schengen *acquis*. Again, bargaining power can explain why the Schengen states were willing to accept the Danish exception; the reasons for the Danish reservation, however, are most often explained by identity-related factors in combination with high ratification hurdles, an argument we will return to in the section of constructivist explanations for integration in the AFSJ. Thus, it should be underlined that, in our view, purely economic reasons cannot satisfactorily account for the Danish preferences in the AFSJ.

As already highlighted, a combination of weak interdependence and strong bargaining power can explain the pattern of opt-outs. In addition, due to the fact that the Schengen Agreement entails some positive externalities for the laggards, they have little incentive to stop the others moving ahead (cf. Kölliker 2001). For example, the Schengen Agreement also expedites the transport of British goods on the continent.

The new Eastern European member states had to accept the *acquis* of the AFSJ as a part of the accession package (Vachudova 2000). Due to their geographic location, they bear a non-negligible amount of the costs of the Schengen and the Dublin Convention since, for instance, the common visa policy makes exchanges with their relations with their Eastern neighbours more cumbersome (cf. Jileva 2002). At the same time, Schengen facilitates contacts with the other EU member states. Currently, Bulgaria's and Romania's bid for membership of the Schengen Area is still pending, with some old members demanding further reforms from these countries. These countries bid for membership, however, once again underlines that the benefits of Schengen seem to outweigh the costs for new member states. Cyprus, finally, remains an exception. Since 1974, this island de facto has been partitioned into the Republic of Cyprus in the South and a Turkish controlled area in the North. A complete implementation of Schengen would demand setting up an EU external border on the middle of this island, entailing strong negative effects for Turkish Cypriots. Therefore, Cyprus is unlikely to become a full member of the Schengen Area before the resolution of the Cyprus dispute.

As to the question of external differentiation, we again find some important overlaps between liberal intergovernmentalism and supranationalism, as we shall see. Interdependence can explain why Norway, Iceland, Switzerland, and Liechtenstein wanted to join the Schengen Area. The Dublin asylum system would entail negative externalities in the form of increased demands for asylum in these states. The reason for this is that asylum seekers whose pleas are declined by Dublin Convention states would have to apply for asylum in other European states; remember that the Dublin Convention aimed at preventing 'asylum shopping' in the member states. In economic parlance, the Convention represents a narrowing of the supply of asylum, increasing the demand for asylum for the other suppliers. In response, those states had incentives to join the regime.

In line with liberal intergovernmentalism, the outcomes of the Schengen negotiations also reflect the weak bargaining power of non-EU member states. Non-EU Schengen states are only associated with the decision-making procedures. Representatives of these countries participate in mixed committees that meet alongside the working parties of the EU Council. They can contribute to informal consultations, but they do not have a formal right to vote. Therefore, their influence is effectively limited. Especially for Switzerland, this procedure seems like a bitter pill, given the dynamic character of the Schengen Agreement and Switzerland's traditional reluctance *vis-à-vis* dynamic international treaties (cf. Wichmann 2009: 653).

Supranationalism

For supranationalists, transnational exchanges are the main driving force of integration. Governmental actors respond to demands from 'below' – (transnational) society – and from 'above' – the supranational actors. Once integration is put into action in a policy area, rule density can fuel further integration dynamics. In addition, functional linkages between different policy areas can lead to spillovers into related fields, an argument initially put forward by neofunctionalism. The following expectations relate the AFSJ to supranationalism.

- According to supranationalism, advances in integration in justice and home affairs during the 1980s and 1990s are a functional consequence of previous integration in other sectors (functional spillover). Transnational interest groups and policy networks, together with effective policy entrepreneurship of supranational actors, should play an important role in the process of integration. In addition, the substantive policies of justice and home affairs should mirror the interests and capacities of transnational socio-economic groups and supranational actors.
- For supranationalists, horizontal and vertical differentiation should reflect variation in the transnational exchanges across countries and across policies. Incentives for cooperation and integration should vary between different states and policies accordingly.
- Supranationalism would predict horizontal and vertical differentiation to decrease over time. Outsiders should be driven towards closer participation, and belated policies such as police and judicial cooperation in criminal matters should follow the integrative patterns of functionally and institutionally neighbouring policies.

Formation and development of the AFSJ: transnational networks and spillover

Historically, different actors have promoted a more coordinated European approach to justice and home affairs. With the rise of terrorism and trans-border criminal activity in the 1970s, national experts from the different interior ministries were eager to coordinate their efforts to combat crime more closely. Functional reasons thus induced early cooperation in this area; drug traffic or terrorism does not stop at a state's border, but national persecution often lagged behind the criminals' mobility. Over time, after first informal contacts had been established, members of police and interior security forces formed transnational networks of security experts. In justice and home affairs, public and governmental rather than private actors pressed for more

European-wide coordination. Inside these transgovernmental networks of experts, the different actors became increasingly familiar with their international partners and their practices. One can imagine that trust increased and socialization occurred accordingly. At the same time, it is noteworthy that such transgovernmental networks may also bring about a policy bias, since the experts forming these epistemic communities are likely to share common ideas and worldviews. In the AFSJ, this is often criticized by liberal activists – who argue that security issues often dominate human rights questions. For instance, Guiraudon (2003) argues that migration control experts used the European level strategically in order to foster their domestic goals. European cooperation, in fact, emphasized the kind of technical solutions that required their expertise, and therefore experts in the interior ministries had good reasons to 'venue shop' at the international level. Accordingly, in substantive terms, cooperation in the AFSJ is often argued to correspond relatively closely to the preferences of these transgovernmental security networks.

On the other hand, we find less support for the supranationalist expectation that supranational actors played a central role in the early integration process of the AFSJ. While the EC agreed on the desirability of promoting integration in justice and home affairs, its capacity to shape integration actively in this area was clearly limited before the late 1990s. Since the policy area was not included in the treaties before Maastricht and, once justice and home affairs was part of the Treaty, it remained in the 'intergovernmental' third pillar. As a consequence, the Commission's power was severely restricted and its role in this policy area strongly depended on the member states' will. For instance, in the early 1980s five member states had successfully called on the ECJ to challenge a Commission decision on immigration coordination in the EC, denying the legal grounds for activities in this area (Baldwin-Edwards 1997: 498). Its capacity to push the policy agenda ahead autonomously was thus clearly limited in this area. Similarly, since the Schengen Agreement was initially created under international and not EC law, the Commission hardly possessed any influence apart from symbolic support of the regime.

Since the early 1990s, the Commission – supported by the Council – has started to intensify its activities in justice and home affairs. In particular, with the transfer of policies to the first pillar, the Commission was authorized to propose new pieces of legislation and it duly made use of its newly-acquired rights. Data from the Commission's PreLex Homepage shows that from 1999 to June 2009 the Commission's Directorate General (DG) Justice and Home Affairs and the DG Freedom, Security and Justice have issued more than 500 proposals. The European Council also mandated the Commission to implement the Hague Programme (cf. Craig and Búrca 2008: 247). Over time, the

Commission thus gained stronger means with which actively to shape the policy agenda in matters relating to justice and home affairs.

The development of justice and home affairs broadly corresponds to the supranationalist expectation that transnational activity is a driving force of cooperation and integration. Given the enormous swell of immigration that followed the fall of the Iron Curtain in the late 1980s, migration questions became pressing for European publics and politicians seeking election or re-election (cf. Monar 2001: 753). Especially in Germany, the issue of immigration was high on the public agenda in the early 1990s; surveys underline that European publics supported – and, indeed, continue to support – more cooperation in this area (cf. Lavenex 2010: 475).

The Schengen Agreement can be considered an example of how economic motivations can drive integration in the area of justice and home affairs. In fact, business criticized the tedious and time-consuming border controls – which, it was argued, hindered the movement of persons and goods (cf. Lavenex and Wallace 2005: 460). We thus see a linkage between policy areas in this case of justice and home affairs, and the freedoms of the single market – and, in particular, with the goal of reaching a 'Europe without frontiers'. By delaying transport, border controls impeded transnational trade. In line with this liberalization logic, the Schengen Convention explicitly expressed its goal to 'facilitate the transport and movement of goods' at the common borders between the 'contracting parties'. This supports the supranationalist expectation that spillover dynamics did, indeed, bring the issue of Schengen on the integrationist agenda.

Supranationalism argues that the integration of one policy area often has effects on related policy areas, inciting political actors to change their original preferences. And there are more examples for such spillover dynamics in the AFSJ. For instance, there is a close issue-specific linkage between the free movement of persons fostered by the Schengen regime and internal security questions. By abolishing border controls between the signatory states, the members of the Schengen regime gave up their capacity to control immigration and to limit transnational (organized) crime at their borders. From such a perspective, the Schengen Agreement created a security vacuum. In turn, the possible negative effects of market integration raised societal and administrative demands for a closer cooperation in interior security policies (cf. Kaunert 2005: 464; Vachudova 2000). Gehring (1998) sees Schengen as an example of 'negative integration' that entails 'positive integration' in related issue areas – such as, for example, asylum policy. The Dublin Convention is thus a functionalist reponse to Schengen. In our view, the functionalist logic that links market integration via the Schengen Agreement to the Dublin Convention fits nicely into the framework of supranationalism, and corresponds to the temporal ordering of integration that this theory would predict.

Finally, it should be noted that, besides raising security concerns, an increase in transnational exchange also brings transnational judicial questions to the fore. According to Art. 81 of the Lisbon Treaty, the 'Union shall develop judicial cooperation in civil matters having cross-border implications, based on the principle of mutual recognition of judgments and of decisions in extrajudicial cases'. Judicial cooperation in civil matters aims at establishing closer cooperation between the authorities of member states and to eliminate obstacles derived from incompatibilities between the various legal and administrative systems. An important example of such conflicts related to an increase of transnational exchanges is the issue of international divorces (cf. Box 8.2 for more details on this issue).

Box 8.2   *Enhanced cooperation in practice: divorce rules*

According to the Commission, each year about a 170,000 divorces in the EU involve international couples (European Voice 2010). This raises the question of which national law applies in international divorces. Great differences between and the complexity of national conflict-of-law rules make it very difficult for international couples to predict which law will apply to their divorce or legal separation proceeding. Take the example of an Austrian woman marrying a British man in the UK. The couple lives in Austria with their son. The husband then returns to the UK and the wife demands a divorce. However, because there is no uniform rule, she does not know which law applies to her divorce. Can she obtain a divorce under Austrian law, or does UK law apply? This example has been used by the Commission to explain why it is in favour of strengthening legal certainty and predictability in the area of divorce rules. In order to prevent 'litigation shopping', the Commission first proposed EU-wide rules on divorce (Rome III regulation) in 2006. After no consensus was reached among all 27 member states, 10 member states decided to move ahead and asked the Commission to make use of the 'enhanced cooperation' procedure. Correspondingly, the European Commissioner for justice, fundamental rights, and citizenship, Viviane Reding, issued a proposal for enhanced cooperation in divorce rules in March 2010 (COM (2010) 105). Under the EU treaties, enhanced cooperation allows nine or more countries to move forward on a measure that they consider important but that is otherwise blocked by a minority of member states. In the particular case – that, by the way, was the first time that the Commission made use of the enhanced cooperation procedure since its introduction in the Treaty of Amsterdam – a main goal of the Commission's proposal was to enhance transparency by defining which country's law applies when couples cannot agree themselves.

Horizontal and vertical differentiation

How does supranationalism account for internal and external differentiation in the Schengen border regime? In general, from a supranationalist perspective, horizontal integration is promoted by dense transnational exchanges. If the density between transnational exchanges varies between different European countries, supranationalism expects horizontal differentiation. Transnational exchanges should thus be stronger between members of the Schengen group than between Schengen insiders and outsiders. In our view, the argument partly holds for the UK, Ireland, and Greece in the 1980s.

During the 1980s, Greece had no land borders with EC member states and, accordingly, the implementation of the Schengen regime in Greece would have been restricted to harbours and airports, and passengers holding EC member state passports. From a Greek perspective, the Schengen Agreement would therefore not have contributed to facilitating transnational exchanges to any appreciable degree. The case of the UK is similar. Since travelling to this island state was more complex than crossing borders on the continent, the costs of maintaining border controls were not conceived as a particular hindrance for transnational exchanges. The Irish were less concerned about the security effects of the Schengen Agreement, but they wanted to maintain the Common Travel Area with the UK. Since the UK is Ireland's closest economic partner, this would have entailed costs that the Irish were not willing to accept. One could thus argue that transnational exchanges can, at least partly, explain the reluctance of Greece, Ireland, and the UK. The explanation, however, does not consistently fit the case of Denmark. In the 1980s, the Schengen Area threatened Danish membership of the Nordic Passport Union. In order to scrap its borders to the south, Denmark would have needed to establish new borders to the north (cf. Zaiotti 2011: 106). But, in the meantime, the other former members of the Nordic Passport Union have all become parts of the Schengen Area, and this argument therefore no longer holds. Thus it is difficult to explain Danish reluctance primarily with a different structure of transnational exchanges.

At the same time, the transnational exchange explanation again fits the patterns of external differentiation in the Schengen regime rather well. Norway and Switzerland are closely linked to the European Communities; they participate to a very large degree in the EU's internal market; and there is an enormous amount of transnational exchange between the EU member states and these countries. The case of Iceland also corresponds to the logic of transnational exchanges driving integration. As a member of the Nordic Passport Union, this country had strong incentives to join the Schengen Area together with its former partners, thereby avoiding discrimination.

The AFSJ, finally, is also characterized by vertical differentiation. While the sector at large has been a latecomer, there still remain some noticeable differences of vertical integration between its policies. Supranationalists would expect a deeper integration of those policies that are more closely linked to transnational exchanges. Arguably, the selection of policies transferred from the third to the first pillar at Amsterdam roughly match these expectations, but more in-depth research would be needed to better understand the different trajectories of, for instance, judicial cooperation in civil matters as compared with police and judicial cooperation in criminal matters.

From differentiation to uniformity?

Supranationalism expects differentiation to decrease over time. This expectation can partly be corroborated. With a view to vertical integration, we find that most policies relating to this area have fallen under the ordinary legislative procedure since the Treaty of Lisbon. At the same time, it is important to stress that matters relating to internal security and interior policies are much more likely to be communitarized if they relate to transnational issues. For the time being, there is no question of setting up a common EU police, although Europol already provides some common infrastructure and the border agency Frontex is executing operational tasks in the field of border security.

In terms of horizontal integration, external differentiation is likely to remain, since the probability of Norway and Switzerland becoming EU members is low for the time being. However, with Iceland's bid for membership, external differentiation could decrease. Internal differentiation has clearly decreased when comparing the 1980s with the first decade of the new millennium. Comprising five states at its inception, the Schengen Area now includes all member states, with the exception of the UK and Ireland (leaving aside Denmark's special status).

All in all, the supranationalist record in explaining vertical and horizontal integration in the AFSJ is mixed. In this sector, the impact of supranational actors has been negligible, until recently. Instead, governmental actors were more decisive. The comparatively late beginnings of integration of this sector are broadly in line with supranationalist expectations. As compared with other sectors – e.g. the single market – the AFSJ raises fewer demands for integration from transnational societal actors. At the same time, supranationalists have fewer difficulties in explaining the dynamics of vertical integration of this sector once it has formally been incorporated into the institutional corpus of the EU. Institutional ties can reinforce cooperation, and the merits of working together become more obvious to the actors. In addition, spillover dynamics can inform us about the temporal patterns of integration of different issue areas. However, from a supranationalist perspective it is less clear why the UK and Ireland persistently remain outsiders of 'Schengeland' and why Denmark holds to its particular status in the AFSJ. We will take up these questions in the next section, which deals with constructivism.

Constructivism

Constructivism offers theoretical alternatives to the rationalist explanations put forward by supranationalism and intergovernmentalism. It introduces a broader perspective on what motivates actors; most importantly, constructivists question the importance of utility-maximization and, instead, emphasize the significance of values, ideas, and identities for explaining social behaviour. Second, for constructivists social interactions can have a transformative impact on actors' ideas, preferences, and identities through learning, persuasion, and socialization. From a constructivist perspective, we can derive the following propositions on the development of the AFSJ:

- The emergence and development of justice and home affairs is driven by inter-subjectively shared ideas and identities. At first, internal security-oriented epistemic communities formulated ideas on how best to combat transnational crime. Later, the idea of a European identity and the goal of a united Europe incited pro-Europeans to accompany the four freedoms with the abolishment of border controls. Finally, a discourse of securitization and an institutionalization of these policies over time promoted deeper integration.
- For constructivists, different national identities can best explain internal horizontal differentiation. Countries with pro-European identities are more likely to support the AFSJ than Eurosceptic countries. Since elites are usually assumed to hold stronger preferences for EU integration, a constraining public opinion matters most in states in which referendums are used.
- Vertical differentiation results from different degrees of ideational support for different European policies. Policies with stronger links to national identities should lag behind those policies that are more functional in character.
- For constructivists, differentiation in the AFSJ should decline over time because of socialization and learning.

Formation and development of the AFSJ: shared ideas and inclusive identities

According to constructivists, an ideational consensus emerged between national experts from the interior ministries in the 1970s. These experts shared the causal idea that the fight against crime demanded closer cooperation between the different European state administrations. Initially, however, these actors did not envisage a communitarization of justice and home affairs. At the same time, the Trevi and the Pompidou groups offered arenas for the exchange of information and policy ideas. Over time, security-oriented transnational epistemic communities emerged that ultimately opened the road to further integration. Monar (2001) calls these groups early 'laboratories' for integration.

During the 1980s, a quaint coalition between pro-Europeanists and security experts emerged. We have already depicted the removal of border controls as an instance of negative integration supported by pro-Europeanists. As a consequence, interior ministries demanded European measures in order to compensate for emerging security lacks. As already mentioned, these experts are sometimes said to have used the European level to circumvent the more restrictive national institutions and to establish their ideas on how best to fight crime on a European level. Security experts managed to frame the AFSJ as a highly technical sector and embed it in a broader discourse of securitization. A whole range of different agencies – such as Frontex, the EU's agency for intelligence-driven coordination in the area of border security; or Europol – fulfil executive tasks in the AFSJ; often beyond close parliamentary scrutiny. Large technical systems such as the Schengen Information System or the Eurodac fingerprint database are used to coordinate the actions on the control of visas and border-crossings. For non-experts, such technical and administrative measures are often hard to understand and disentangle.

Constructivists also draw our attention on the discourses used to promote the AFSJ. For example, the renaming of the policy area from 'justice and home affairs' in the Maastricht Treaty to the AFSJ underlines that European security proponents were increasingly seeking legitimacy and support for their actions. In European negotiations, supporters of deeper integration made use of European principles such as 'burden-sharing' or the 'policy of solidarity' (cf. Jileva 2002: 83–4) in order to persuade their more reluctant partners to support their demands. Similarly, a discourse of a 'European public order' or a 'single space' aims at institutionalizing security ideas on the European level (cf. Kaunert 2005; Monar 2006: 497). Zaiotti (2011) speaks of a new 'culture of border control' to underline the importance of a new understanding and practice of frontier relations in Europe.

Differentiated horizontal integration

Another important question we need to answer is why some states participate in the AFSJ, and why others have decided to opt out. On the domestic level, constructivism has identified national identities, values, and norms as important factors for understanding whether countries participate in European integration. Take, for instance, the introduction of EU citizenship in Maastricht. This symbolic step, adding a European dimension to national citizenship, was not uniformly applauded by all actors. After the first negative Maastricht referendum, the Danish government demanded that European citizenship should not apply to Danish citizens. While this matter was later resolved at Amsterdam, some authors have explained the Danish opt-out from EC citizenship in Maastricht by referring to a conflict between Danish and EU citizenship (cf. Hansen 2002). Given the strong linkage between the nation and the state in Denmark, the idea of holding an EU citizenship in this regard can be conceived as endangering national and cultural identity. In fact, during the referendum campaign those against emphatically invoked threats to the cultural concept of the Danish nation state (Hansen 2002: 69). Euroscepticism is strong in Denmark. In *Eurobarometer* surveys, Denmark generally ranks amongst the most eurosceptic states. In addition, the institutional ratification hurdles in Denmark are high, and referendums tend to empower the public *vis-à-vis* the more Europhile elites. In line with the expectations formulated by Hooghe and Marks (2008), the Maastricht provisions relating to justice and home affairs split the Danish public. During the campaign for the Maastricht referendum, the 'yes' vote was advocated by centre parties ranging from the Social Democrats on the left, to the Liberal Party on the right; the 'no' vote was promoted by the most right-wing party, the Party of Progress, by the Socialist People's Party and two social movements (the 'People's Movement against the EC' and the 'June Movement'). Thus, the parties at the extremes of the political spectrum successfully mobilized against further European integration. In their campaign, they depicted Maastricht as a threat to Danish identity. Such considerations have so far hardly been incorporated in supranationalist and liberal intergovernmentalist accounts of European integration and, therefore, constructivism can importantly contribute to our understanding of horizontal differentiation.

In the previous sections, we reviewed intergovernmentalist and supranationalist arguments on why certain countries were opposed to the Schengen Area. We argued, for instance, that Denmark faced higher costs than the Netherlands since, for example, the Schengen Area was conceived as a threat to the Nordic Passport Union. Also, for the UK the removal of border controls potentially entails negative consequences for internal security without the benefits of rendering transnational exchanges more efficient. At the same time, it is often argued that Ireland, for example, was not against the Schengen Area in principle, but wanted to maintain its Common Travel Area with open borders to the UK. So, why is the UK more reluctant than Ireland and other EU member states *vis-à-vis* the Schengen Area? The British public usually ranks amongst the most Eurosceptic publics in the EU. European issues enjoy a high salience in the UK and, in addition, not even the elites strongly support European integration. Neither the Tories nor Labour are fervent European federalists. Therefore, the permissive consensus and the identification with the EU were always rather limited in the UK. While its geographical location puts the UK in a different situation when it comes to questions of internal security, the abolition of border controls also has a strong symbolic meaning that clashes with the UK's ideal of sovereignty and independence. Accordingly, the Schengen Area can be considered a threat to its status and identity as an 'island nation'. For example, Wiener (1999) finds that the idea of the Schengen Area did not resonate with British identity, and entrenched national principles and practices in the UK.

In contrast to the negative reception of justice and home affairs in the UK, this policy area generally enjoys strong public support in most other member states. For instance, in a 2004 *Eurobarometer* survey 71 per cent of respondents affirmatively answered the question of whether the policy on the prevention and fight against crime would be more effective if it were decided jointly at the European Union level, rather than at the level of individual member states. On the question of whether rules for asylum seekers should be the same throughout the European Union, 85 per cent affirmed their agreement (*Flash Eurobarometer* 2004). Thus, while such policies might restrict national independence on the one hand, immigration and organized crime are sensitive issues in national political debates and electoral campaigns, on the other. This underlines that the resonance of European policy proposals with national identities and ideas on security can determine a country's participation in the AFSJ.

While constructivism is well-equipped for explaining internal differentiation in the AFSJ, it has greater difficulty in explaining the demand of non-EU member states for cooperation in the AFSJ. For instance, we find little evidence for identity-related reasons for Norway, Iceland, Switzerland, and Liechtenstein to wish to join the Schengen Area. Traditionally, these countries are conceived to be rather eurosceptic, and rationalist explanations linked to previous agreements on the free movement of persons between those states and the EU in our view can better explain their desire for participation. Their accession to the Schengen Area seems far from a love match.

Finally, according to constructivism we should expect that the number of opt-outs should decrease over time. This is not corroborated by recent developments, and the scenario that the Schengen 'laggards' engage in closer cooperation seems less likely than ever. The rise in migration from Northern Africa, following the Arab spring of 2011 has put border controls high on the EU's agenda. In spring 2011,

France had controlled borders with Italy; Denmark returned to using systematic customs controls at its borders with Germany. There is thus an ongoing tension between the two constructivist logics of, on the one hand, policy learning and socialization and, on the other hand, a politicized protection of national sovereignty rights. At the time of writing, the trend seems to point towards increasing anti-integrationist concerns. In general, this tension also makes constructivist predictions on the future developments of the AFSJ relatively uncertain.

Conclusion

In this chapter, we analyzed integration of different policies falling under the heading of the AFSJ. In our view, the AFSJ is one of the most complex policy areas of the EU. Integration in this policy area started belatedly but has developed rapidly since the 1990s. Most issues of the EU's former third pillar have been communitarized, and only police and judicial cooperation in criminal matters do not in total fall under the ordinary legislative procedure. But, even in this least-integrated field of police and judicial cooperation in criminal matters, the Commission after the Treaty of Lisbon has gained the right to issue legislative proposals. In addition, measures relating to these policies have become subject to the judicial review of the ECJ. This underlines the deep degree of integration of the AFSJ. Adler-Nissen (2011: 1104) finds that 'cooperation in justice and home affairs has shifted from taboo to totem'.

The evaluation of the explanatory and predictive capabilities of supranationalism, intergovernmentalism, and constructivism again produces balanced results. All three accounts can contribute to explaining vertical integration in this sector. We identified transnational exchanges and interdependence as important reasons for integration. Supranationalism has taught us about the importance of establishing links between different policies and understanding endogenous dynamics of integration. In line with the functional spillover argument, the free movement of persons has triggered demands for integration in justice and home affairs. Liberal intergovernmentalism, on the other hand, draws our attention to the importance of bargaining power for understanding the outcomes in the AFSJ. The comparatively comfortable position of Denmark, the UK, and Ireland in a context of unanimous decision-making allowed them opt-outs and opt-ins in this policy area. Liberal intergovernmentalism can also explain why non-EU member states such as Norway or Switzerland have joined the Schengen Agreement and the Dublin Convention. These regimes imposed external costs on the neighbouring states – for instance, by making 'asylum shopping' more difficult – and rationalist explanations can satisfactorily account for the integration demands of these other-wise rather reluctant partners. Finally, constructivism can add to our understanding of the patterns of internal differentiation. Reluctance in the AFSJ is often due to heterogeneity of identities and ideas amongst EU member states and their populations. For instance, economic con-siderations alone can hardly explain the hesitant position of Denmark.

On the downside, supranationalism has difficulties in explaining the opting-out of some member states from the AFSJ, and there is not much support for strong Commission activity in this area. Liberal intergovernmentalism, on the other hand, does not offer a dynamic story of integration by establishing functional linkages between dif-ferent policies. In addition, it does not clearly specify the positions we should expect of different member states. It cannot satisfactorily account for why certain states decided to opt-out from parts of the AFSJ's policy portfolio. Constructivism, finally, has difficulties in for-mulating clear predictions on cooperation in this issue area. While it can explain why certain countries behave more reluctantly than others, it refrains from establishing the conditions of integration. Judging the pros and cons of the different theoretical accounts, the chapter, all in all, highlights that we can consider the three theoretical accounts as complementary to one another. To conclude, this chapter has shown that the AFSJ has some interesting potential for bringing our under-standing of European integration forward. In our view, the AFSJ there-fore merits stronger attention from the theoretical literature than it has so far received.

Chapter 9

Conclusion: Integration and Differentiation in the European Union

In the 1950s, the European integration project started with six European states creating a community to coordinate the production and distribution of coal and steel and, a few years later, to set up a common market. Since then the European Union has increased to include 28 member states by 2013 and to cover most areas of modern governance more or less tightly. At first, most policies were only loosely coordinated but, over time, have become progressively more communitarized by the increasing the powers of supranational actors such as the European Commission, the EP, and the ECJ, and by loosening the grip of individual member states on policy decisions. In this book, we named the two institutional dynamics that characterize the EU integration process: horizontal and vertical integration. Horizontal integration refers to the territorial extension of the EU's policy regimes; vertical integration captures the depth or centralization of supranational decision-making in different policy areas.

The patterns of vertical and horizontal integration generally show a development towards an 'ever closer' and an 'ever wider' Union. At the same time, our survey of policy areas has revealed that European integration is not uniform. Rather, it is characterized by strong differentiation across policy areas and space. The EU, as a system of differentiated integration, exhibits vertical and horizontal differentiation. On the one hand, vertical differentiation means that different policy areas or policies display different temporal patterns and degrees of integration. While market issues have, for instance, been communitarized since the founding of the EEC, justice and home affairs have lagged behind and only began to achieve a similar depth of integration since the 1990s (with some policies in the AFSJ still being decided intergovernmentally). While the member states of the eurozone have delegated all their monetary responsibilities to the ECB in Frankfurt, in questions relating to common defence the supranational actors for the most part remain more or less side-lined. Horizontal differentiation, on the other hand, means that the ideal of 'ever closer union', which emphasizes complete and exclusive participation of EU member states in each individual policy area, is being increasingly challenged. As to the horizontal dimension, we have distinguished external from internal differentiation, and external and internal differentiation combined. External horizontal differentiation is present if all EU member states participate in a specific policy and, in addition, at least one state that is not a member of the EU also participates. Internal differentiation means that one or more EU member states have decided to refrain from participation in one integrated policy area. If non-member states 'opt in' and EU member states 'opt out', we have a situation of external and internal horizontal differentiation in the policy area concerned.

Why is a perspective of differentiated integration helpful for studying the EU? In order to analyze the EU's policies and politics, it is useful to have a solid understanding of the nature of the beast. Differentiation is sometimes used in federal states – for example, nullification is a corresponding idea in US constitutional history; in Germany there have been debates on a so-called '*Abweichungsrecht*' (divergent legislation) that allows exceptions for some German *Länder*, and in Canada the 'notwithstanding clause' of the Canadian Charter of Rights and Freedoms grants provinces temporal opt-outs from the application of this very Charter. Yet, uniformity is still generally the rule in nation states. At the same time, the EU has a far more centralized political system and covers far more policy areas than any other international organization (see Figure 1.1). Since the literature traditionally uses different conceptual and theoretical tools and instruments to study states and international organizations, this long-standing conceptual tension between state and international organization has given rise to some important debates on how best to approach the EU and its history. In our view, the concept of differentiated integration can help to relax this tension by shifting the analytical focus to policy areas as core units of analysis. Focusing on policy areas, their level of centralization and their horizontal extension allow us analytically to disentangle some important theoretical integration puzzles. Technically speaking, a perspective of differentiated integration invites us to systematically exploit variation in the EU for the sake of improving explanation. Differentiated integration should therefore allow us to obtain a better analytical grip on the integration history of the EU. By analyzing integration advances together with resistances or drawbacks, we hope to improve our knowledge of the mechanisms of integration.

In this concluding chapter, we will first systematically review and compare the findings of our empirical chapters on the single market, the EMU, defence policy, and the AFSJ. We will use the empirical background to compare and discuss the performance of different integration theories. We will argue that none of the integration theories can fully account for the complex empirical reality that we find in the empirical chapters. In fact, despite their competitive claims, there is no clear 'winner' emerging from our analysis of the policy areas. We therefore distil and discuss the strengths and weaknesses of the different theories, but also identify often overlooked common ground between the different approaches. Finally, we will formulate some suggestions for a possible synthesis of integration theories.

Theoretical synthesis is often considered to be an opportunity to make theoretical progress possible. While there is an ongoing debate on the practicability and usefulness of theoretical synthesis (see Fearon and Wendt 2002; Hellmann 2003; Katzenstein and Sil 2008), we advance some ideas on how to synthesize EU integration theories. We show possibilities for the combination of constructivist and rationalist approaches. For example, we build constructivist logics into frameworks commonly used by the rationalist literature. In addition, we tentatively define possible scope conditions under which specific theories should perform best. Scope conditions are those conditions that specify when the different assumptions and hypotheses about integration preferences and negotiations are most likely to hold. They tell us, for instance, under which conditions supranational actors are most relevant and which ideational preferences matter most. In doing so, we build on earlier work in integration theory. One major inspiration is Paul Pierson's (1996) historical institutionalist model of path-dependent European integration; the other is Liesbet Hooghe and Gary Marks' (2008) postfunctionalist approach to integration. We suggest that both institutional path-dependencies at the supranational level and identity politics at the domestic level can be understood as extensions of an intergovernmentalist baseline model that play out over time and under specific scope conditions.

Differentiated Integration in the European Union

Our empirical chapters on the single market, the EMU, defence policy, and the AFSJ revealed a series of interesting patterns of integration (Table 9.1). First, the policy areas vary with regard to the timing of supranational integration. European integration started with the common market in the 1960s. The decision to create a supranational monetary policy followed in the early 1990s to be followed by AFSJ a few years later. In the case of defence policy, however, it is an open question whether member states will ever agree to supranational rather than intergovernmental integration.

In terms of vertical integration, EMU is the most centralized policy area, with all major monetary policy competencies delegated to the autonomous European system of central banks (note, however, that fiscal policy has remained at the level of intergovernmental cooperation). Single market issues are decided by joint decision-making, which

Table 9.1   *Ordering integration and differentiation across policy areas (ranging from '1' as 'early or high' to '4' as 'late or low')*

	Timing of supranational integration	Vertical integration	Horizontal integration	Horizontal differentiation
Internal market	1	2	1	External
Monetary union	2	1	4	Internal
Defence	3	4	3	Weak internal
AFSJ	4	3	2	External and internal

also makes a highly centralized policy area. Since the late 1990s, the AFSJ has gradually shifted from an intergovernmental mode of decision-making towards the 'community method'. Only issues relating to policing and judicial cooperation in criminal matters are decided unanimously, with limited powers granted to the EP. Defence policy remains rather loosely coordinated between the participating governments and thus lags behind the other policy areas; yet, member state governments are gradually stepping up joint defence and institutional capacities. Turning to horizontal integration, the single market assumes the top spot: it unites all 27 member states with the three members of the EEA. At the other end of the spectrum, only 17 states participate in the eurozone. The AFSJ and defence fall between these two poles.

Finally, all our policies display different forms of horizontal differentiation. The single market is externally differentiated, with the EEA states participating in addition to all EU member states. Switzerland participates more selectively in the single market using bilateral treaties, and Turkey through the Customs Union. At the same time, except for a limited transition period for new member states (relating, for instance, to specific products or, in the case of Eastern enlargement, to the freedom of labour movement), there is no internal differentiation in the Internal Market. In contrast, monetary union is internally differentiated with some EU member states unwilling, and others not permitted or unable, to join the eurozone. Defence is the least differentiated policy area in our sample because only Denmark has opted out. These findings suggest that differentiation necessitates some degree of vertical integration. For example, in the single market external differentiation in the form of the EEA followed the deepening of the market enacted by the '1992' programme. In fact, the EFTA states increasingly feared exclusion from the single market after the SEA. The AFSJ, finally, shows a unique pattern of internal and external horizontal differentiation, in that some non-EU member states participate in the Schengen and Dublin regimes of border control and asylum policy, whereas certain EU member states have opted out (and opt in selectively).

In sum, we find substantive variation in both horizontal and vertical integration and in differentiation across our four policy areas. We will now turn to our integration theories and assess their performance on the basis of the empirical cases presented.

Evaluating the Theories

In the empirical chapters, we applied different integration theories to individual policy areas. We will now assess their relative performance in these different policy areas. In order to do so, we take up a slightly extended version of the framework presented in the introduction to Part I. We first distinguish a demand side of integration from a supply side. Whereas 'demand' is about the actors' preferences regarding integration, 'supply' refers to how negotiations translate the constellation of preferences into an integration outcome – the extent to which a policy area is integrated vertically and horizontally. We will first briefly recall the theoretical predictions for our different theoretical dimensions before scrutinizing the fit of the integration theories to the empirical outcomes. As always, such a comparative exercise demands some degree of simplification, and we lose specificity for the sake of generalization.

Assumptions and expectations

Our framework prompts us to ask the following questions:

- Who are the actors that demand integration? And who are the key actors on the supply side?
- What kinds of preferences do these actors hold? Are these preferences material or ideational? Are they exogenous or endogenous to previous integration dynamics?
- How do the actors interact? Are their interactions primarily about bargaining and the exchange of threats and promises, or do the actors exchange arguments and try to persuade one another?
- What roles do resources – and, in particular, power – play, and which constraints matter for explaining integration processes?

Table 9.2 summarizes the assumptions of the integration theories.

Intergovernmentalism attributes integration to the interests of governments (and powerful societal interests) to preserve and increase their autonomy and efficiency in the face of international interdependence.

Table 9.2   *Analytical framework of integration theories (see also Table PI.3)*

	Intergovernmentalism	Supranationalism	Constructivism
Actors (demand)	Governments (and domestic society)	Transnational society and supranational actors	Not specified
Actors (supply)	Governments	Supranational actors, governments	Supranational actors, governments, publics
Preferences	Material (exogenous)	Material (endogenous)	Ideational (endogenous)
Interactions	Hard bargaining	Soft bargaining	Arguing
Power/constraints	Bargaining power	Institutions	Identities and norms

Correspondingly, variation in vertical and horizontal integration results from variation in international interdependence, in the compatibility of governments' preferences, and in the politicization of issues and interstate relations across policies and countries. *Supranationalism* explains integration as a response to rising transnational exchanges and demands supported by supranational organizations. Variation in vertical and horizontal integration reflects variation in the intensity of transnational exchanges and in the capacity of the EU's supranational organizations across policies and countries. Finally, *constructivism* regards integration as a response to international ideational consensus and a reflection of international community. It accounts for variation in vertical and horizontal integration by variation in the strength of community ideas (international ideational consensus and the institutionalization of ideas) and politicization across policies and countries.

Table 9.3 summarizes the expectations of the integration theories regarding the timing and extent of vertical integration, as well as horizontal integration and differentiation.

In order to evaluate the theories we will now compare their predictions with the empirical patterns that we find in our policy case studies along these different dimensions. We will turn to the timing and trajectory of vertical integration and differentiation, before summarizing the results from our analyses on horizontal integration and differentiation.

Table 9.3   *Expectations of integration theories*
(see Table P2.2 for more detail)

	Intergovernmentalism	*Supranationalism*	*Constructivism*
More vertical and horizontal integration depends on ...	stronger/wider international interdependence	stronger/wider transnational interactions	Stronger/wider legitimacy and consensus
	stronger/wider preference compatibility	stronger supranational actors	lower politicization
	lower autonomy costs		

Vertical integration and differentiation

In the case of the single market, supranationalist analyses of integration demonstrated that transnationally operating businesses and economic interest groups were the main *demandeurs* of integration. Their objective was to destabilize domestic rules and regulations hindering the free exchange of goods and services in order to reap (material) gains from integration. Supranational actors – most notably the Commission and the ECJ – readily provided supranational rules for self-interested reasons, and played a crucial role in advancing both 'negative' and 'positive' integration. According to liberal intergovernmentalism, economic interest groups are also accorded a central role on the demand side of integration, but – contrary to supranationalism – they direct their demands primarily to national governments, which are then also the main suppliers of supranational rules in the intergovernmental negotiations preceding the SEA. Yet, interest group pressure alone did not suffice to trigger demand for integration; it took the convergence of the economic policy preferences of the governments in France, Germany, and the UK in the mid-1980s that preceded the adoption of the single market programme. In sum, those actors that expected to benefit most from liberalization lobbied either their respective governments or supranational actors, such as the Commission, to support their demands.

Even though economic interest groups also voiced demand for monetary integration to reap material benefits from the absence of exchange rate risks and capital controls, the demand for monetary integration was less pronounced than the demand for market integration. This was due mainly to two factors. First, monetary policy was initially (until the early 1970s) embedded in a global policy regime. Second, the macroeconomic preferences of governments diverged sharply. As a result, the demand for integration within the Community framework remained rather low. Other than in the case of market integration, which was negotiated in the context of a 'permissive consensus' and relatively low autonomy costs, monetary integration is constrained by politicization, as it entails autonomy as well as identity costs to states and governments. For example, the Deutsche Mark was considered a national symbol of successful post-war economic recovery and stability in West Germany and, hence, a cornerstone of Germany's postwar national identity. With regard to autonomy costs, the delegation of monetary policy to an independent central bank threatened to restrict the macroeconomic toolkits of national governments. Despite these obstacles to monetary integration, why did it come about in the end? In line with liberal intergovernmentalist expectations, the convergence of monetary policy preferences of the German and French governments made the breakthrough towards EMU possible.

Supranationalists, on the other hand, were able to demonstrate that the Commission, non-governmental actors (such as transnational corporations and interest groups), and transgovernmental actors, (most notably the central bankers of the EC member states meeting in the so-called 'Delors Committee') proposed EMU as a functionally 'necessary' step to reduce the transactions costs of trade and to counter risks associated with liberalized capital markets (e.g. currency speculation and currency instability). The timing of EMU can thus be accounted for best by its temporal proximity to the adoption of the single market programme and the concomitant abolition of capital controls. Moreover, governments and supranational actors alike were guided by the joint expectation and belief that market integration would benefit from monetary integration.

In defence matters, interest groups and supranational actors play a much less pronounced role (the field of defence procurement being an exception). Since societal interests are generally less important in this policy area, governments have more leverage to push ahead or – even more common in this policy area – to step on the brakes. After the early failure of the EDC, defence policy did not reach the level of inter-governmental cooperation until the turn of the millennium, and it is highly unlikely that it will move to higher levels of vertical integration in the near future. Since European interdependence in the area of security and defence has remained relatively low, socio-economic interest groups do not voice demand for integration in security and defence matters. European governments have depended – and, arguably, still do – less on each other for achieving security and military effectiveness than on the USA. Transgovernmental exchanges have taken place in the context of NATO, rather than Europe. Moreover, defence policy is arguably a policy area where identity and autonomy costs are considered particularly pronounced. Given the potential for politicization, even under conditions of high interdependence during the Cold War, it has always remained an intergovernmental policy. In turn, supranational actors, such as the Commission and the EP, have only very limited capacities to advance integration in this field. Yet, we have also seen that, in past decades, close contacts and interactions among security and defence officials have fostered the development of a common European outlook in matters of common security and defence issues.

The AFSJ falls between the poles of the single market and defence. Demand for integration was voiced by governments, as well as by non-governmental actors. The first actors to demand integration were domestic bureaucrats in the Interior ministries of the EU member states. In the 1980s, businesses that operated transnationally criticized the tedious and time-consuming border controls that were considered to obstruct the smooth movement of persons and goods. The Schengen border regime explicitly addressed these obstacles. Responding to the demands from private interest groups, governments also supported integration in order to reap the joint gains from fully realizing the 'four freedoms'. Supranational actors, the Commission, the EP, and the ECJ had relatively limited capacities to affect the course of integration initially: Schengen was not formally part of the treaties before Amsterdam, and when justice and home affairs were introduced as the 'third pillar' of the Maastricht Treaty, decision-making remained intergovernmental. With the transfer of certain JHA policies to the 'first pillar', the Commission was authorized to propose new pieces of legislation and it made use of its newly-acquired rights.

Our results are thus generally in line with the expectations that more interdependence, transnational interactions, and preference compatibility, together with lower autonomy costs and politicization, produce earlier and higher vertical integration. In market integration, the conditions for early integration were very conducive. Trade is the area of high transnational exchange and international interdependence *par excellence*. It is also an area of low autonomy and identity costs for liberal democracies. It is a hallmark of liberal democracies that the state does not control the market directly. It regulates the market, but state ownership of economic enterprises is very limited. Trade has traditionally been the most liberalized and open kind of cross-border activity and transnational exchange. By integrating the market, governments therefore lose relatively little autonomy. Moreover, markets do not qualify as strong symbols of national identity. Finally, the founding members of the EEC were similar in terms of their economic structure and wealth. This similarity facilitated preference convergence. These characteristics of market integration contrast starkly with the policy areas that were integrated at a later stage. Macroeconomic policies and policies of border control, immigration, internal security, and defence have traditionally been exclusive domains of the state, and transnational exchanges and interactions in these areas have been more limited than in trade. The supranational integration of these policies causes a substantial loss of autonomy for the participating states. Giving up the national currency, control of borders and migration, and the national army are also likely to create strong concerns about the preservation of national identities.

If these characteristics explain why these policies were integrated later than the market, why were they integrated at all? In our empirical analyses, we found strong linkages between different policy areas. Integration of one policy area creates a new institutional environment to which actors adapt. We thus find that, in order to understand demand for integration, previous integration needs to be considered. Several 'waves of spillover' have emanated from initial market integration.

First, the deepening of market integration through the internal market programme of the SEA resulted from increased interdependence generated by economic relations in the Common Market, the harmonization policies of the Commission, the jurisdiction of the ECJ, and the convergence of economic preferences in the major member states of the Community. In a second step, monetary union received a boost from the abolition of capital controls that was part of the Internal Market programme and was facilitated by the convergence of macroeconomic preferences, which had partly been the result of networking and learning at the European level. Whereas the member states had preserved formal sovereignty over monetary policy, monetary integration was helped by the fact that the de facto autonomy of the member states in monetary affairs had long been severely damaged. Similarly, national control over borders and migration came under pressure by the freedom of movement of workers, agreed on in the context of the Internal Market programme.

Further policies became subject to a third wave of spillover produced by monetary integration and the liberalization of border controls. The fact that fiscal policy was not supranationally integrated alongside monetary policy can be explained in line with our framework by weaker interdependence, weaker preference convergence, and higher autonomy costs. The same can be said about the reason why the liberalization of border controls was not accompanied by supranational police and justice competences. The sovereign debt crisis we are currently witnessing has, however, exposed the incompatibility of strong monetary integration with weak fiscal integration, raised fiscal interdependence between the eurozone countries considerably, and boosted initiatives to strengthen supranational capacities in the area of budget surveillance. Less dramatically, the EU has also stepped up police and judicial integration in the AFSJ since the turn of the millennium.

The logic of functional linkages or spillover, of course, is at the heart of supranationalist theory. Spillover occurs, when the integration of one policy area produces externalities that affect neighbouring policy areas, thereby creating new demands for integration. While supranationalism accounts well for such endogenous preferences and the dynamics of the integration process, liberal intergovernmentalism is less well-suited to capture this dynamic process fully and, hence, the trajectory of integration. This is largely due to its focus on specific intergovernmental conferences. On this issue, we broadly side with Pierson (1996). As a historical institutionalist, he argues that 'snapshots' of social processes at a single point in time can lead to distortions, in that they overlook the feedback processes linking integration attempts and outcomes over time, and he therefore recommends conceptualizing European integration as a 'moving picture'. While constructivist integration theory, too, assumes that actors' preferences are endogenous to their interactions, our analysis finds limited evidence for socialization or internalization. They are 'constrained' rather than 'converted' (Parsons 2003:18) by previous integration outcomes and their effects. On the issue of whether integration preferences are endogenous or exogenous, and whether endogenous preferences are created by institutional constraints or socialization, we thus find that supranationalism outperforms the other integration theories.

Horizontal integration and differentiation

How do our theories perform to account for horizontal differentiation? The internal market is a case of particularly early and high vertical integration; and it is a case of particularly wide horizontal integration, too. Transnational economic exchanges not only tend to be more intense and dense than other transnational exchanges; they also tend to cover a wider geographical space. 'Globalization' is most pronounced in international trade. Market integration generates negative externalities for EU outsiders and produces 'geographical spillover'. The desire to obtain full access to the Internal Market in order to avoid trade diversion and discrimination has been one of the most important reasons for non-member countries to seek accession to the EU, and for the EU to increase from six to 27 members. But short of enlargement, market integration has led to external differentiation, of which the establishment of the EEA, which incorporates the EFTA countries into the EU's Internal Market, is an important example. Akin to EU candidate countries, EFTA states faced negative externalities from the Single Market project, fearing discrimination through diversions in trade and investments. They took up the Commission's idea of negotiating a global agreement that would ensure access to the Single Market resulting in the EEA agreement, which coincides – with a small time lag – with the deepening of the European integration project through the single market programme.

The lack of internal differentiation can be attributed to the low level of political contestation of issues pertaining to market integration. As the autonomy and identity costs of market integration are relatively low, there is no reason for governments to forego the benefits of market integration and seek opt-outs. For the same reason, the high-level capacities of supranational actors in this policy area have been accompanied by a 'permissive consensus' and have not created identity-driven popular backlashes. As the case of the EEA illustrates, high interdependence with the EU leads to demand for external differentiation. Yet, two situations of external differentiation need to be distinguished where high levels of demand meet different supply conditions. In the first case, high interdependence coincides with eurosceptic majorities in non-EU member states, such as in Norway or Switzerland. In these countries, the accession of their country to the EU has been repeatedly rejected by popular referendums. At the same time, however, they have adopted a large majority of Internal Market rules in order to gain unrestricted access to the vast market in their neighbourhood on which they depend for most of their exports and imports. In the second case, countries such as Turkey or Serbia have not been admitted by the EU member states because their governments have long been – and still are, to some extent – unwilling to meet the EU's identity-based political conditions for membership, which has stirred domestic opposition in the EU member states. Nevertheless, they have been associated with the Internal Market because of their strong economic interdependence with the EU and because the EU regards association as a way to tie these countries to its practices and values. In sum, whereas the absence of internal differentiation in the Internal Market is an effect of high interdependence and low levels of political contestation, external differentiation is a way to deal with high interdependence in spite of high levels of political contestation over a membership perspective.

What explains internal differentiation and the lack of uniform integration in EMU? In the case of the common currency, we have shown that internal differentiation comes in two forms. First, there are those EU member states that have deliberately opted out from EMU: Denmark, Sweden, and the UK. Other states were perhaps more willing, but less capable. Most of the new member states that have acceded to the EU after the 2004 and 2007 enlargement rounds have not joined EMU. Variation between these countries can be mainly explained by differential interdependence – the smaller, more trade-dependent new member states have been willing to work harder toward fulfilling the conditions for EMU membership than the larger and less trade-dependent ones. When it comes to account for the opt-outs of Denmark, Sweden, and the UK, explanations based on levels of economic interdependence and macroeconomic preferences are not convincing, since these three member states do not differ critically from the EU member states that decided to join EMU. In line with our analysis of vertical integration, we find that monetary policy integration is much more susceptible to autonomy and identity concerns than is market integration. The autonomy and identity concerns associated with the supranational centralization of monetary policy and the concomitant abdication of national currencies enable us to illuminate why monetary policy integration is characterized by internal differentiation rather than uniform integration. High levels of vertical integration generate heightened opposition in countries where concerns about national autonomy and identity tend to be particularly prevalent. Politicization or the 'constraining dissensus' expressed *vis-à-vis* EMU triggered opt-outs in Denmark, the UK, and Sweden – countries with eurosceptic populations that had joined the EU mostly out of economic necessity and not out of ideational commitment to supranational integration. In sum, the comparatively high level of exclusive national identities and opposition to supranational integration, in combination with strong domestic ratification constraints, are common features of the three opt-out countries and sets them apart from the other member states.

How can we account for the interesting pattern of internal *cum* external differentiation in the case of the Schengen Area? We argued that variation in interdependence and domestic identity concerns (euroscepticism) are responsible for differentiation. In questions that touch upon domestic security issues, integration is likely to be affected by a 'constraining dissensus', whereby attempted integrative measures may trigger eurosceptic responses among domestic constituents (most notably in Denmark and the UK). Just as in the case of the Internal Market, external differentiation is a response to interdependence in the face of identity-based accession constraints. Norway and Iceland are members of the Schengen Area because of their traditional passport union with Denmark, Sweden, and Finland; and Switzerland and Liechtenstein have joined the Schengen Area because they are surrounded by Schengen member countries. For these two countries the market logic also applies, since Liechtenstein is a member state of the EEA and Switzerland has enacted the free movement of persons with the EU in the bilateral treaties. In the case of Switzerland, membership in the Schengen border control 'regime' (as well as in the Dublin asylum 'regime') can also be explained by negative externalities due to the closer cooperation of other European states in these policy areas. For example, due to the Dublin Convention limiting the possible locations in which to apply for asylum, Switzerland has increasingly become a place for so-called 'asylum shopping'.

Last, why do we find little horizontal differentiation in security and defence policy? On the one hand, the low level of vertical integration imposes only limited autonomy or identity costs on partaking governments. Counterfactually speaking, we would expect to see more internal differentiation if there were an initiative to form a European army. The Danish opt-out reflects a strong popular resentment towards EU integration in general. Moreover, the domestic discourse on European security and defence cooperation was not compatible with the domestically held (majority) view that the integration project is, first and foremost, an economic enterprise.

The pattern and variation of horizontal integration and differentiation we found in our analysis of core policy areas thus point to a mix of explanatory factors proposed by the integration theories. With regard to external differentiation, intergovernmentalism and supranationalism point to the externalities that integration produces and the effects they have on 'outsiders'. These externalities create incentives for non-EU member states to be selective when considering integration in individual policy areas, such as the Internal Market or the Schengen Area. The fact that these externalities do not lead non-member countries to join or to be admitted to the EU has, however, often to do with high identity and autonomy costs and the concomitant politicization highlighted by constructivism and (realist) intergovernmentalism. Whereas some countries are not admitted because they do not fulfil the EU's normative requirements of liberal democracy, others reject membership in a supranational organization because of popular concerns about national identity and sovereignty. These concerns are also the main factors of internal differentiation.

Our analysis of horizontal differentiation has, furthermore, demonstrated the importance of domestic ratification procedures – especially in those countries that make use of referendums to ratify EU treaties. Referendums have been a major source of both external differentiation (when electorates rejected accession treaties, as in Norway) and internal differentiation (e.g. when the Danish voters rejected the Maastricht Treaty). The importance of ratification is implicitly acknowledged by liberal intergovernmentalism, since utility-maximizing politicians should take the positions of their constituency into oaccount. Supranationalism, on the other hand, generally neglects the mechanisms of ratification in its functionalist logic of integration. As, for example, Hooghe and Marks (2008) have argued, there is a gap between a more functionalist understanding of integration from political elites and a more identity-related approach from the public that increasingly is becoming aware of European matters. The preferences that matter thus can vary along institutional contexts, but also over time, as we will show in more detail. While material cost-benefit calculations were decisive for many years in most of the Western European countries, there is an increasing reluctance towards integration that is often based on identity concerns. This is a constructivist message that has long been neglected by the traditional intergovernmentalist and supranationalist theories of European integration. Both material and ideational factors determine integration.

In summary, we find partial support for all our integration theories in the empirical chapters. There is not a single 'winner' emerging from this overview that can best explain vertical and horizontal integration and differentiation in all the policy areas that we analyzed. All theories contribute to understanding some parts of the complex puzzle of European integration, but are less convincing in explaining others. Based on this assessment, we will now suggest a synthesis of the integration theories.

A Synthetic Framework

In our empirical analysis we found that no single theory offers an exclusively valid, complete, or completely convincing explanation of integration and differentiation in all four policy areas. First, the factors and explanations overlapped partly so that it proved difficult to attribute the evidence to a single theory. Second, each theory revealed strengths and weaknesses. These comparative advantages and disadvantages, however, seem to be of a systematic nature and showed themselves in similar fashion across the policy case studies. In this final chapter, we therefore make an attempt to draw on the respective strengths to propose a synthetic integration theory framework and provide a comprehensive explanation of integration and differentiation in the EU. The synthetic framework we propose consists of common ground and scope conditions. *Common ground* refers to those assumptions and hypotheses that are shared or at least not explicitly contested by the three theories. *Scope conditions* are those conditions that specify when the different assumptions and hypotheses about integration preferences and negotiations are most likely to hold.

Common ground

Beyond the analytical framework based on demand and supply conditions of integration, we see common ground in an *intergovernmental core* that is explicitly or implicitly shared by all theories. Governments are the key actors. Whereas it is debated who else is relevant for European integration, the theories agree that governments cannot be left out of the picture. However they may be formed and informed, the integration preferences of governments and their constellation play a central role in explanations of integration and differentiation. And, ultimately, it is the governments that negotiate and make decisions to transfer formal competencies from the nation-state to the EU, to admit new member states or make agreements with non-member countries, and to differentiate integration across countries and policies. This claim is intuitive, since formal steps of European integration are based on international treaties that require the consent of all participating states. This implies that explanations for integration need to be based on the preferences, negotiations, and decisions of governments.

This *formally intergovernmental* framework does not, however, necessarily entail support for *intergovernmentalism in substance.* To say that government preferences matter does not mean that governments define their preferences autonomously and unconstrained by previous integration outcomes, as intergovernmentalism assumes. Neither does a focus on intergovernmental negotiations and decisions imply that these negotiations and decisions are unconstrained by other actors or the institutional context of the negotiations. The assumption that governments are formally the key actors of European integration is compatible with the assumption that the same governments are heavily influenced and constrained by domestic or supranational actors, as well as their ideational and institutional environment. A formally intergovernmental framework therefore does not automatically invalidate supranationalist or constructivist integration theory. However, it does allow us to formulate supranationalist and constructivist hypotheses in terms of what governments want and do.

There is substantive common ground, too. Several conditions of integration are either stipulated explicitly or accepted implicitly by intergovernmentalism, supranationalism, and constructivism.

Interdependence. For intergovernmentalism, international interdependence is the fundamental cause of integration. As governments realize that unilateral policy options do not yield desired results, they engage in multilateral cooperation and integration to obtain economic and security benefits they could not achieve otherwise. According to supranationalism, transnational exchanges and transactions are a major driving force of integration, generating demand for international rules. To the extent that transnational exchanges are both a cause and a manifestation of international interdependence, the two factors can be equated with each other. This is most obvious in the case of transnational economic exchanges, which result from welfare benefits that countries derive from foreign trade and investment, and which increase their sensitivity and vulnerability to their international environment. Both intergovernmentalism and supranationalism stipulate that interdependence generates demand and support for integration. Constructivism does not explicitly theorize interdependence, but is compatible with the idea that interdependence produces demand for integration.

Both intergovernmentalism and supranationalism stipulate that interdependence promotes vertical and horizontal integration. Differences in interdependence, then, promote vertical and horizontal differentiation: different degrees of interdependence across policy sectors produce different levels of integration, and different degrees of interdependence across countries explain the variation in demand for opt-outs. At the same time, however, all theories agree that interdependence is not sufficient to bring about integration.

Convergence of preferences. One factor that conditions the relationship between interdependence and integration is the constellation of governmental preferences. Interdependence does not automatically lead to common interests. For intergovernmentalism, the convergence of national (and mainly material) preferences is therefore a key condition of integration. Constructivists agree that common preferences are relevant, but focus on international ideational consensus as a necessary condition for interdependence to produce integration. Supranationalists would not object to the key role of common or compatible preferences, but emphasize that it is transnational interest groups, supranational organizations, and the spillovers of earlier integration steps that help create this convergence. Vertical and horizontal integration thus depend on the extent of preference convergence among governments and societies. Vertical differentiation is the result of differences in the level of convergence across policies. The propensity of a country to steer clear of or opt out from integration is a function of the distance of its material or ideational preferences from the mainstream: preference outliers are most likely to stay out or opt out. The result is horizontally differentiated integration.

Politicization. Whereas the convergence of preferences facilitates integration, politicization creates obstacles. For (realist) intergovernmentalism, the autonomy costs of integration produce reluctance among governments and societies to support further integration. For constructivists, it is the identity costs of integration that provide obstacles for further integration: the concern that integration dilutes or dissolves national identity and the institutions that symbolize it. Although politicization does not feature prominently in supranationalist theory, neofunctionalists assumed that integration would start with technical, low-politics issues. All theories hypothesize that politicized policies are integrated later and at a lower level than non-politicized policies. They also produce greater horizontal differentiation. Countries with stronger autonomy or identity concerns are more likely to be constrained by politicization, seek opt-outs from integration, or remain outside the EU altogether.

In simple terms, the common ground in integration theory can be formulated as follows: *conditional on preference convergence and low politicization, interdependence promotes integration.* In other words, in highly politicized policy areas, it requires higher interdependence and a higher degree of preference convergence to produce integration. This common ground, however, masks disagreement about the nature of preferences, the causes of politicization, and the origins of interdependence. Moreover, a major issue remains highly contested: the relevance of supranational actors and institutions for explaining integration negotiations and outcomes.

Scope conditions

Scope conditions can make such contested causal claims compatible. We distinguish two sets of scope conditions. The first set refers to competing claims regarding integration preferences (demand), the second to different assumptions and hypotheses about integration negotiations (supply). For the scope conditions of demand, we ask under which conditions the preferences of governments are more likely to be exogenous or endogenous, material or ideational, and rooted in the government itself or based on the preferences of other actors. The scope conditions regarding actors and material or ideational preferences have already been proposed by Andrew Moravcsik (1998: 36, 486–9); the scope on exogenous and endogenous preferences is broadly in line with supranationalism.

In general terms, we can stipulate that *governmental preferences are influenced by the preferences of those actors who are both most affected and most powerful.* Governments are the relevant actors, and governmental preferences are most relevant where integration primarily affects the autonomy, competences, or resources of the state or state bureaucracies. Societal actors are the relevant actors, and societal preferences are most relevant where integration affects interests of powerful societal actors. In line with this argument, we find that interest groups are more active in market issues than in justice or home affairs. Whether the preferences of national or transnational society are more relevant depends on the degree to which social or interest groups in different countries are similarly affected, have compatible interests, and are organized in transnational interest groups. Again, the very active European Round Table of Industrialists illustrates the importance of transnational interest groups in the 1980s. If we assume, finally, that supranational actors are generally highly affected by integration, their influence on governmental preferences depends mainly on their expertise and administrative resources.

Integration preferences become more endogenous as integration progresses. Remember that exogenous preferences are defined as preferences that are not influenced by the integrated rules and supranational institutions. Endogenous preferences are those that have been changed as a result of prior integration steps and their effects. Quite logically, governmental preferences are exogenous at the beginning of the integration process because there is no organization or prior step of integration from which endogenous preferences could result. As integration progresses, however, competences are transferred to the European level, supranational actors are created, policies are removed from the exclusive purview of national governments, and additional countries become part of the integration process. These developments make it more likely that the preferences of governments are shaped and constrained by integration. An example is the deepening of market integration in the 1980s, or the establishment of the third pillar, JHA, in the Treaty of Maastricht. *Ceteris paribus*, governments become more affected by the integration process and relatively less affected by purely domestic development, or events in the larger international sphere. This scope condition does not mean that governments' preferences will at some point become exclusively, or even predominantly, endogenous; neither does it mean that preferences will become increasingly integration-friendly. It only implies that the balance shifts in favour of integration-induced options and preferences.

Material preferences are the more relevant, the higher and the more certain the material costs and benefits of integration. This argument concerns both the security and autonomy implications of integration (realist intergovernmentalism) and the consequences for national wealth (liberal intergovernmentalism). Conversely, ideational preferences gain ground if integration has no implications for national wealth or security, or if these implications are weak, indirect, remote, or unclear. In addition, however, *ideational preferences also become the more prominent, the more that integration affects core symbols, institutions, and ideas that define collective identities.* This scope condition follows from constructivist integration theory. As a consequence, it is difficult to predict whether material or ideational preferences prevail where integration affects both material conditions and identities clearly and strongly. It is also difficult to predict preferences where material interests call for more integration, whereas ideas produce opposition, or the reverse. If we assume, however, that governments are loss-aversive, we may still conclude that governments will be reluctant to accept material losses of integration in return for ideational gains, and vice versa.

Another set of scope conditions concerns integration negotiations. Under which conditions are these negotiations more or less intergovernmental, characterized by hard and soft bargaining or arguing? Under which conditions is intergovernmental bargaining power constrained by the normative and institutional context of negotiations? We suggest that the actors, modes, and constraints of integration negotiations depend on the stage and level of integration, as well as on the extent of politicization.

Purely intergovernmental negotiations and unconstrained bargaining are most relevant at the beginning of the integration process and at low levels of centralization. Under these conditions, supranational institutions do not exist, or are too weak to play an important role in the negotiations or to constrain the bargaining behaviour or bargaining power of the governments. In addition, the 'permissive consensus' of citizens gives governments a high level of discretion in integration negotiations. This changes once integration reaches a significant level of centralization. At this point, supranational organizations have acquired sufficient capacities and expertise to become important (if mainly informal) players in integration negotiations; and intergovernmental bargaining is constrained by existing (status quo) rules, increasing costs of exit, and institutionalized norms.

Yet, supranational institutionalization and bargaining constraints work most strongly in areas of low politicization, in which the 'permissive consensus' remains intact and governments can negotiate and make agreements in the absence of domestic public attention and scrutiny. In areas of high politicization, however, European policies become contentious and citizens are mobilized. Under this condition, governments are constrained by the threat of non-ratification and by actors who are not part of the EU policy-making process and do not follow European norms and habits of negotiating behaviour. We thus add two further scope conditions. On the one hand, *integration negotiations become more supranationally institutionalized and constrained as integration progresses in areas of low politicization.* On the other hand, however, *integration negotiations become more domestically contested and constrained as integration progresses in areas of high politicization.*

Which conclusions can we draw from these scope conditions for the explanation of integration and differentiation? Supranationalism and intergovernmentalism disagree on the causal relevance of prior steps of integration and the capacity of supranational actors. If we use the state or level of integration as a scope condition, this disagreement can be solved.

- At the initial stage of integration in a policy area, or at low levels of centralization, the capacity of supranational organizations and the endogenous effects of integration are weak. Therefore, integration depends on exogenous interdependence, intergovernmental preference constellations, and bargaining power as expected by intergovernmentalism.
- The dynamic shifts, however, once a critical state of integration is reached. Supranational organizations are established and acquire considerable capacity; and the rules of integration begin to constrain or shape governmental preferences and bargaining behaviour. At this stage, the spillover and community-building mechanisms proposed by supranationalism and constructivism gain in strength; expand integration to new policy areas, new countries, and higher

levels of centralization; and reduce or avoid differentiation. The more powerful the Commission, the Parliament, the Court, and other supranational organizations, the better they are capable of centralizing issue areas, preventing opt-outs, and overcoming differentiated integration where it exists. If that were the only scope condition, we would see the inexorable drive towards centralization and supranational state-building that is associated with early supranationalist theory.

There is, however, an alternative second logic highlighted by both realist intergovernmentalists and constructivists: the logic of politicization. As integration progresses, it becomes increasingly intrusive, expands into core areas of state autonomy and national identity, and triggers adverse reactions by actors that value autonomy and identity. Politicization shifts the locus of integration negotiations from the international to the domestic level. Negotiations become domestically embedded and constrained. As a result, we expect to see more horizontal differentiation in highly politicized areas, more vertical differentiation between policies of high and low politicization, and a reduced pace of vertical integration overall.

Summary

We found the *common ground* of the three integration theories in the proposition that, conditional on preference convergence and low politicization, interdependence promotes integration. On the basis of our discussion of *scope conditions*, we added that, once integration reaches a critical level of centralization, the further path of integration bifurcates. If politicization remains low, i.e. in areas of weak autonomy and identity relevance, integration is stabilized as a result of supranational enforcement capacities and supranational constraints on intergovernmental bargaining. Moreover, various spillover processes promote endogenous interdependence and preference convergence, and thus further integration. By contrast, in those policy areas or countries that are particularly sensitive to autonomy and identity concerns, integration heightens sensitivity, generates opposition to (further) integration, and leads to divergence in governmental preferences. Under these circumstances, integration either stagnates, or further integration is accompanied by further differentiation.

Figure 9.1 illustrates the synthetic and dynamic model of integration. The first part of the diagram shows the common ground at the initial stage of integration (T1). Interdependence generates demand for integration, particularly if government preferences are compatible and politicization remains weak. The initial integration outcome creates spillover and institutionalization effects that generate additional inter-

266

Figure 9.1 *A synthetic model of integration*

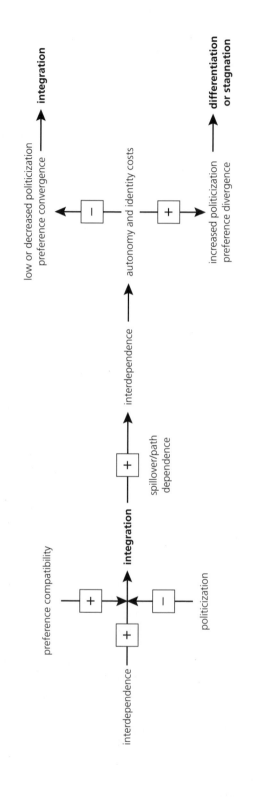

dependence, calling for more integration at time T2. Depending on the autonomy and identity costs that governments and citizens perceive to result from the spillover effects, the integration path bifurcates at time T3. Under the condition that the perceived autonomy and identity costs of further integration steps are low, preferences remain compatible or converge, and politicization remains weak or even decreases. As a result, we are likely to see further integration in order to deal with spillover and institutionalization effects. If, however, the perceived autonomy and identity costs are high, preferences are likely to diverge and politicization increases. Integration either stagnates at the status quo level or becomes more differentiated as it progresses.

Where Do We Go From Here?

Despite repeated claims that European integration has run its course and reached a 'constitutional equilibrium', the EU remains a vibrant political system that is constantly in flux. In this book, we surveyed the theoretical literature on regional integration and applied integration theories to different policy areas in the EU. Our special focus has been on differentiation. Based on our analysis, we think that differentiation has become a core feature of the EU that is likely to persist in the years to come. Comprising 28 member states in 2013, with the likelihood of even more states joining the EU in the future, heterogeneity is likely to grow. So are the pressures for further deepening resulting from the financial crisis and the flaws of the eurozone design. Differentiation can, at least in part, reconcile the tension created by deepening and widening.

At the time of writing, European integration seems an ambiguous affair. With an unexpected level of integration having already been attained, there are growing functional incentives for even deeper integration. At the same time, European publics have become increasingly sensitive to, and reluctant about, integration. Over time, the politicization of integration has moved from the geographical peripheries to the centre of the EU. These challenges are paradigmatically illustrated by the current euro crisis. The Greek financial crisis, on the one hand, underlines the inescapable interdependence between the member states and, due to this, the functional imperatives of working together. On the other hand, citizens seem more reluctant than ever to pay the price for integration. Citizens in the wealthier member states worry about the fate of their financial contributions, citizens in Greece fear the loss of their national autonomy. The current crisis underlines that solidarity among the citizens of the EU is much weaker than in the national context, and even seemingly outdated national clichés survive and resurface. Institutionally, the eurozone has reached a critical point, as the status quo of 2010 proved untenable for solving the dilemmas at hand.

Our analysis prompts three broad predictions in the current situation. First, theoretical considerations and empirical evidence suggest that the crisis will not lead to disintegration. The exit of Greece from the eurozone and, to an even greater extent, the breakdown of the euro would be a novel development in the history of European integration, so far characterized by 'ever deeper' and 'ever wider' integration. Theoretically speaking, the 'sunk costs' of integration and the high risk of 'spillbacks' – i.e. negative repercussions in other policy areas and European international relations on the whole (Lindberg and Scheingold 1970: 137) – lead us to expect that EU governments will do whatever they can to save the eurozone. Second, however, whatever EU governments will do to save the eurozone and resolve other problems in European integration is likely to increase politicization. Each new step of integration – even if it appears to be dictated by the necessities of the situation – is likely to have high autonomy and identity costs, and to trigger politicization and domestic mobilization. And, even if further integration results from this process, it is likely to generate new differentiation or deepen that which already exists.

Our final, and probably least controversial, prediction is that the current crisis emphasizes the need for integration theory and its further elaboration. It demonstrates, in our view, the practical importance of theoretical understanding of the mechanisms of regional integration. Theorizing integration is not *art pour l'art* but, rather, an important condition for successfully shaping international cooperation in a turbulent twenty-first century.

References

Abbott, Kenneth W. and Duncan Snidal (1998) 'Why States Act through Formal International Organizations', *Journal of Conflict Resolution* 42(1): 3–32.

Adler-Nissen, Rebecca (2009) 'Behind the Scenes of Differentiated Integration: Circumventing National Opt-Outs in Justice and Home Affairs', *Journal of European Public Policy* 16(1): 62–80.

Adler-Nissen, Rebecca (2011) 'Opting Out of an Ever Closer Union: The Integration Doxa and the Management of Sovereignty', *West European Politics* 34(5): 1092–113.

Alter, Karen J. and Sophie Meunier-Aitsahalia (1994) 'Judicial Politics in the European Community. European Integration and the Pathbreaking', *Cassis de Dijon* Decision. *Comparative Political Studies* 26(4): 535–61.

Aspinwall, Mark and Gerald Schneider (2000) 'Same Menu, Separate Tables: The Institutionalist Urn in Political Science and the Study of European Integration', *European Journal of Political Research* 38: 1–36.

Baldwin-Edwards, Martin (1997) 'The Emerging European Immigration Regime: Some Reflections on Implications for Southern Europe', *Journal of Common Market Studies* 35(4): 497–519.

Baldwin, Richard E. (1995) 'A Domino Theory of Regionalism', in *Expanding Membership of the European Union*, ed. Richard E. Baldwin, Pertti Haaparanta and Jaako Kiander. Cambridge: Cambridge University Press: 25–47.

Barnett, Michael N. and Martha Finnemore (1999) 'The Politics, Power, and Pathologies of International Organizations', *International Organization* 53(04): 699–732.

Bartolini, Stefano (2005) *Restructuring Europe. Centre Formation, System Building, and Political Structuring between the Nation-state and the European Union*. Oxford: Oxford University Press.

Battistelli, Fabrizio and Pierangelo Isernia (1993) 'Europa und die Integrationstheorien. Obsoleszenz oder Wachstumskrise?', in *Die Europäische Option. Eine interdisziplinäre Analyse über Herkunft, Stand und Perspektiven der europäischen Integration* (ed.) Armin von Bogdandy. Baden-Baden: Nomos: 171–98.

Beyers, Jan (2005) 'Multiple Embeddedness and Socialization in Europe: The Case of Council Officials', *International Organization* 59: 899–936.

Börzel, Tanja A. (2005) 'Mind the Gap! European Integration between Level and Scope', *Journal of European Public Policy* 12(2): 217–36.

Buono, Laviero (2009) 'From Tampere to The Hague and Beyond: Towards the Stockholm Programme in the Area of Freedom, Security and Justice, *ERA-Forum* 10(3): 333–42.

Burgess, Michael (1989) *Federalism and European Union. Political Ideas, Influences, and Strategies in the European Community 1972–1987*. London: Routledge.

269

Burley, Anne-Marie and Walter Mattli (1993) 'Europe Before the Court: A Political Theory of Legal Integration', *International Organization* 47(01): 41–76.

Cameron, David (1992) 'The 1992 Initiative: Causes and Consequences', in *Euro-Politics: Institutions and Policymaking in the 'New' European Community*, (ed.) Alberta Sbragia. Washington, DC: Brooking: 23–74.

Cameron, David R. (1995) 'Transnational Relations and the Development of European Economic and Monetary Union', in *Bringing Transnational Relations Back In. Non-State Actors, Domestic Structures and International Institutions*, (ed.) Thomas Risse-Kappen. Cambridge: Cambridge University Press: 37–78.

Caporaso, James (1998) 'Regional Integration Theory: Understanding our Past and Anticipating our Future', *Journal of European Public Policy* 5(1): 1–16.

Caporaso, James A. and John T.S. Keeler (1995) 'The European Union and Regional Integration Theory', in *The State of the European Union*, ed. Carolyn Rhodes and Sonia Mazey. Boulder, CO: Lynne Rienner. 29-62.

Carrubba, Clifford J., Matthew Gabel, and Charles Hankla (2008) 'Judicial Behavior under Political Constraints: Evidence from the European Court of Justice', *American Political Science Review* 102(4): 435–52.

Checkel, Jeffrey T. (1999) 'Social Construction and Integration', *Journal of European Public Policy* 6(4): 545–60.

Checkel, Jeffrey T. (2001) 'Why Comply? Social Learning and European Identity Change', *International Organization* 55(03): 553–88.

Christiansen, Thomas, Knut Eric Joergensen and Antje Wiener (eds) (2001) *The Social Construction of Europe*. London: Sage.

Clark, William Roberts, Matt Golder and Sonia Nadenichek Golder (2002) 'Fiscal Policy and the Democratic Process in the European Union', *European Union Politics* 3(2): 205–30.

Commission of the European Communities, Directorate-General for Economic and Financial Afairs (1990) 'One Market, One Money: An Evaluation of the Potential Benefits and Costs of Forming an Economic and Monetary Union', *European Economy*, 44, available at http://ec.europa.eu/economy_finance/publications/publication_ summary7520_en.htm.

Cooley, Alexander and Henrik Spruyt (2009) *Contracting States. Sovereign Transfers in International Relations*. Princeton: Princeton University Press.

Craig, Paul and Gráinne De Búrca (2008) *EU Law. Text, Cases and Materials*. 4th edn. Oxford: Oxford University Press.

Crombez, Christophe (1996) 'Legislative Procedures in the European Community', *British Journal of Political Science* 26(2): 199–228.

Cusack, Thomas (2001) 'Partisanship in the Setting and Coordination of Fiscal and Monetary Policies', *European Journal of Political Research* 40: 93–115.

Delgado, Francisco J. and María José Presno (2010) 'Tax Policy Convergence in the EU: an Empirical Analysis', *Rivista de Economía Mundial* 26: 53–83.

Deutsch, Karl W. (1954). *Political Community at the International Level: Problems of Definition and Measurement*. Garden City, NY: Doubleday.

Deutsch, Karl W. (1957) *Political Community and the North Atlantic Area: International Organization in the Light of Historical Experience*. Princeton, NJ: Princeton University Press.

Dinan, Desmond (2004) *Europe Recast: A History of European Union.* Basingstoke: Palgrave Macmillan.

Donahue, John D. and Mark A. Pollack (2001) 'Centralization and its Discontents: The Rhythms of Federalism in the United States and the European Union', in *The Federal Vision. Legitimacy and Levels of Governance in the United States and the European Union*, ed. Kalypso Nicolaidis and Robert Howse. Oxford: Oxford University Press: 73–112

Donnelly, Shawn (2010) *The Regimes of European Integration: Constructing Governance of the Single Market.* Oxford: Oxford University Press.

Duchêne, Francois (1994) *Jean Monnet. The First Statesman of Interdependence.* New York and London: Norton.

Dyson, Kenneth, and Kevin Featherstone (1999) *The Road to Maastricht: Negotiating Economic and Monetary Union.* Oxford: Oxford University Press.

Farrell, Henry and Adrienne Héritier (2003) 'Formal and Informal Institutions under Codecision: Continuous Constitution-Building in Europe', *Governance* 16(4): 577–600.

Farrell, Henry and Adrienne Héritier (2004) 'Interorganizational Cooperation and Intraorganizational Power: Early Agreements under Codecision and their Impact on the Parliament and the Council', *Comparative Political Studies* 37(10): 1184–212.

Fearon, James D. and Alexander Wendt (2002) 'Rationalism v. Constructivism: A Sceptical View', in *Handbook of International Relations*, ed. Walter Carlsnaes, Thomas Risse and Beth A. Simmons. London: Sage: 52–72.

Finke, Daniel (2009) 'Domestic Politics and European Treaty Reform: Understanding the Dynamics of Governmental Position-Taking', *European Union Politics* 10(4): 482–506.

Finnemore, Martha (1996) *National Interests in International Society.* Ithaca, NY: Cornell University Press.

Fligstein, Neil (2008) *Euroclash. The EU, European identity, and the future of Europe.* Oxford: Oxford University Press.

Fligstein, Neil and Iona Mara-Drita (1996) 'How to Make a Market: Reflections on the Attempt to Create a Single Market in the European Union', *American Journal of Sociology* 102(1): 1–33.

Fligstein, Neill and Alec Stone Sweet (2001) 'Building Europe: From the Treaty of Rome to the Constitution of Policy Domains', in *The Institutionalization of Europe*, ed. Alec Stone Sweet, Wayne Sandholtz and Neill Fligstein. Oxford: Oxford University Press.

Fligstein, Neill and Alec Stone Sweet (2002) 'Constructing Polities and Markets: An Institutionalist Account of European Integration', *American Journal of Sociology* 107(5): 1206–43.

Frey, Bruno S. and Reiner Eichenberger (1996) 'FOCJ: Competitive Governments for Europe', *International Review of Law and Economics* 16: 315–27.

Garrett, Geoffrey (1992) 'International Cooperation and Lnstitutional Choice: The European Community's Internal Market', *International Organization* 46(02): 533–60.

Garrett, Geoffrey, Daniel R. Kelemen and Heiner Schulz (1998) 'The

European Court of Justice, National Governments, and Legal Integration in the European Union', *International Organization* 52(1): 149–76.

Gehring, Thomas (1998) 'Die Politik des koordinierten Alleingangs. Schengen und die Abschaffung der Personenkontrollen an den Binnengrenzen der Europäischen Union', *Zeitschrift für Internationale Beziehungen* 5(1): 43–78.

George, Steven (1990) *'An Awkward Partner: Britain in the European Community*. Oxford: Oxford University Press.

Giegerich, Bastian and William Wallace (2010) 'Foreign and Security Policy: Civilian Power Europe and American Leadership', in *Policy-Making in the European Union*, ed. Helen Wallace, Mark A. Pollack and Alastair R. Young. Oxford: Oxford University Press: 431–55.

Grieco, Joseph M. (1996) 'State Interests and International Rule Trajectories: A Neorealist Interpretation of the Maastricht Treaty and European Economic and Monetary Union', *Security Studies* 5(3): 261–306.

Gstöhl, Sieglinde (1994) 'EFTA and the European Economic Area or the Politics of Frustration', *Cooperation and Conflict* 29(4): 333–66.

Gstöhl, Sieglinde (2000) 'The European Union after Amsterdam: Towards a Theoretical Approach to (Differentiated) Integration', in *The State of the European Union. Risks, Reform, Resistance, and Revival*, ed. Maria G. Cowles and Michael Smith. Oxford: Oxford University Press: 42–63.

Gstöhl, Sieglinde (2002) *Reluctant Europeans. Norway, Sweden, and Switzerland in the process of integration*. Boulder, CO: Lynne Rienner.

Guiraudon, Virginie (2003) 'The Constitution of a European Immigration Policy Domain: A Political Sociology Approach', *Journal of European Public Policy* 10(2): 263–82.

Haas, Ernst B. (1958) *The Uniting of Europe: Political, Social and Economic Forces, 1950–57*. Stanford, CA: Stanford University Press.

Haas, Ernst B. (1961) 'International Integration: The European and the Universal Process', *International Organization* 15(3): 366–92.

Haas, Ernst B. (1968) *The Uniting of Europe. Political, Social, and Economic Forces 1950–1957*. Stanford, CA: Stanford University Press.

Haas, Ernst B. (1975) *The Obsolescence of Regional Integration Theory*, Berkeley, CA: Institute of International Studies.

Haas, Ernst B. (2001) 'Does Constructivism Subsume Neo-functionalism?', in *The Social Construction of Europe*, ed. Thomas Christiansen, Knut Eric Joergensen and Antje Wiener. London: Sage.

Haas, Peter M. (1992) 'Introduction: Epistemic Communities and International Policy Coordination', *International Organization* 46(01): 1–35.

Hall, Peter A. and Rosemary C.R. Taylor (1996) 'Political Science and the Three New Institutionalisms', *Political Studies* 44(4): 936–57.

Hansen, Lene (2002) 'Sustaining Sovereignty: The Danish Approach to Europe', in *European Integration and National Identity: the Challenge of the Nordic States*, ed. Lene Hansen and Ole Waever. London: Routledge: 50–87.

Heipertz, Martin and Amy Verdun (2010) *Ruling Europe: The Politics of the Stability and Growth Pact*. Cambridge: Cambridge University Press.

Hellmann, Gunther (2003) 'Are Dialogue and Synthesis Possible in International Relations?', *International Studies Review* 5(1): 123–53.

Héritier, Adrienne (2007) 'Mutual Recognition: Comparing Policy Areas', *Journal of European Public Policy* 14(5): 800–13.

Hill, Christopher and Karen Smith (2000) *European Foreign Policy: Key Documents*. London: Routledge.

Hitchcock, William I. (1997) 'France, the Western Alliance, and the Origins of the Schuman Plan, 1948–1950', *Diplomatic History* 21(4): 603–30.

Hitchcock, William I. (1998) *France Restored: Cold War Diplomacy and the Quest for Stability in Europe, 1945–1954*. Chapel Hill, NC: University of North Carolina Press.

Hix, Simon (1994) 'The Study of the European Community: The Challenge to Comparative Politics', *West European Politics* 17(1): 1–30.

Hix, Simon (2002) 'Constitutional Agenda-Setting Through Discretion in Rule Interpretation: Why the European Parliament Won at Amsterdam', *British Journal of Political Science* 32(2): 259–80.

Hix, Simon (2005) *The Political System of the European Union*, 2nd edn. Basingstoke: Palgrave Macmillan.

Hobolt, Sara Binzer (2009) *Europe in Question. Referendums on European Integration*. Oxford: Oxford University Press.

Hoffmann, Stanley (1966) 'Obstinate or Obsolete? The Fate of the Nation State and the Future of Western Europe', *Daedalus* 95(4): 861–98.

Hoffmann, Stanley (1982) 'Reflections on the Nation-State in Western Europe Today', *Journal of Common Market Studies* 21(1): 21–38.

Hooghe, Liesbet (2005) 'Several Roads Lead to International Norms, but Few Via International Socialization: A Case Study of the European Commission', *International Organization* 59(04): 861–98.

Hooghe, Liesbet and Gary Marks (2001) *Multi-level Governance and European Integration*. of *Governance in Europe*. Lanham, MD: Rowman & Littlefield.

Hooghe, Liesbet and Gary Marks (2003) 'Unraveling the Central State, but How? Types of Multi-Level Governance', *American Political Science Review* 97(2): 233–43.

Hooghe, Liesbet and Gary Marks (2005) 'Calculation, Community and Cues: Public Opinion on European Integration', *European Union Politics* 6(4): 419–43.

Hooghe, Liesbet and Gary Marks (2008) 'A Postfunctionalist Theory of European Integration: From Permissive Consensus to Constraining Dissensus', *British Journal of Political Science* 39(01): 1–23.

Hosli, Madeleine O. (2005) *The Euro. A Concise Introduction to European Monetary Integration*. Boulder, CO: Lynne Rienner.

Howorth, J. (2001) 'European Defence and the Changing Politics of the European Union: Hanging Together or Hanging Separately?,' *Journal of Common Market Studies,* 39(4): 765-89.

Howorth, J. (2004) 'Discourse, Ideas and Epistemic Communities in European Security and Defence Policy', *West European Politics,* 27(1): 29-52

Howorth, Jolyon (2005) 'From Security to Defence: the Evolution of the CFSP', in *International Relations and the European Union*, ed. Christopher Hill and Michael Smith. Oxford: Oxford University Press: 179–204.

Hug, Simon and Thomas König (2002) 'In View of Ratification: Governmental Preferences and Domestic Constraints at the Amsterdam Intergovernmental Conference', *International Organization* 56(2): 447–76.

Jabko, Nicolas (1999) 'In the Name of the Market: How the European Commission paved the way for Monetary Union', *Journal of European Public Policy* 6(3): 475–95.

Jabko, Nicolas (2006) *Playing the Market: A Political Strategy for Uniting Europe, 1985–2005*. Ithaca, NY: Cornell University Press.

Jachtenfuchs, Markus and Beate Kohler-Koch (1996) 'Regieren im dynamischen Mehrebenensystem', in *Europäische Integration*, ed. Markus Jachtenfuchs and Beate Kohler-Koch. Opladen: Leske & Budrich: 15–44.

Jileva, Elena (2002) 'Larger than the European Union: The Emerging EU Migration Regime and Enlargement', in *Migration and the Externalities of European Integration*, ed. Sandra Lavenex and Emek M. Ucarer. Lanham, MD: Lexington Books: 75–89.

Joerges, Christian and Jürgen Neyer (1997) 'From Intergovernmental Bargaining to Deliberative Political Processes: The Constitutionalisation of Comitology', *European Law Journal* 3(3): 273–99.

Johnson, Juliet (2008) 'The Remains of Conditionality: The Faltering Enlargement of the Euro Zone', *Journal of European Public Policy* 15(6): 826-41.

Johnston, Alastair Iain (2001) 'Treating International Institutions as Social Environments', *International Studies Quarterly* 45(4): 487–515.

Jones, Seth (2007) *The Rise of European Security Cooperation*. Cambridge: Cambridge University Press.

Kaelberer, Matthias (1997) 'Hegemony, Dominance or Leadership? Explaining Germany's Role in European Monetary Cooperation', *European Journal of International Relations* 3(1): 35–60.

Kaiser, Wolfram (2001) 'Institutionelle Ordnung und strategische Interessen. Die Christdemokraten und "Europa" nach 1945', in *Das Europäische Projekt zu Beginn des 21. Jahrhunderts*, (ed.) Wilfried Loth. Opladen: Leske & Budrich.

Kaiser, Wolfram (2007) *Christian Democracy and the Origins of the European Union*. Cambridge: Cambridge University Press.

Kaiser, Wolfram and Brigitte Leucht (2008) 'Informal Politics of Integration. Christian Democratic and Transatlantic Networks in the Creation of the ECSC Core Europe', *Journal of European Integration History* 14(1): 35–49.

Katzenstein, Peter J. (1997) 'United Germany in an Integrating Europe', in *Tamed Power. Germany in Europe*, (ed.) Peter J. Katzenstein. Ithaca, NY: Cornell University Press. 1–48.

Katzenstein, Peter and Rudra Sil (2008) 'Eclectic Theorizing in the Study and Practice of International Relations', in *The Oxford Handbook of International Relations*, ed. Christian Reus-Smit and Duncan Snidal. Oxford: Oxford University Press: 109–30.

Kaunert, Christian (2005) 'The Area of Freedom, Security and Justice: The Construction of a 'European Public Order', *European Security* 14(4): 459–83.

Keohane, Robert O. (1984) *After Hegemony: Cooperation and Discord in the World Political Economy*. Princeton, NJ: Princeton University Press.

Keohane, Robert O. and Joseph Nye (1977) *Power and Interdepence: World Politics in Transition*. Boston: Little, Brown.

Keukeleire, Stephan and Jennifer MacNaughtan (2008) *The Foreign Policy of the European Union*. Basingstoke: Palgrave Macmillan.

Kölliker, Alkuin (2001) 'Bringing Together or Driving Apart the Union? Towards a Theory of Differentiated Integration', *West European Politics* 24(4): 125–51.

Kölliker, Alkuin (2006) *Flexibility and European Unification: The Logic of Differentiated Integration*. Lanham, MD: Rowman & Littlefield.

Koremenos, Barbara, Charles Lipson and Duncan Snidal (2001) 'The Rational Design of International Institutions', *International Organization* 55(04): 761–99.

Kostakopoulou, Theodora (2006) 'Security Interests. Police and Judicial Cooperation', in *The Institutions of the European Union*, ed. John Peterson and Michael Shackleton. Oxford: Oxford University Press: 231–51.

Lavenex, Sandra (2009) 'Switzerland's Flexible Integration in the EU: A Conceptual Framework', *Swiss Political Science Review* 15(4): 547–75.

Lavenex, Sandra (2010) 'Justice and Home Affairs. Communitarization with Hesitation', in *Policy-Making in the European Union*, ed. Helen Wallace, Mark A. Pollack and Alastair R. Young. Oxford: Oxford University Press: 457–77.

Lavenex, Sandra and William Wallace (2005) 'Justice and Home Affairs. Towards a "European Public Order"?', in *Policy-Making in the European Union*, ed. Helen Wallace, William Wallace and Mark A. Pollack. Oxford: Oxford University Press: 457–80.

Leuffen, Dirk (2007) *Cohabitation und Europapolitik. Politische Entscheidungsprozesse im Mehrebenensystem*. Baden-Baden: Nomos.

Leuffen, Dirk (2009) 'Does Cohabitation Matter? French European Policy-Making in the Context of Divided Government', *West European Politics* 32(6): 1140–60.

Lewis, Jeffrey (2003a) 'Informal Integration and the Supranational Construction of the Council', *Journal of European Public Policy* 10(6): 996–1019.

Lewis, Jeffrey (2003b) Institutional Environments and Everyday EU Decision Making', *Comparative Political Studies* 36(1–2): 97–124.

Lewis, Jeffrey (2010) 'How Institutional Environments Facilitate Co-operative Negotiation Styles in EU Decision-making', *Journal of European Public Policy* 17(5): 648–64.

Lindberg, Leon N. (1963) *The Political Dynamics of European Economic Integration*. Stanford, CA: Stanford University Press.

Lindberg, Leon N. and Stuart A. Scheingold (1970) *Europe's Would be Polity: Patterns of Change in the European Community*. Englewood Cliffs, NJ: Prentice-Hall.

Lindner, Johannes and Berthold Rittberger (2003) 'The Creation, Interpretation, and Contestation of Institution – Revisiting Historical Institutionalism', *Journal of Common Market Studies* 41(3): 445–73.

Lipgens, Walter (1982) *A History of European Integration*. Oxford: Clarendon Press.

Majone, Giandomenico (1996) *Regulating Europe*. London: Routledge.

Manners, Ian (2002) 'Normative Power Europe: A Contradiction in Terms?', *Journal of Common Market Studies* 40(2): 235–58.

March, James G. and Johan P. Olsen (1999) *Rediscovering Institutions. The Organizational Basis of Politics.* New York: Free Press.

Marks, Gary, Liesbet Hooghe and Kermit Blank (1996) European Integration since the 1980s: State-Centric versus Multi-Level Governance', *Journal of Common Market Studies* 34: 343–78.

Mattli, Walter (2005) 'Ernst Haas's Evolving Thinking on Comparative Regional Integration. of Virtues and Infelicities', *Journal of European Public Policy* 12(2): 327–48.

McNamara, Kathleen R. (1999) 'Consensus and Constraint: Ideas and Capital Mobility in European Monetary Integration', *Journal of Common Market Studies* 37(3): 455–76.

McNeely, Connie L. (1995) *Constructing the Nation-State. International Organization and Prescriptive Action.* Westport, CT: Greenwood Press.

Mérand, Frédéric. (2006) 'Social Representation in the European Security and Defence Policy', *Cooperation and Conflict* 41(2): 131–52.

Mérand, Frédéric (2008) *European Defence Policy: Beyond the Nation State.* Oxford: Oxford University Press.

Meyer, Christoph O. (2005) 'Convergence Towards a European Strategic Culture? A Constructivist Framework for Explaining Changing Norms', *European journal of International Relations* 11(4): 523–49.

Milner, Helen V. (1997) *Interests, Institutions, and Information Domestic Politics and International Relations.* Princeton, NJ: Princeton University Press.

Milward, Alan S. (1984) *The Reconstruction of Western Europe, 1945–51.* Berkeley, CA: University of California Press.

Milward, Alan S. (1994) *The European Rescue of the Nation State.* London: Routledge.

Milward, Alan Steele and George Brennan (1992) *The European Rescue of the Nation State.* Berkeley, CA: University of California Press.

Monar, Jörg (2001) 'The Dynamics of Justice and Home Affairs: Laboratories, Driving Factors and Costs', *Journal of Common Market Studies* 39(4): 747–64.

Monar, Jörg (2006) 'Cooperation in the Justice and Home Affairs Domain: Characteristics, Constraints and Progress', *Journal of European Integration* 28(5): 495–509.

Moravcsik, Andrew (1991) 'Negotiating the Single European Act: National Interests and Conventional Statecraft in the European Community', *International Organization* 45(1): 19–56.

Moravcsik, Andrew (1993) 'Preferences and Power in the European Community: A Liberal Intergovernmentalist Approach', *Journal of Common Market Studies* 31(4): 473–524.

Moravcsik, Andrew (1998) *The Choice for Europe. Social Purpose and State Power from Messina to Maastricht.* Ithaca, NY: Cornell University Press.

Moravcsik, Andrew (1999) 'A New Statecraft? Supranational Entrepreneurs and International Cooperation', *International Organization* 53(2): 267–306.

Moravcsik, Andrew (2000) 'De Gaulle between Grain and Grandeur: The Economic Origins of French EC Policy, 1958–1970', *Journal of Cold War Studies* 2(2): 3–43.

Moravcsik, Andrew (2005) 'The European Constitutional Compromise and the Neo-functionalist Legacy', *Journal of European Public Policy* 12(2): 349–86.

Moravcsik, Andrew (2007) 'The European Constitutional Settlement', in *Making History. European Integration and Institutional Change at Fifty*, ed. Sophie Meunier and Kathleen R. McNamara. Oxford: Oxford University Press: 23–50.

Moravcsik, Andrew and Kalypso Nicolaïdis (1999) 'Explaining the Treaty of Amsterdam: Interests, Influence, Institutions', *Journal of Common Market Studies* 37(1): 59–85.

Mörth, Ulrika (2003) *Organizing European Cooperation – The Case of Armaments*. Lanham, MD: Rowman & Littlefield.

Mörth, Ulrika and Malena Britz (2004) 'European Integration as Organizing: The Case of Armaments', *Journal of Common Market Studies* 42(5): 957–73.

Nelson, Douglas (1988) 'Endogenous Tariff Theory: A Critical Survey', *American Journal of Political Science* 32(3): 796–837.

Neve, Jan-Emmanuel de (2007) 'The European Onion? How Differentiated Integration is Reshaping the EU', *Journal of European Integration* 29(4): 503–21.

Niemann, Arne and Philippe C. Schmitter (2009) 'Neo-functionalism', in *Theories of European Integration*, ed. Antje Wiener and Thomas Diez. Oxford: Oxford University Press: 45–66.

Nye, Joseph S. (1971) *Peace in Parts: Integration and Conflict in Regional Organization*. Boston, MA: Little Brown & Co.

Ojanen, Hanna (2006) 'The EU and NATO: Two Competing Models for a Common Defence Policy', *Journal of Common Market Studies* 44(1): 57–76.

Olsen, Gorm Rye (2007) 'Denmark and the ESDP', in *The North and the ESDP: The Baltic States, Denmark, Finland and Sweden*, ed. Klaus Brummer. Gütersloh: Verlag Bertelsmann Stiftung: 22–33.

Parsons, Craig (2002) 'Showing Ideas as Causes: The Origins of the European Union', *International Organization* 56(1): 47–84.

Parsons, Craig (2003) *A Certain Idea of Europe*. Ithaca, NY: Cornell University Press.

Parsons, Craig (2010) 'Revisiting the Single European Act (and the Common Wisdom on Globalization)', *Comparative Political Studies* 43(6): 706–34.

Pastor-Castro, Rogelia (2006) 'The Quai d'Orsay and the European Defence Community Crisis of 1954', *History* 91: 386–400.

Peers, Steve (2007) *EU Justice and Home Affairs Law*. 2nd edn of *Oxford EC Law Library*. Oxford: Oxford University Press.

Pierson, Paul (1996) 'The Path to European Integration: A Historical Institutionalist Perspective', *Comparative Political Studies* 29(2): 123–63.

Pierson, Paul (1998) 'The Path to European Integration: A Historical-Institutionalist Analysis', in *European Integration and Supranational Governance*, ed. Wayne Sandholtz and Alec Stone Sweet. Oxford: Oxford University Press: 27–58.

Pierson, Paul (2000) 'Increasing Returns, Path Dependence, and the Study of Politics', *American Political Science Review* 94(2): 251–67.

Pierson, Paul (2004) *Politics in Time. History, Institutions, and Social Analysis*. Princeton, NY: Princeton University Press.

Plümper, Thomas and Christina Schneider (2007) 'Discriminatory Membership and the Redistribution of Enlargement Gains', *Journal of Conflict Resolution* 51(4): 568–87.

Pollack, Mark A. (1997) 'Delegation, Agency, and Agenda Setting in the European Community', *International Organization* 51(1): 99–134.

Pollack, Mark A. (2003) *The Engines of Integration: Delegation, Agency and Agenda Setting in the Europen Union*. Oxford: Oxford University Press.

Posen, Barry (2006) 'European Union Security and Defense Policy: Response to Unipolarity?', *Security Studies* 15(2): 149–86.

Puchala, Donald J. (1971) 'Of Blind Men, Elephants and International Integration', *Journal of Common Market Studies* 10(3): 267–84.

Putnam, Robert D. (1988) 'Diplomacy and Domestic Politics: The Logic of Two-Level Games', *International Organization* 42(3): 427–60.

Reynolds, Christopher (2010) *Understanding the Emergence of the European Security and Defence Policy: A Historical Institutionalist Analysis*. Baden-Baden: Nomos.

Risse, Thomas (2000) '"Let's Argue!": Communicative Action in World Politics. *International Organization* 54(01): 1–39.

Risse, Thomas, Daniela Engelmann-Martin, Hans Joachim Knopf and Klaus Roscher (1999) 'To Euro or Not to Euro? The EMU and Identity Politics in the European Union', *European Journal of International Relations* 5(2): 147–87.

Risse, Thomas and Mareike Kleine (2010) 'Deliberation in Negotiations', *Journal of European Public Policy* 17(5): 708–26.

Rittberger, Berthold (2005) *Building Europe's Parliament. Democratic Representation Beyond the Nation-State*. Oxford: Oxford University Press.

Rittberger, Berthold and Frank Schimmelfennig (2006) 'Explaining the Constitutionalization of the European Union', *Journal of European Public Policy* 13(8): 1148–67.

Rosamond, Ben (2000) *Theories of European integration*. New York: St Martin's Press.

Rosamond, Ben (2007) 'The Political Sciences of European Integration: Disciplinary History and EU Studies', in *Handbook of European Union Politics*, ed. Knut Erik Joergensen, Mark A. Pollack and Ben Rosamond. London: Sage: 7–30.

Rosato, Sebastian (2011) *Europe United. Power Politics and the Making of the European Community*. Ithaca, NY: Cornell University Press.

Ruane, Kevin (2000) *The Rise and Fall of the European Defence Community. Anglo-American Relations and the Crisis of European Defence, 1950–55*. Basingstoke: Palgrave Macmillan.

Sandholtz, Wayne (1993) 'Choosing Union: Monetary Politics and Maastricht', *International Organization* 47(1): 1–39.

Sandholtz, Wayne and John Zysman (1989) '1992: Recasting the European Bargain', *World Politics* 42(1): 95–128.

Scharpf, Fritz Wilhelm (1999) *Governing in Europe: Effective and Democratic?* Oxford: Oxford University Press.

Schimmelfennig, Frank (2001) 'The Community Trap: Liberal Norms,

Rhetorical Action, and the Eastern Enlargement of the European Union', *International Organization* 55(1): 47–80.

Schimmelfennig, Frank (2003a) *The EU, NATO and the Integration of Europe. Rules and Rhetoric*. Cambridge: Cambridge University Press.

Schimmelfennig, Frank (2003b) 'Strategic Action in a Community Environment', *Comparative Political Studies* 36(1–2): 156–83.

Schimmelfennig, Frank (2009) 'Entrapped Again: The Way to EU Membership Negotiations with Turkey', *International Politics* 46(4): 413–31.

Schimmelfennig, Frank (2010) 'The Normative Origins of Democracy in the European Union: Toward a Transformationalist Theory of Democratization', *European Political Science Review* 2(2): 211–33.

Schimmelfennig, Frank and Andrew Moravcsik (2009) 'Liberal Intergovernmentalism', in *European Integration Theory*, ed. Antje Wiener and Thomas Diez. Oxford: Oxford University Press: 67–87.

Schimmelfennig, Frank and Ulrich Sedelmeier (eds) (2005) *The Politics of European Union Enlargement: Theoretical Approaches*. London: Routledge.

Schmitter, Philippe C. (1969) 'Three Neo-Functional Hypotheses about International Integration', *International Organization* 23(01): 161–6.

Schmitter, Philippe C. (1996) 'Imagining the Future of the Euro-Polity with the Help of New Concepts', in *Governance in the European Union*, ed. Gary Marks, Fritz W. Scharpf, Philippe C. Schmitter and Wolfgang Streeck. London: Sage.

Schneider, Christina J. (2009) 'Conflict, Negotiation and European Union Enlargement', Dissertation, Universität Konstanz, 2006. Cambridge: Cambridge University Press.

Schneider, Gerald and Lars-Erik Cederman (1994) 'The Change of Tide in Political Cooperation: A Limited Information Model of European Integration', *International Organization* 48(4): 633–62.

Schön, Harald (2008) 'Identity, Instrumental Self-Interest and Institutional Evaluations: Explaining Public Opinion on Common European Policies in Foreign Affairs and Defence', *European Union Politics* 9(1): 5–29.

Smith, Michael E. (1998) *Europe's Foreign and Security Policy*. Cambridge: Cambridge University Press.

Stone Sweet, Alec (2004) *The Judicial Construction of Europe*. Oxford: Oxford University Press.

Stone Sweet, Alec and Thomas L. Brunell. (1998) 'Constructing a Supranational Constitution: Dispute Resolution and Governance in the European Community', *American Political Science Review* 92(1): 63–81.

Stone Sweet, Alec, Neill Fligstein and Wayne Sandholtz (2001) 'The Institutionalization of European Space', in *The Institutionalization of Europe*, ed. Alec Stone Sweet, Wayne Sandholtz and Neill Fligstein. Oxford: Oxford University Press: 1–28.

Stone Sweet, Alec and Wayne Sandholtz (1997) 'European Integration and Supranational Governance', *Journal of European Public Policy* 4(3): 297–317.

Stone Sweet, Alec and Wayne Sandholtz (1998) 'Integration, Supranational Governance, and the Institutionalization of the European Polity', in *European Integration and Supranational Governance*, ed. Wayne Sandholtz and Alec Stone Sweet. Oxford: Oxford University Press: 1–26.

Stubb, Alexander (2002) *Negotiating Fexibility in the European Union. Amsterdam, Nice and Beyond*. Basingstoke: Palgrave.

Stubb, Alexander C. (1996) 'A Categorization of Differentiated Integration', *Journal of Common Market Studies* 34: 283–95.

Thomas, Daniel (2009) 'Explaining the Negotiation of EU Foreign Policy: Normative Institutionalism and Alternative Approaches', *International Politics* 46(4): 339–57.

Thomas, Daniel C. (2006) 'Constitutionalization through Enlargement: the Contested Origins of the EU's Democratice Identity', *Journal of European Public Policy* 13(8): 1190–210.

Tovias, Alfred (2006) 'Exploring the "Pros" and "Cons" of Swiss and Norwegian Models of Relations with the European Union', *Cooperation and Conflict* 41(2): 203–22.

Tranholm-Mikkelsen, Jeppe (1991) 'Neo-functionalism: Obstinate or Obsolete? A Reappraisal in the Light of the New Dynamism of the EC', *Millenium: Journal of International Studies* 20(1): 1–22.

Tsebelis, George (1994) 'The Power of the European Parliament as a Conditional Agenda Setter', *American Political Science Review* 88(1): 128–42.

Vachudova, Milada Anna (2000) 'Eastern Europe as Gatekeeper: The Immigration and Asylum Policies of an Enlarging European Union', in *The Wall Around the West: State Borders and Immigration Controls in North America and Europe*, ed. Peter Andreas and Timothy Snyder. Lanham, MD: Rowman & Littlefield: 153–72.

Varwick, Johannes, and Jana Windwehr (2007) 'Norwegen und Schweiz als Modellfälle für differenzierte Integration', *Aus Politik und Zeitgeschichte* 43: 15–20.

Verdun, Amy (1999) 'The Role of the Delors Committee in the Creation of EMU: an Epistemic Community?', *Journal of European Public Policy* 6(2): 308–28.

Waever, Ole (2009) 'Discursive Approaches', in *European Integration Theory*, ed. Antje Wiener and Thomas Diez. Oxford: Oxford University Press: 163–80.

Wallace, Helen, William Wallace and C. Webb (eds) (1983) *Policy-Making in the European Community*. Chichester: Wiley.

Wallace, William (1983) 'Less than a Federation, More than a Regime: The Community as a Political System', in *Policy-Making in the European Community*, ed. Helen Wallace, William Wallace and C. Webb. Chichester: Wiley: 403–36.

Walsh, James I. (2000) *European Monetary Integration and Domestic Politics: Britain, France, and Italy*. Boulder, CO: Lynne Rienner.

Weber, Steven (1994) 'Origins of the European Bank for Reconstruction and Development', *International Organization* 48: 1–38.

Weiss, Moritz. (2011) *Transaction Costs and Security Institutions. Unravelling the ESDP*. Basingstoke: Palgrave Macmillan.

Wichmann, Nicole (2009) '"More In Than Out": Switzerland's Association With Schengen/ Dublin Cooperation', *Swiss Political Science Review* 15(4): 653–82.

Wiener, Antje (1999) 'Forging Flexibility – the British "No" to Schengen', *European Journal of Migration and Law* 1(4): 441–63.

Wilks, Stephen (2010) 'Competition Policy. Towards an Economic Constitution?'. in *Policy-Making in the European Union*, ed. Helen Wallace, Mark A. Pollack and Alastair R. Young. Oxford: Oxford University Press: 133–55.

Wolf, Dieter and Bernhard Zangl (1996) 'The European Economic and Monetary Union: "Two-Level Games" and the Formation of International Institutions', *European Journal of International Relations* 2(3): 355–93.

Young, Alastair R. (2010) 'The Single Market. Deregulation, Reregulation, and Integration', in *Policy-Making in the European Union*, ed. Helen Wallace, Mark A. Pollack and Alastair R. Young. Oxford: Oxford University Press: 107–31.

Zaiotti, Ruben (2011) *Cultures of Border Control: Schengen and the Evoluation of European Frontiers*. Chicago, IL: University of Chicago Press.

Index